TRAV
NEW MEXICO

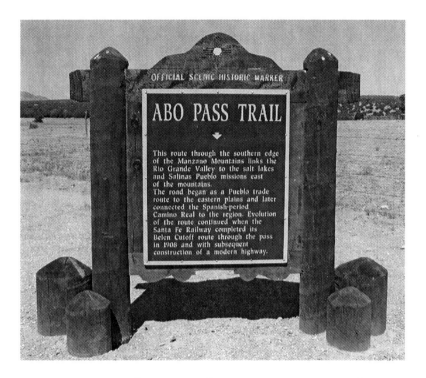

A Guide to the Historical
and State Park Markers

Phil T. Archuletta and Sharyl S. Holden

SUNSTONE
PRESS
SANTA FE

Sunstone books may be purchased for educational, business, or sales
promotional use. For information please write: Special Markets Department,
Sunstone Press, P.O. Box 2321, Santa Fe, New Mexico 87504-2321.

Library of Congress Cataloging-in-Publication Data:

Archuletta, Phil T., 1946–
    Traveling New Mexico: a quide to the historical and state park markers
/ by Phil T. Arculetta & Sharly S. Holden.
        p. cm.
    ISBN: 0-86534-400-0 (pbk.)
        1. Historical markers—New Mexico—Guidebooks. 2. Parks—New
Mexico—Guidebooks. 3. New Mexico—History, Local. 4. New Mexico—
Guidebooks. 5. Automobile travel—New Mexico—Guidebooks. I. Holden,
Sharyl S., 1963– II. Title.

F797. A73 2003
917.8904'54—dc   2003045442

Published in   SUNSTONE PRESS
                    Post Office Box 2321
                    Santa Fe, NM 87504-2321 / USA
                    (505) 988-4418 / *orders only* (800) 243-5644
                    FAX (505) 988-1025
                    www.sunstonepress.com

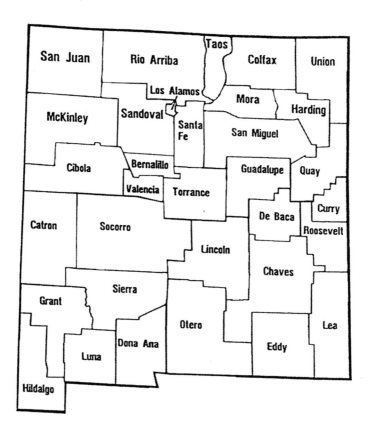

State Motto: "It Grows as it Goes"
State Song: "Oh Fair New Mexico", "Así es Nuevo Méjico"
State Flower: "Yucca"
State Tree: "Pinon"
State Bird: Chaparral ("Road-runner")
State Animal: Black Bear"

New Mexico
Land of Enchantment

New Mexico State Parks

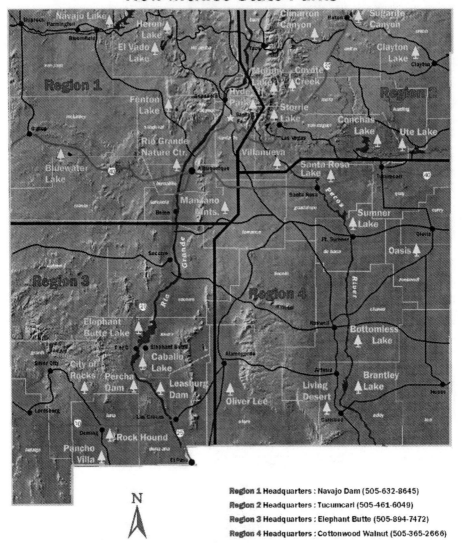

Region 1 Headquarters : Navajo Dam (505-632-8645)
Region 2 Headquarters : Tucumcari (505-461-6049)
Region 3 Headquarters : Elephant Butte (505-894-7472)
Region 4 Headquarters : Cottonwood Walnut (505-365-2666)

Energy, Minerals and Natural Resources Department

4

Introduction

The historical marker program designed to inform the traveling public of the different points of interest to visit in New Mexico, began in 1935. The agencies involved were the State Tourism bureau, the New Mexico Highway Commission and the National Parks Service. These agencies contributed to the beginning program.

The historical markers were manufactured by the State Highway department and the New Mexico Prison Industries. The vigas were constructed according to the drawings of the State Highway Department, and the sign panels were printed by an employee of the Highway Department, Sotenes Delgado. These panels were painted with yellow backgrounds, black and red letters, and a green border. The famous Delgado Printing on the historical markers has been maintained through all the history of the historical marker project.

The Highway Department, in cooperation with the Travel and Tourism Department, has been responsible for the costs relating to the historical marker project. The Highway department manufactured and installed the historical markers whereever the cultural properties review committee designated for a historical marker to be installed. In 1968, there were approximately 263 historical markers throughout the state, and approximately 22 New Mexico State Park markers.

By 1981, the project had grown to 287 historical markers and 38 New Mexico State Park markers. At the present time, there are over 500 historical markers.

In 1980, the New Mexico Highway Department was advised by the Federal Transportation Agency that all historical markers in the State of New Mexico were to be changed so that they could comply with the Manual of Uniformed Control Devices colors. Because the historical markers were recreational type signs and not warning signs, the colors had to be changed from yellow, black, red and green, to brown and white. The exception were the Entrance signs to New Mexico. They would remain the original colors of yellow, black, red and green, as those were some of the colors of the New Mexico Flag.

By 1981, a Cultural Properties Review Committee which had representatives from the National Parks, State Parks, Department of Tourism, Department of Economic Development, the New Mexico Historical Society, and the Office of New Mexico Historical Culture, was formed. The Cultural Review

Committee approved the text of each marker. A contract was awarded to Ojo Caliente Craftsman, through Phil T. Archuletta, to redesign and manufacture the new style of markers for the Highway Department.

In 1994, P&M Signs, Inc. in Mountainair, New Mexico, under the direction of Phil T. Archuletta and Maybel G. Ocaña, was awarded the first state contract to manufacture the historical marker components for the highway department. By March of 1999, P&M Signs, Inc. was awarded a new state contract to manufacture and install the historical markers for all six highway districts of the state. Under the contract, P&M Signs, Inc.'s job task was to log and map all the historical markers in the State of New Mexico and to manufacture and install the historical markers in District 4. At the present time, some of the historical markers have been taken down, because of deterioration or vandalism and no longer exist in some of these communities. To preserve the work of historians from 1935 to present, the signs have been logged and recorded into this book for preservation for the future generations to enjoy.

How to use this book

What is the easiest way to use this book? That is a good question and one that the authors have puzzled over when adapting the information into a practical and useful guide. There are different ways to use it. If you know where you are, you can look up the sign on the corresponding county map to locate the number, then find the corresponding number behind that county map to find out more information on that particular Historical Marker.

If you are not sure where you want to go, browse through the book and read about the signs within a particular county or along a specific route. Then spend the day searching out where the signs physical locations are. You will get a brief history lesson as well as enjoy the beautiful country side.

With luck, you will enjoy just browsing through this book, and hopefully learn a little bit about this enchanting state, New Mexico.

New Mexico Department of Energy, Minerals and Natural Resources

Table of Contents

24. San Juan / 259

A. City of Bloomfield / 260
B. Aztec / 261
C. Aztec Ruins National Monument / 262
D. Farmington / 263
E. Hogback / 264
F. Shiprock / 265
G. Beclabito Dome / 266
H. Salmon Ruin / 267
 I. Chaco Culture National Historical Park / 268
J. Blanco Trading Post / 269

25. San Miguel / 270

A. Watrous / 271
B. La Cueva National Historic District / 272
C. Storrie Lake State Park / 273
D. Camp Maximiliano Luna / 274
E. New Mexico Highlands University / 275
F. Las Vegas / 276
G. Hogbacks / 277
H. Villanueva State Park / 278
 I. Pecos / 279
J. Glorieta Battlefield / 280
K. Pecos National Historic Monument / 281
L. Conchas Lake State Park / 282
M. Puertocito de la Piedra Lumbre / 283
N. Strike Valley / 284
O. Hermit's Peak / 285

26. Sandoval / 286

A. Pueblo of Zia / 287
B. Vasquez de Coronado's Route / 288
C. Fenton Lake State park / 289
D. Pueblo of Jemez / 290
E. Jemez State Monument / 291
F. Soda Dam / 292
G. Valle Grande / 293
H. Colorado Plateau / 294
 I. Cuba / 295
J. San Juan Basin / 296
K. Jicarilla Apache Reservation / 297
L. Continental Divide / 298

M. Alameda / 299
N. Pueblo of Sandia Nafiat / 300
O. Bernalillo / 301
P. Pueblo of Sandia / 302
Q. Las Placitas / 303
R. La Angostura / 304
S. Pueblo of San Felipe / 305
T. Pueblo of Santo Domingo Kiua / 306
U. Pueblo of Santo Domingo / 307
V. Pueblo of Chochiti / 308
W. La Bajada / 309
X. Pueblo Revolt Tricentennial / 310
Y. Kearney's Route / 311

27. Santa Fe / 312

A. Galisteo Pueblo / 313
B. Galisteo Basin / 314
C. Southern Rockies / 315
D. Garden of the Gods / 316
E. Cerrillos / 317
F. Gold and Turquoise / 318
G. La Bajada / 319
H. Bicentennial Celebration / 320
H. La Bajada / 320
 I. South End of the Rockies / 321
J. Canoncito at Apache Canyon / 322
K. Seton Village / 323
L. Santa Fe on the Camino Real / 324
M. Agua Fria / 325
N. San Isidro Catholic Church / 326
O. Pueblo of Tesuque / 327
P. Santa Fe Opera / 328
Q. Pueblo Revolt Tricentennial / 329
R. Pueblo of Nambe / 330
S. Bandelier National Monument / 331
T. Jemez Mountains / 332
U. Pueblo of San Ildefonson / 333
V. Puye Ruins / 334
W. Chimayo / 335
X. Santuario De Chimayo / 336

28. Sierra / 337

A. Elephant Butte Dam / 338
B. Elephant Butte Lake State Park / 339
C. Truth or Consequences / 340
D. Geronimo's Springs / 341
E. Caballo Mountains / 342
F. Percha Creek Bridge / 343

Bernalillo County

Created in 1852 as one of the nine original counties, this county was named after the settlement of Bernalillo.

County Seat: Albuquerque
Communities: Chilili, Tijeras,
                     Cedar Crest,
                     Alameda,
                     Rio Rancho

Petroglyph National Park

1,169 Square Miles

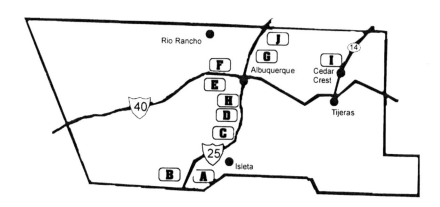

Pueblo of Isleta Tuei

This Southern Tiwa Pueblo is said to have derived its name from the frequent flooding of the Rio Grande, which surrounded the village, giving it the appearance of a little island. Isleta was noted for the excellence of its crops and orchards. The western branch of the Camino Real crossed the river north of here.

Isleta means "little Island" in Spanish, but Isleta Pueblo is hardly little, having an area of 211,002 acres and a population of greater than three thousand. It was during the Pueblo Revolt that many of the people from Isleta fled to Hopi settlements in Arizona. After the rebellion was over and people returned, they brought Hopi mates and half-Hopi children. When some members from Laguna and Acoma Pueblos joined the Isleta community in the eighteen hundreds, friction developed with the slight differences of religion and customs. To settle this problem two smaller communities, Oraibi and Chicale were created near the main pueblo of Isleta.

Agriculture is still the principal occupation of the Isleta People. With the legalization of gambling for the Indians, the Isleta people have succeeded in establishing the Isleta Gaming Palace. They also have year round golf, fishing, picnicking and RV Campsites.

Isleta Pueblo
P.O. Box 1270
Isleta Pueblo NM 87022
(505) 869-3111

NM 147 South of Isleta Pueblo
MM 1.7

1-A

Pueblo of Isleta

Isleta, or "little island" in Spanish, is the largest of the Rio Grande pueblos. Many Isletans moved to El Paso with the Spanish during the 1680 Revolt: others resettled the pueblo around 1710. Parts of the mission San Agustin de la Isleta, date from about 1613.

Today, the tribe has invested itself in modern living and offers many recreational activities catering to tourists and local visitors alike. From a championship 27 hole golf course, to campgrounds complete with trails for hiking and lakes for fishing to a modern air conditioned gambling casino-restaurant, Isleta Pueblo offers something for everyone.

The Pueblo also follows traditional values. Bread baking ovens called "hornos", compliment nearly every yard. Ladies can be seen baking bread daily and many local stores carry the bread, if you're lucky enough to get there before it is all gone.

Farmers and gardeners around the Pueblo grow blue corn and sell the ground corn meal from roadside stands and local shops. Blue cornmeal lends a unique flavor and color to goods baked with it. Growing more and more popular, are blue corn tortilla chips, also available locally.

Alfalfa, winter wheat, and corn are farmed around the valley in Isleta. Cattle, sheep, and horses are raised primarily by Isleta ranchers.

The Isleta Reservation is divided north/south by both Bernalillo and Valencia Counties, respectively. It directly adjoins Los Lunas at the northwestern village limits.

NM 314 in Pueblo of Isleta
MM 14.8

1-B

Los Padillas

Los Padillas is an extended family settlement which was resettled in 1718 by Diego de Padilla. His grandparents had lived on the site prior to the 1680 Pueblo Revolt at which time they were forced to abandon it. In the 1790 census the town, referred to as San Andres de los Padillas, had a population of 168. This is the site of the old Los Padillas School, originally built in 1901 and replaced in 1912.

Los Padillas is the southern-most community in the South Valley of the greater Albuquerque metropolitan area. The Los Padillas Land Grant was established before there was an Albuquerque.

The small community is located on the flood plain of the middle Rio Grande Valley, and is considered rural. It has a diverse ecosystem containing endangered Bosque (Riverside cottonwood forest), with precarious surface and ground water sources.

Many of the families residing here have lived continuously in this community for more than three centuries, where there's a blend of tradition and modern ways.

Farming is still a major land use. Small track farms grow chile, corn, squash, tomatoes, and fruit. Alfalfa is the major crop. There are several dairies and feed lots present as well.

South on Isleta Blvd on Los Padillas St
MM 0.6

1-C

Pajarito

In the 17th Century, the Spanish established a series of farming and ranching communities, called estancias, along the Western bank of the Rio Grande. The Camino Real normally followed the east bank of the river, but a western branch of the road along what is now Isleta Boulevard to incorporate their estancias and later communities such as Pajarito (Little bird) and nearby Los Padillas.

The South Valley comprises nearly a third of the area of Albuquerque. From Central Avenue south, it moves slowly from urban to semi-urban to the open rural ranchos of Parjarito and Los Padillas communities. There are 39 square miles of the South valley and adjacent mesa slopes, and they represent diversity in land use and rich culture and history.

The South Valley has clear cultural and ethnic traditions. Its rich history and cultural traditions find expression in place names and in past settlements, first by Pueblo Indians, then by Spanish and Mexican, and finally by Anglo settlers.

The history of settlement in the South Valley began about 12,000 years ago with bands of nomadic hunters and gatherers entering the area. Archeological evidence indicates that the first pueblo builders entered the valley of the Rio Grande over 600 years ago.

Isleta Blvd.
North of Los Padillas in Pajarito

1-D

Albuquerque
On the Camino Real

Spanish settlers had lived here before the Pueblo Revolt of 1680, but the area was resettled when the "Villa de Alburquerque" was founded in 1706. In addition to promoting colonization, the new town was intended to provide protection from attacks by Indians in Rio Abajo, or lower Rio Grande Valley. Population 331,767. Elevation 5,310 feet.

Just imagine what the city of Albuquerque looked like 2,000 years ago. The environment was very different, cooler and wetter. Shallow lakes called playas were on the west mesa, and a large lake, Lake Estancia lay to the east of the Mountains. A wide variety of exotic animals lived here then—mammoths, saber-toothed tigers, and dire wolves. Paleo-Indian lifestyle was centered on the hunting of large game, but there was still a need to collect plants and seeds, and the people moved their campsites often and over great distances.

As the climate of the Southwest gradually changed to become more like the deserts, the exotic animals hunted by the Paleo-Indians died off, and so did the Indians' nomadic way of life.

Corn became the dietary staple, and the presence of good agricultural land a necessary condition for the establishment of a village to grow the corn. Water was needed for both domestic use and to raise the crops. Corn depletes nitrogen from the soil, but the Puebloans planted beans, which are nitrogen fixing, in the same field. They also grew squash; and where the growing season was long enough, planted cotton as well.

Despite the relative sophistication of pueblo agriculture, the desert environment did not allow a living by farming alone. Prehistoric Puebloans, as did their ancestors, gathered a variety of wild plants including piñon nuts, Indian rice grass, and cacti. Hunting was also important because animal meat provided fat and a source of protein other than beans.

In Albuquerque 4 miles from Central and Coors
on Old Hwy 66

1-E

Rio Grande Rift

Albuquerque is situated at the juncture of two major blocks in the earth's crust. One block, the Sandia Mountains, is tilted upward toward the east along the Sandia fault. West of the fault, the Rio Grande rift has dropped downward forming a great trough which has subsided 26,000 feet from the rim of the mountains.

The geological history of this area is almost as fascinating as the cultural heritage. The city's familiar mountain/valley/mesa trough shape is long and complex, extending hundreds of millions of years into the past. The story unfolds as a fascinating scenario involving a series of dramatic earth changes.

Long ago, this valley was relatively flat and a shallow sea advanced into most of New Mexico. As this sea retreated and evaporated, muds and sands were deposited by rivers on a vast flood plain inhabited by dinosaurs. It was nearly 250 million years ago and deciduous trees such as oak and maple became common in the local environments.

Over 150 million years later, another sea advanced across New Mexico leaving a thick layer of marine shales and flood plain deposits. This later became the Tijeras Coal Basin.

With generalized tension, stretching of the Earth's crust, fracturing of the sedimentary layers and the bedrock caused the area in Albuquerque to sink as blocks on either side lifted. This huge grave-like trough, called a "rift" was formed.

This rift can be followed for more than 600 miles from Mexico to Northern Colorado.

Northwest of Intersection
of I-40 and I-25 on West I-40

1-F

Albuquerque

In 1706, New Mexico Governor Francisco Cuervo y Valdez founded the new Villa de Albuquerque (now Albuquerque), which became the principle settlement of the Rio Abajo, or lower river district. Here, the Camino Real wound its way through a series of farming and ranching communities and led to a nearby ford which linked the Camino Real to settlements on the west bank of the Rio Grande.

Albuquerque was founded near the Rio Grande by Captain Hurtado, Father Juan Minguez, and 252 original settlers who acquired land from the Spanish government on a provisional basis.

The railway provided access to a new market for Albuquerque's exports (Kansas City) and to materials from the east. Commercial plaster and window glass changed the appearance of Albuquerque's houses, but milled lumber was particularly sought after. The lumber was used in building construction, but especially for boardwalks. Flooding along Railway Avenue was so common that boardwalks and building entrances were built as much as five feet above ground level. The architectural style that emerged, called "New Mexico Territorial", was an odd blend of Hispanic and Anglo traditions. During the Territorial Period, and for some time after statehood, the preferred way of building was Anglo. Thus, the first buildings on the University of New Mexico campus were red brick and would not have been out of place in New York or Maryland.

Albuquerque's clean air and high altitude were important to another aspect of the city's growth. In the first part of the 20th century, the city became a Mecca for those suffering from tuberculosis. The sanitariums, most notably Presbyterian Hospital, were built on the outskirts of the city. The city eventually grew to encompass them. The provision of health services has been an important aspect of Albuquerque's economy.

Further progress for the city, and its continued growth, were assured by the U.S. military with the establishment of Kirtland Air Force Base and Sandia Laboratories and Base.

Albuquerque Chamber of Commerce
P.O. Box 25100
Albuquerque, NM 87125
505-764-3700

Exit 157A on Rio Grande Blvd.
Off of Romero Street in Old Town Plaza

1-G

Old Town Plaza
On the Camino Real

The center of Albuquerque's Old Town, the plaza dates from the early 18th century. San Felipe de Neri Church was established in 1706, but construction of the present structure was begun in 1793. In March 1862, General Henry H. Sibley and his Texas volunteers occupied Albuquerque and raised the Confederate flag here.

In 1706, following the re-conquest of the area, Don Francisco Cuervo y Valdez, 28th colonial governor, founded an administrative unit or villa which he named San Francisco De Alburquerque in honor of Don Francisco Fernandez de la Cueva Enriquez, Duque de Alburquerque, the 34th viceroy of New Spain, and resident in Mexico City. The viceroy, fearing the displeasure of King Philip V of Spain because the new villa had not been authorized by him, changed the name to San Felipe De Alburquerque, in honor of the king. The Anglo-American colonists later dropped the "r" in the second syllable.

The new villa was founded on the edge of meadows of the Rio Grande at a place where the river could be forded by ox carts and near good pasturage and timber. The original settlement consisted of 12 families who had come from Bernalillo. The original settlement was in what is now Old Town.

The plan of Hispanic settlements like Albuquerque, consisted of a church and buildings arranged around a plaza in a rectangular or square formation. This arrangement offered protection, a stockade against attacks by nomadic Indians or possibly against another rebellion on the part of the pueblos. The church in Albuquerque, San Felipe de Neri, was built on the north side of the plaza, where it still stands today, surrounded by a few public buildings and houses.

Thus, it is no accident that life in New Mexico reflects Spanish heritage to a greater extent than the English heritage characteristic of the eastern part of the country, since Spanish culture was dominant for a longer period of time. Many people of Hispanic descent can trace the New World history of their families back more than 300 years.

In Old Town Plaza
in Albuquerque

1-H

Tijeras Canyon

This pass between the Sandia and Manzano Mountains has been a natural route for travel between eastern New Mexico and the Rio Grande Valley since prehistoric times. Known as Canon de Carnue in the Spanish colonial period, it takes its present name from the village of Tijeras, Spanish for "scissors."

Genizaros served as military personnel, protecting colonists and Pueblo Indians from attacks by nomadic Indians, who had, by this time, acquired the horse and were thus a real threat. Some Genizaros were captive "barbarous Indians," some were Pueblo Indians, and some were low-class mestizos. As reward for their military service, Genizaros were given land and homes in barrios within Spanish settlements or were given land to form their own Hispanic communities.

The Genizaro communities were often strategically placed to protect Spanish colonial administrative centers. Thus the village of Carnue in Tijeras Canyon was a Genizaro community, guarding Albuquerque from Comanche raiders coming from the east. Belen was a Genizaro community guarding Albuquerque from the south. If such communities were successful and were not destroyed by raiders, the population lived a "Hispanicized" way of life and considered themselves Spanish.

On Hwy NM 337-N
Just West of Tijeras MM 7.5

1-I

Catron County

Catron County was named for New Mexico's first United States Senator and famous Santa Fe Attorney, Thomas B. Catron. The largest county in New Mexico, it was created February 25, 1921.

County Seat: Reserve.
Communities: Luna, Quemado, Datil
Glenwood, Mogollon.

6,898 Square Miles

Very Large Array

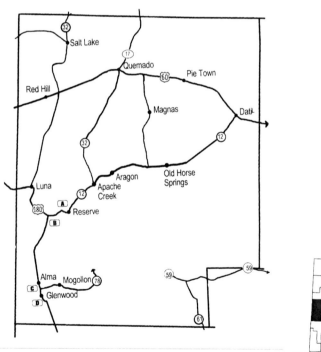

Reserve

Located in the San Francisco Valley, Reserve was named Upper San Francisco Plaza by its original Hispanic settlers in 1874. The name was later changed to Reserve in recognition of the U.S. Forest Service headquarters located here. Apaches made frequent attacks on the community, which lay within Apache hunting lands. Population 600. Elevation 5,765 feet.

Reserve is located in the heart of the Gila National Forest Service on the Arizona/New Mexico border. With over a half million acres of wild, rugged mountains, the Gila National Forest is the oldest wilderness area in the United States.

Reserve is the county seat of Catron County, the largest county and also the smallest population. There are Indian ruins, petroglyphs and historical old west sites to explore, as well as hiking, hunting, fishing and camping.

On February 25, 1921, Catron became a county. It was named after a famous attorney and Santa Fe political leader, Thomas B. Catron. Reserve has a population of about 650, and retains the true flavor of a western town.

Reserve Chamber of Commerce
P.O. BOX 415
Reserve, New Mexico 87830
Phone: (505)533-6116

NM hwy 12 in Reserve
MM 7.2

2-A

Wild Horse Mary
Rustling Hideout

Life in the wild west was never easy, nor safe. Women who were left on their own had an even harder time. They had very few choices when it came to making a living. Many became soiled doves, or ladies of the night.

A brave few sought a bit more excitement. Rustling cows was a dangerous, but highly profitable occupation. Capture a few head, alter the brand, then sell them. No one would be the wiser.

No one, except the owner whose cows were missing. Now he would be more than a little put out that his livelihood was being driven off in the night. So, he would hire guards and trackers to hunt down his missing livestock.

Woe to those who were found with stolen livestock. It was a good way to find a quick and painful death. It didn't matter if you were a man or a woman, either.

On Hwy 180 South of Reserve

2-B

Mogollon

The mountains and the town were named for Juan Ignacio Flores Mogollón, governor of New Mexico from 1712 to 1715. The name also is applied to the Pueblo Indians who abandoned the area in the early 1400s. These mountains were inhabited by Apaches until the late 19th century.

The Mogollon were the least densely populated of the major prehistoric peoples of the Southwest Tradition. Around 200 BC they expanded into the mountains of southeastern Arizona and southwestern New Mexico from the high plateaus of south-central New Mexico. Here they began creating multi-storied buildings as their pit houses became more complex.

They selected easily defensible home sites on promontories near their fields on steep slopes and intermountain valleys. Although they practiced rudimentary farming, their retention of age-old subsistence patterns, relying on native plants and animals, distinguished them from the other major southwestern cultural groups.

A branch of the Mogollon called the Mimbres thrived in southwestern New Mexico between 1000 and 1130 AD. They were famous for their ceramics, including magnificent painted ceremonial bowls adorned with geometric and pictorial designs.

Anthropologists believe that, sometime between 900 and 1100 AD, the Anasazi cultural dominance consumed much of the Mogollon culture, merging traits from both. Total abandonment of these areas, however, did not occur until about 1450. It is believed that this hybrid tradition contributed to the cultural background of the Hopi, Zuni and Acoma.

On US 180 South to Silver City
MM 47.1

2-C

The Catwalk

This steel causeway follows two pipelines which supplied water and water power to the old town of Graham where gold and silver ores were milled from nearby mines in the 1890s. The causeway clings to the sides of a sheer box canyon in Whitewater Creek and is accessible by a foot trail from the Whitewater picnic ground.

Once a hideout for Indians and desperados, Whitewater Canyon was the entrance to a rich gold and silver mine discovered around 1889. In 1893, miners built a four-inch metal pipeline, reaching three miles up into the canyon to supply water for the operation of the mill's electric generators. It also furnished water to the 200 townspeople.

Four years later, an 18-inch pipeline was built parallel to run an even larger generator. As washouts and leaks demanded repairs, the repairmen called it the "catwalk." In 1935–36, the Civilian Conservation Corps built the original Catwalk Trail, constructed entirely of wood. The mines were worked until 1942.

In 1962, falling under the Forest Service's jurisdiction, the catwalk was built with the present day steel. It was designated a national recreation trail in December of 1978. The day after it received it's designation, it was wiped out in a flood. The national designation provided funds for the repairs.

NM 180 Just South of Glenwood
MM 50

2-D

Chavez County

Chavez was created in 1889 and named for Col. Jose Francisco Chavez, a native of Bernalillo and delegate to Congress.

County Seat: Roswell
Communities: Lake Arther, Hagerman
Dexter, Mesa, Elkins

6,095 Square Miles

Bottomless Lakes State Park

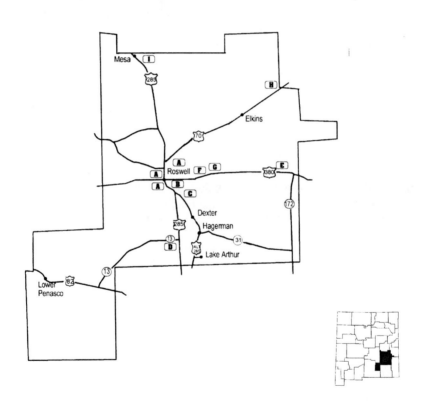

Roswell

Roswell was a watering place for the Pecos Valley cattle drives of the 1870's and 1880's. It was incorporated in 1891 and is seat of Chaves County, named for Col. J. Francisco Chaves, Civil War soldier and delegate to the U.S. Congress from the Territory of New Mexico. In the 1930's, Dr. Robert Goddard conducted experiments in liquid fuel rocket flights here. Population 50,000. Elevation 3,612 feet.

It was the cattle industry that originally sired settlement in the Pecos Valley when John S. Chisum founded the Jinglebob Ranch in 1878. Chisum established his headquarters on the now-dry South Spring River, six miles from the tiny trading post of Rio Hondo, soon to be renamed Roswell.

Captain Joseph C. Lea, an early settler and merchant, first platted Roswell in 1885, and brought stability to the area after the trials of the Lincoln County War.

The Chavez County seat, and the fourth largest city in the state, the city lies on the west edge of the Llano Estacado in the rich and fertile Pecos Valley. What started as a rowdy little cowtown in the 1800s, where cowboys drove their cattle on the Chisum Trail, Roswell has grown into an agricultural center with cotton, alfalfa, chile, pecans, sheep and cattle production, and is the largest mozzarella cheese manufacturing plant in the nation using 4 million pounds of milk daily.

The town was named for Roswell Smith, the father of a professional gambler, and is the home of the new Mexico Military Institute. Dr. Robert H. Goddard, the father of space exploration, made his rocket experiments in the city between 1930-41, and it was also near Roswell that a supposed Unidentified Flying Object crashed in 1947.

Roswell Chamber of Commerce
131 West 2nd
P.O. Drawer 70
Roswell, NM 88202-0070
505-623-5695

{1} Hwy 285 South of Roswell
    MM 105.6
{2} South 285 MM 105.6   {3}US 285 S. Jct W/US 70   **3-A**
North of Brasher Intersection   MM 115.5

Roswell Pioneer Plaza

This plaza incorporates two of downtown Roswell's most historic buildings. East of this location is the Chavez County Courthouse, built in 1911. It is one of the best surviving examples of courthouses built in the Beaux Arts Revival "monumental civic style" architecture. The nearby Conoco service station was built in the 1920's. It is one of the few remaining architecturally intact gasoline stations from this early period of New Mexico's transportation history.

Roswell's Pioneer Plaza is dedicated to those who helped create this impressive city, including John S. Chisum, rancher and businessman who created a great cattle empire in the Pecos Valley. His ranch headquarters was located near where Roswell was platted out. His legend lives on when a statue of him on horseback was installed in the Plaza in the late 1990's.

Another Pioneer of Roswell was Robert Hutchings Goddard. He had a dream of exploring Mars which was fueled, as a youngster, by a serialized version of H.G. Wells' War of the Worlds. His early experiments caught the eye of Charles Lindbergh. Lindbergh arranged for funding and made it possible for Goddard to work on rocketry full time and on a much larger scale. In need of open spaces and good year round weather, he came to Roswell. It was a place where they would neither bother anyone nor would anyone bother them.

In the Summer of 1930, the Goddards and a crew of four arrived on a small farm on the edge of Roswell. They built a launch tower about 10 miles outside of town. Over the next 12 years, Goddard and his crew made major strides in rocket propulsion as well as the practical matters of launch control, stabilization, tracking, and recovery.

Before he could finish his work, a World War II contract required him to return to Annapolis, Maryland where he died. After the war, he was posthumously awarded a Congressional Medal and several patents for his work.

Roswell Museum & Art Center
Robert H. Goddard Planetarium
100 W. 11' St.
Roswell, NM 88202
Phone #624-6744.

Hwy 285 Roswell

3-B

32

Chisum's South Spring Ranch

In 1875, John S. Chisum, the "Cattle King of the Pecos," made this the headquarters of a cattle ranching empire which extended for 150 miles along the Pecos River. In that year, 80,000 cattle bore his famous Jinglebob earmark. After Chisum's death, the ranch was acquired by J.J. Hagerman.

After earning enough capital taking cattle to the markets in Arizona, John S. Chisum purchased South Spring Ranch three miles South of Roswell. It consisted of 40 acres, a now dry South Spring and a large adobe house. He tore down the old adobe house and built an adobe/frame house with four rooms on each side of an open hallway. Underneath the hall was an acequia which helped to keep the house cool during the hot summer.

There were porches on both the front and the back of the house so he could sit in the shade at any hour of the day. He also built a separate room at the back of the house so that his cowboys could have their dances, "and won't cut up my Axminster carpets with their boots."

John Wayne, legendary actor, starred in a movie about the life of John S. Chisum. The movie, "Chisum". Filmed in 1970, and directed by Andrew V. McLaglen, the movie is a tribute to John S. Chisum's involvement with the Lincoln County War.

Hwy 285
South of Roswell

3-C

Civilian Conservation Corps
Lake Arthur Campsite

The Civilian Conservation Corps was established to provide employment for the nation's young men during the Great Depression of the 1930's. More than 50,000 were enrolled in the program in New Mexico between 1933 and 1942. CCC enrollees at the Lake Arthur camp improved grazing lands, and developed water sources for livestock and wildlife.

Established in 1933 by President Franklin Delano Roosevelt, the Civilian Conservation Corps was created for the conservation of the country's natural resources and to provide employment for young men during the Great Depression. More commonly known as CCC, it helped about 3 million unemployed and unmarried men between the ages of 17 and 23 to have work.

Across the nation, these men lived in camps and worked on projects including reforestation, construction of fire-observation towers, laying of telephone lines, and development of state parks.

The enrollees to the camp received clothing, food, a place to sleep, job training and $30 per month in wages. One of the agreements the men had to make was to send at least $22 of his wages home every month.

The program was concuded in 1942, but had managed to improve the morale, health and education of millions of young men and their families.

US 285   MM 80
South of Artesia

3-D

34

Llano Estacado

Nomadic Indians and countless buffalo herds dominated this vast plain when the Vasquez de Coronado expedition explored it in 1541. Later it was the focus of Comanchero activity, and in the 19th century it became a center for cattle ranching. The name LLANO ESTACADO, or stockaded plains, refers to the fortress like appearance of its escarpment.

When the Rocky Mountains were forming, sediments collected here, forming this amazingly huge, and relatively flat mesa. Water eroded deep arroyos and canyons and left this level surface.

When viewed from space, this flat land is like a huge table. It was covered with natural grasses and the pioneers had to follow stakes to navigate the "sea of grass".

The test on these two markers was misinterpreted. Llano Estacado does not refer to the escarpments, but to the stakes themselves.

On US 380 East of Roswell
MM 201.3

3-E

Goodnight-Loving Trail

This famous old cattle trail, running 2000 miles from Texas to Wyoming was blazed in 1866 by Charles Goodnight and Oliver Loving. In New Mexico, the trail followed the Pecos River north to Fort Sumner, where the government needed beef to feed the Navajos at the Bosque Redondo Reservation.

Oliver Loving was born in frontier Kentucky in 1812. He spent his entire life living dangerously and has been called "The Dean of Texas Trail Drives". He earned the title through his fearless drives of large longhorn herds through territory where no others had gone before.

Former Texas Ranger, Col. Charles Goodnight began gathering a herd in 1866 to take on the trail. He knew that "whole of Texas would start north for the market" that year, making a jam on those routes headed North. As an alternative, he came up with a daring plan to move his herd south then west below the main Comanche territory, then across the Pecos and into New Mexico before heading to the gold fields of Denver.

As Goodnight was putting his outfit together, he happened upon Oliver Loving's Camp. The two discussed the plan. Loving told Goodnight about the horrors, hazards, and problems he would face. Goodnight, still determined to make the journey, agreed to let Loving go with him.

A handshake between two honorable men, more valuable than any paper contract, made the two men partners. They left the Texas Frontier on June 6th, 1866, with 2000 head of mixed cattle and 18 armed men to blaze a trail that went down into history as the Goodnight-Loving Trail, a very profitable venture.

US 380 MM 167
West of Roswell

3-F

Bottomless Lakes State Park

Bordered by high red bluffs, the seven small lakes at the park were formed when circulating later dissolved gypsum and salt deposits into underlying rock formations creating a network of underground cavities. The roofs of some of those caverns collapsed under their own weight, and the resulting sink holes filled with water. Some of the lakes are stocked with trout and swimming is permitted in Lea Lake. There are also hiking trails, visitor center displays and skin diving opportunities.

More than a hundred years ago, when the cowboys drove their cattle along the nearby Goodnight-Loving Trail, the cowboys attempted to find out how deep these lakes were. They would tie rocks to their lariats and slowly let out the length as the rocks sank into the greenish blue color.

As one lariate would end, another would be tied on and still the bottom was never found. The reason was not because the lakes are bottomless, but because the lariats were swept aside by underwater currents. The deepest of the lakes is about 90 feet and each of these small lakes was formed when circulating underground water dissolved salt and gypsum deposits to form underground caverns. As the roofs of the caverns collapsed, the formed sinkholes filled with water.

Only one of the lakes, Lea Lake, is large enough to support swimming and other water recreational activities.

There is a visitors' center, and nature trails, overnight campsites and drinking water.

Bottomless Lakes State Park
HC 12, Box 1200
Roswell, NM 88201
505-624-6058

US 380 West of Roswell
MM 165

3-G

Pecos Valley

Plains bordering east side of Pecos Valley. Caprock escarpment, west edge of Llano Estcado, staked Plains, 15 miles to northeast on horizon. Capitan Mountains and Sierra Blanca on western skyline are east edge of basin and range province. Railroad "Mountain" low east-west ridge 5 miles to south is igneous dike. Elevation 4,110 feet.

The rich plentiful grassland of the Llano Estacado beckoned many people to come west and homestead in the early years of the 20th century. The nearby small town of Elida was a trading center for ranchers before Portales was settled. Its Post Office was established in 1902 and serves this small, close knit community today.

Kenna was first established in 1902–1906. It changed its name to Urton in 1906–1907, then back to Kenna in 1907. W.G. and George Urton, ranchers from Missouri, were the reason for the brief name change. It was known as Kenna's Camp prior to building the railroad, and the stages found this a convenient stop to transfer mail and passengers. The Vice-president of the railroad was named E.D. Kenna and it's logical that this is the reason the name was changed back to Kenna.

Ranching is still the major economic base for these two small communities. The Pecos River Valley, fertile and with the necessary water to produce crops, is just a too far to try to irrigate from here. This arid area is more suitable to cattle than sheep.

US 70 North MM 390
30 Miles from Clovis

3-H

Mesa and Pecos Valley

Pecos Valley section of Great Plains province stretches westward to foothills of Capitan, Jicarilla, and Gallinas Mountains. Southern High Plains, 50 miles to the east, capped by water-bearing Ogalalla Formations: Poquita Mesa just to the east is remnant. Nearby depressions are sinkholes in porous Permian limestones. Elevation 4,500 feet.

The Pecos River flows over 900 miles through eastern New Mexico and Western Texas. Its watershed covers nearly 40,000 square miles by the time it drains into the Rio Grande River. The river has cut a narrow canyon over 1,000 feet deep in the final 125 miles of its travel.

The Ogallala Formations to the east are a part of the huge Ogallala Aquifer (a natural underground reservoir of water) which stretches from New Mexico and Texas northward through Oklahoma, Colorado, Kansas, Nebraska and Wyoming.

The word Mesa comes from the Spanish language and means "table". The flat top look to the formation reminded early explorers of a table. Near the top of the Mesa is a layer of harder rock which acts as a protective cap for the softer, erodible layers beneath it.

The sinkholes nearby are formed by the slow erosion of the underlying Permian limestone. As the limestone is disolved by rain water flowing underground, the surface slowly collapses into the void left behind.

The Permian limestone of the region was formed 230 to 280 million years ago as massive reef barriers grow around seamounts and volcanic islands during the time of the Pangaea Supercontinent. The limestone formations stretch from eastern New Mexico into western Texas.

Hwy 285 North
Messa Rest Area MM 150

3-I

Cibola County

Inscription Rock

Named for the Cibola National Forest, Cibola County is New Mexico's newest county, created in 1981.

County Seat:: Grants
Communities: Milan, Fenton Lake,
                         Laguna, Seboyeta

4,180 Square Miles

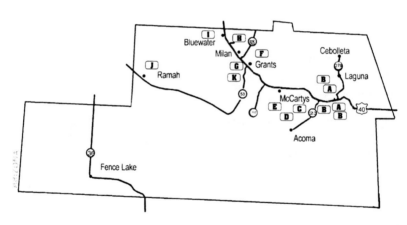

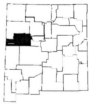

San Jose De La Laguna Mission

The picturesque mission church of San José de la Laguna was built around 1706 by Fray Antonio Miranda and shows the single-aisle floor plan commonly used in pueblo churches. It has been repaired many times, and acquired its distinctive white stucco exterior in 1977.

Built by pueblo workers under the direction of Fray Antonio Miranda in 1706, the church has a single aisle with two rows of seats from either side of the aisle. This was a common way to build the missions.

The church contains a beautiful and well-preserved altar screen made between 1800 and 1808 by a folk artist known only as the "Laguna santero." The interior walls are mud-plastered and white-washed, and the floor is made of packed earth. The handsome wooden ceiling is laid in a herringbone pattern.

Built within the spectacular views and natural beauty of the Laguna Pueblo area, the San Jose de Laguna Mission is the pueblo's centerpiece. This church, however, is wonderfully preserved.

I-40 West of Albuquerque At Laguna Pueblo
MM 114.5

I-40 East Bound
MM 113.5

4-A

Pueblo of Laguna

Keresan-speaking refugees from Santo Domingo, Ácoma, Cochití, and other pueblos founded Laguna after the Pueblo Revolt of 1680 and the Spanish reconquest of 1692. Named by the Spaniards for a marshy lake to the west, the pueblo still occupies its original hilltop site today.

Laguna is the largest keresan speaking pueblo with around 8,000 members. They prize thinking above all other attributes and value intellectual activity and education. The Pueblo conducts a scholarship program insuring advance study for many of the young people, making them among the best educated of all of New Mexico's pueblos.

The pueblo comprises six major villages, Laguna, Paguate, Encinal, Mesita, Seama, Paraje, scattered over a wide area. The discovery of one of the world's richest uranium fields was located on the reservation. Many of the men became miners. Livestock grazing has been a more traditional occupation, and traditional crafting of pottery has been re-established recently.

Visitors to the Laguna community will enjoy Casa Blanca Commercial Center. Located just off I-40, it offers a large supermarket and a number of shops where the handicrafts of the pueblo may be purchased.

Pueblo of Laguna
PO Box 194
Laguna Pueblo, NM 87026
Tel (505) 552-6654

I-40 West Bound
MM 114.5

I-40 East Bound
MM 113.5

I-40 East Bound
MM 102.2

4-B

Pueblo of Acoma

Built atop a great mesa for defensive purposes, Ácoma has been continuously occupied since the 13th century. A dramatic battle between the Ácomas and Oñate's forces occurred here in 1599. The mission church of San Esteban was built between 1629 and 1641, and today looks much as described by Fray Francisco Atanasio Domínguez in 1776.

Known as "Sky City," the Pueblo of Acoma is situated on a 367-foot-high sandstone rock mesa. It is considered to be one of the oldest inhabited villages in the United States. There are over 400 houses on the mesa, but only a few are inhabited today.

Acoma was nearly destroyed when Governor Juan de Oñate sent 70 of his men to retaliate for the killing of 13 Spanish soldiers by the Acomas when the soldiers tried to steal grain from the pueblo storehouses in 1598. As a restitution of peace, the San Esteban del Rey Mission was built in 1629 and completed in 1640 under the guidance of Friar Juan Ramirez.

The Acomas are well known for their thin-walled pottery which can be seen on display at the Sky City Visitor Center. Both the mission and the pueblo have been designated as Registered National Historical Landmarks.

Sky City Visitor Center
P.O. Box 309
Acoma, NM 87034
Tel: (505)470-0181

I-40 East Bound
MM 102.2

4-C

Pueblo Revolt Tricentennial

The western pueblos of Ácoma and Zuñi took part in the revolt against Spanish rule which broke out on August 10, 1680. During the 1690's refugees from the Río Grande pueblos, escaping from reconquest of their lands, joined with local Keresans to form the Pueblo of Laguna.

Popé was a religious leader from San Juan Pueblo in present-day New Mexico. He organized and led the most successful Indian uprising in the history of the American West.

Provoked by a Spanish crackdown on native religion in 1675, Popé soon began conferring with other disaffected Pueblo leaders, some with Apache ties. They discussed the possibility of a large scale revolt against the Spanish.

Popé offered a vision to the Pueblos, stressing the complete expulsion of the Spanish military and religious authority and a return of Pueblo deities. Popé launched his revolt early in August 1680. He achieved stunning success due to the Pueblos vastly superior numbers. There were more than 8,000 warriors against fewer than 200 armed colonists. Despite language differences and distance, the Pueblos attacked everywhere at once, killing 21 Franciscan friars and more than 400 Spanish colonists.

When Don Diego de Vargas re-conquered New Mexico for Spain in 1692, it did not mean a return to the days before the uprising. Popé's revolt had permanently weakened the political power of the Franciscans. It was after his death that an alliance was made between the Pueblos and the Spanish. Though he would have disagreed with the alliance, he created the conditions for a new culture to emerge in the American Southwest, a blend of Indian and European influences which retains its distinctive character even today.

I-40 East Bound
MM 102.2

4-D

Cebolleta

In 1749 a Navajo mission was established at Cebolleta, and by 1804, Albuquerque area stockmen had built a fortified town for themselves. During the resulting warfare, the Spanish settlers used Los Portales Cave as a refuge. The cave was later converted to a shrine with an altar carved from the living rock.

Fray Alonzo Benavides made an unsuccessful attempt in 1630 to Christianize the Navajos. Benavides found "These of Navajo are very great farmers, for that is what Navajo signifies—great planted fields."

In 1746, Padre Menchero induced several hundred Navajos to settle at Cebolleta, but the Navajos returned to their homes and their lifestyle.

In 1749, Padre Menchero again made another attempt. He re-established the Cebolleta mission as well as a second one at Encinal, but on June 24, 1750, the Indians abandoned the settlements to return to their wilderness.

Lava Beds

This is the narrowest stretch of lava flow that extends almost 25 miles to the southwest where it originated about 1,000 years ago from a volcanic vent. Here the flow fills an old river valley where numerous dry and water-filled pockets are associated with pressure ridges and areas of collapsed lava tubes.

El Malpais National Monument is set within the lava beds produced from eruptions of several volcanoes up until about 800 years ago. Since then, nature has slowly covered them with scattered trees and bushes. The patterns of the molten lava are still easy to recognize, from large flows several feet high to small ripples at the edge of the lava course.

Other parts of the lava lie on land administered by the BLM and some smaller sections are in private ownership. The BLM land contains several lava caves. These caves are formed when a solidified rock crust formed around still-flowing lava. The hot lava later drained away, leaving an empty tunnel.

In sharp contrast, some of the tunnels left by the flowing lava have had water seep into them over the years. The temperature in some of the caves averages about 31 degrees. The water has slowly frozen in huge green layers over the years. An arctic algae has grown giving the ice it's green tint.

The land of Fire and Ice, contrasts that make this well worth a stop.

I-40 West of Laguna
(Marker Missing)

4-F

Grants

Located just north of the great lava bed known as the malpais, Grants began as a coaling station for the Santa Fe Railroad. Around 1880 it was known as Grant's Camp, after the Canadian bridge contractor Angus A. Grant. In 1950, the area's vast uranium deposits were discovered. Population 11,451. Elevation 6,500 feet.

For 220 million years, this area has been hosted a variety of travelers, and many of them were not human. Dinosaurs once roamed the area. Members of the prehistoric Anasazi culture built great settlements north of Grants. As recently as 2000 years ago, the volcanoes that formed the great lava beds were active, spewing rivers of fire that consumed early pueblo dwellers' fields.

In the late 1800's, homesteaders and settlers brought sheep and cattle. Grass for grazing and water were abundant. Logging camps started in the nearby Zuni Mountains.

Three brothers, Angus, Lewis, and John Grant were contracted to build the railroad through this vast area. Base Camps were established during the work westward. First, the area became known as Grant's Camp, then Grant's Station, and finally, just Grants.

Uranium was discovered in the area, and Grants once again "boomed". Mining became an important way of life, providing economic and population growth.

Grants Chamber of Commerce
P.O. Box 297
Grants NM 87020
505-287-4802

Cibola County
I-40 Exit 85 on Santa Fe Blvd
In Grants MM 85.5

4-G

Mount Taylor

One of the great volcanic cones of the Colorado Plateau, Mount Taylor rises to an elevation of 11,301 feet and last erupted some 2 million years ago. Numerous fissure eruptions since that time and as recently as about 1,200 years ago have created lava flows that form malpais or badlands along portions of this route. Elevation here 6,550 feet.

Navajo legend tells the Dineh, or "People", had to pass through three different worlds before emerging into the present world—the Fourth World or Glittering World. So, the Holy People put four sacred mountains in four different directions: Mt. Blanca in the east, Mt. Taylor in the south, San Francisco Peaks in the west, and Mt. Hesperus in the north, thus creating the boundaries of Navajoland. Centuries ago, the Navajo people were taught by the Holy People to live in harmony with Mother Earth and how to conduct their many activities of everyday life. The Dineh believe there are two classes of beings: the Earth People and the Holy People. The earth People are ordinary mortals, while the Holy People are spiritual beings that cannot be seen. Holy People are believed to aid or harm Earth People.

The Navajo people are very dynamic and creative people who strongly believe in the power of the mind to think and create; finding expression in the myriad symbolic creations of the Navajo language, art and ritual ceremonies.

The Navajo language embodies a high prevalence of humor in day to day conversation. Humor transforms difficult and frustrating circumstances into bearable and even pleasant situations. The strong emphasis and value Navajos place on humor is evidenced in the First Laugh rite. The first time a Navajo child laughs out loud is a time for honor and celebration.

Aside from being the mother tongue of the Navajo Nation, the Navajo language also has played a highly significant role in helping the entire nation. During World War II, the Navajo language was used as a code to confuse the enemy. Navajo bravery and patriotism is unequaled. Navajos were inducted and trained in the U.S. Marine Corps to become "code talkers" on the front-line. Shrouded in secrecy at the time, these men are known today as the famed Navajo Code Talkers, proved to be the only code that could not be broken during World War II. Although not all tribal members speak the language fluently, most Navajos have a deep respect for it.

I-40 West of Grants
Marker Missing

4-H

Bluewater Village

This community was founded in 1894 on the site of an earlier homestead and stage coach stop. Irrigation, from Bluewater Lake and its proximity to the railroad and Route 66, allowed development of extensive agricultural fields which earned Bluewater the title, "Carrot Capital of the World." The region became known as the "Uranium Capital of the World" after uranium was discovered nearby in 1950.

Nearby Bluewater Lake State Park is set within rolling hills studded with piñon and juniper trees. The lake is stocked with trout and catfish, offering boating, water-skiing and camping, as well as ice fishing during the winter.

Bird watching is a must at the lake with at least 68 different species of birds calling the park home.

Located on the north flank of the Zuni Mountains in the Las Tusas Basin, the reservoir is in a valley carved from shale and limestone. Hunting for fossils among the limestone is another attraction. There are snails and brachiopod fossils to be found.

The lake has 1,200 surface acres set in a 3,000 acre park. The elevation is 7,400 feet and it reaches an average of 86 degrees during the heat of summer.

Bluewater Lake State Park
P.O. Box 3419
Prewitt, NM 87045
505-876-2391

I-40 West of Grants, Exit 72
MM 72

4-I

El Morro National Monument

Until it was by-passed by the railroad in the 1880s, its waterhole made El Morro an important stop for travelers in the Ácoma-Zuñi region. Numerous inscriptions carved in the sandstone date from the prehistoric, Spanish, Mexican, and Territorial periods in New Mexico's history. An important example is Oñate's inscription, carved in 1605.

The soft sandstone rock is about 200 ft high. One of the earliest inscriptions was that made in 1605 by Juan De Onate, colonizer and Spanish governor of New Mexico.

Elsewhere on the rock are Native American symbols and pictures carved into the rock. The ruins of a prehistoric pueblo are on top of the rock.

There is a visitor's center with archeological objects.

El Morro National Monument
Route 2, Box 143
Ramah, NM 87321-9603
505-783-4226

Hwy 602, then East On US 53
MM 44.9

4-J

San Rafael

San Rafael, formerly known as El Gallo, is located at a spring near the Malpais, the great lava flow to the east. The area was visited by members of Vásquez de Coronado's expedition in 1540. In 1862, it was selected as the original site of Fort Wingate, focus of the campaign against the Navajos.

After repeated Navajo attacks on ranches and settlements, the Army sent Christopher "Kit" Carson to end the attacks once and for all. Carson crossed the Navajo's traditional homeland, burning homes and crops, killing livestock. He would send those who surrendered to him, or those who he captured to a reservation established at Fort Sumner, New Mexico.

After several seasons, the once proud people turned themselves in. Life on the reservation was anything but peaceful. To avoid starving and freezing, the Navajos were often forced to leave the reservation seeking food and fuel. Parties went over 25 miles, trying to avoid Mexicans, Utes and others wanting slave labor.

Finally, peace treaties were signed and the Navajo were allowed to return to a large reservation in New Mexico and Arizona. This often led to conflict with the Hopi who claimed the same land. Less than 2000 members made it back to the reservation alive.

West of Grants Exit 81 on NM 53
MM 83.1

4-K

Colfax County

Senator & Mrs Dorsey

Colfax County has 4 communities which have been the County seat during its long colorful history.

County Seat: Raton
Communities: Angel Fire, Eagle Nest,
              Cimarron, Raton,
              Springer

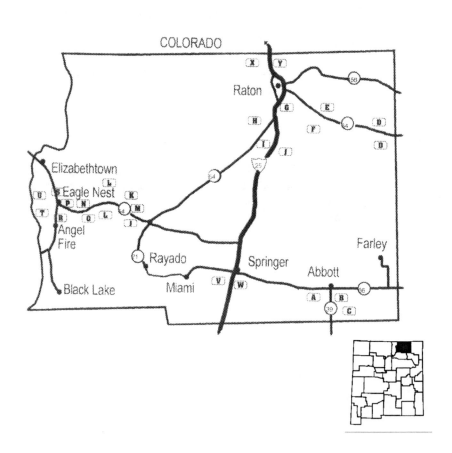

Point of Rocks

Point of Rocks was a major landmark on the Santa Fe Trail. Located in Jicarilla Apache country, it was near here that the party of Santa Fe merchant J.W. White was attacked in 1849. Kit Carson was a member of the military party organized to rescue White's wife and daughter.

Raids were the way of life for many in the old west. The world here was survival of the fittest. One who answered the challenge of the west was Christopher Houston "Kit" Carson. Born the 9th child of 14 on Christmas Eve 1809, Carson left home at age 15 to travel to New Mexico with a wagon train.

When he was 19, he was hired for a fur trapping expedition to California. In spite of his small stature, 5'6", he soon proved himself able and courageous. Like other white trappers, Carson traveled and lived extensively among Indians, learning their ways and being accepted by them. His first two wives were Arapaho and Cheyenne. One of his wives had his daughter in 1836, but the wife died shortly thereafter.

In 1842 Carson met John C. Fremont and over the next several years would guide Fremont to Oregon, California, and through much of the Central Rocky Mountains and the Great Basin. Fremont's widely-read reports of his expeditions made Kit Carson a national hero, presented in popular fiction as a rugged mountain man capable of superhuman feats.

On NM 56
MM 23.7

5-A

The Dorsey Manor

Built by controversial Arkansas Senator Stephen W. Dorsey in the late 1870's and early 1880's this part log and part stone mansion was once a center of social life in the southwest. Since its completion, it has been a unique architectural feature in New Mexico

Just off the Santa Fe Trail in Colfax County lies a 36 room 10,000 square foot log and masonry home. This is part of the legacy left by US Senator Stephen W. Dorsey. His mark has been left on much of Northeastern New Mexico.

Inside the mansion you'll find paintings from Paris, Dorsey's prized stuffed hunting trophies, and a variety of curiosities on display from his sporting lodge.

Built during the late 1880's and 1890's, it was a focal point for social life in Northern New Mexico and a gathering point for some of the United States most powerful men. Today, it sits on expansive grasslands, a forlorn reminder of a vast empire long gone.

Also of interest are the ruins of the smoke house and greenhouse. The green house is thought to be the first one built in the state of New Mexico.

Daily tours of the mansion are available, weather permitting. Call in advance for road conditions and reservations.

(505) 375-2222

on US 56
MM 23.7

5-B

View of the Rockies

Reaching altitudes of more than 13,000 feet, well watered, and forested, the Rocky Mountains are hosts to numerous recreational activities including skiing, fishing, hunting, and camping. To the north can be seen numerous volcanic peaks that lie east of the Rocky Mountains in both Colorado and New Mexico. Elevation here is 6,300 feet.

Treeless grasslands of the High Plains cover the eastern one-third of New Mexico and stretch eastward into the mid-continent. Surface water from the mountains beyond and underground aquifers permit ranching as the principal economic activity. Carbon dioxide gas, a geologic resource, has been discovered and developed in the subsurface.

More than a half billion years ago in the Precambrian era, the core of the Rocky Mountains was formed in ancient ranges and later leveled by erosion. At the close of the Mesozoic era, during the Cretaceous Period more than 75 million years ago, the growth of the Rockies began. Perhaps the best way to describe what happened is to place your hands on a table cloth a few inches apart. Now slide your hands together. The wrinkles formed between your hands would represent the Rocky Mountains.

Through the years, streams and rivers cut canyons and deep gorges through the ranges. During the last Ice Age, snows accumulated on the mountains. Glaciers formed and moved down the valleys, further eroding the mountains. The sculpting of the Rockies by rain, wind, and ice continues today.

Rugged and massive, the Rocky Mountains form a nearly continuous mountain chain in the western part of the North America Continent. Along the crest of the Rockies is the Continental Divide, which separates streams that drain to the east from those that flow to the west.

US 56
MM 23.7

5-C

Capulin Volcano National Monument

An outstanding example of an extinct volcano cinder cone, Capulin Mountain was formed as early as 10,000 years ago. In cinder cones, lava pours from cracks in the base rather than over the top. Capulin itself was the escape hatch for gases that blew lava fragments into the air where they solidified and landed red hot on the cone.

Capulin Volcano, a nearly perfectly-shaped cinder cone, stands more than 1200 feet above the surrounding High Plains of Northeastern New Mexico. The volcano is long extinct, and today the forested slopes provide habitat for mule deer, turkey, black bear and other wildlife. Abundant displays of wild flowers bloom on the mountain each summer.

A two-mile paved road spiraling to the volcano rim makes Capulin volcano one of the most accessible volcanoes in the world. Trails leading around the rim and to the bottom of the crater, allow a rare opportunity to easily explore a volcano.

Capulin Volcano National Monument
P.O. Box 40
Capulin, New Mexico 88414
(505) 278-2201

Capulin Volcano National Monument was established in 1916 to preserve this striking example of a volcanic cinder cone.

Interstate 25 North Bound Lane
Mile Marker 360.4

5-D

Rocky Mountains

The Sangre de Cristo ranges of the Southern Rocky Mountains visible here include the Spanish Peaks in Colorado, and the Culebra and Cimarron Ranges in New Mexico. Reaching altitudes of more than 13,000 feet, the well watered and forested mountains offer numerous recreational activities including skiing, hiking, fishing and climbing.

More than a half billion years ago in the Precambrian era, the core of the Rocky Mountains was formed in ancient ranges and later leveled by erosion. At the close of the Mesozoic era, during the Cretaceous Period more than 75 million years ago, the growth of the Rockies began. Perhaps the best way to describe what happened is to place your hands on a table cloth a few inches apart. Now slide your hands together. The wrinkles formed between your hands would represent the Rocky Mountains.

Through the years, streams and rivers cut canyons and deep gorges through the ranges. During the Ice Age snows accumulated on the mountains. Glaciers formed and moved down the valleys, further eroding the mountains. The sculpting of the Rockies by rain, wind, and ice continues today.

Rugged and massive, the Rocky Mountains form a nearly continuous mountain chain in the western part of the North America Continent. Along the crest of the Rockies is the Continental Divide, which separates streams that drain to the east from those that flow to the west.

An outdoor enthusiasts' paradise, the Rockies have majestic views, challenging cliffs for climbers, and wildlife galore. Winter brings challenging winter sports at many of the local ski areas developed throughout the mountains.

US 64/
MM 36445

5-E

Raton

Once the Willow Springs freight stop on the Santa Fe Trail, the town of Raton developed from A.T.& S.F. repair shops established when the railroad crossed Raton Pass in 1879. Valuable coal deposits attracted early settlers. Nearby Clifton House was a stagecoach stop until the Trail was abandoned after 1879. Population 8,225. Elevation 6,379 feet.

At the base of Raton Pass, just seven miles from the Colorado border lies Raton, the fourth county seat of Colfax County's history.

Raton was founded at the site of Willow Springs, a stop on the Santa Fe Trail. The original 320 acres for the Raton townsite was purchased from the Maxwell Land Grant in 1880. Raton quickly developed as a railroad, mining and ranching center for the northeast part of New Mexico territory and was a principal trading center of the area.

The community, nestled in the foothills of the Rocky Mountains, enjoys pleasant summers, colorful autumns and mild winters. Tourism and mining are major income producing activities for the county. People are drawn to a place where rolling prairies, rimrock mesas and alpine meadows come together. Location and accessibility are among Raton's strongest assets, along with being centered between the major metro areas of Denver, Albuquerque, and Amarillo.

During World War I, Raton's Seaburg European Hotel was the largest Hotel in New Mexico. It is now the location of the El Portal Hotel. The Mary and McCuistion School was first public high school in New Mexico founded in 1884.

Be sure and stop by the Tourist Information Center located on Clayton Highway to learn more about this strong community.

Raton Chamber and Economic Development Council
Tourist Information Center
100 Clayton Highway
P.O. Box 1211
Raton, NM 87740
800-638-6161   505-445-3689

US 64/87
MM 350.0

5-F

Sugarite Canyon State Park

This heavily wooded mountainous park, located on the Colorado-New Mexico border, was formerly the site of a thriving coal camp. There are two fishing lakes in the New Mexico portion of the canyon, and another lake lies just across the border in Colorado. Wild turkey and deer are plentiful in the park vicinity, and facilities include hiking trails and camping/picnicking sites. The colorful history of the canyon and region is described in the visitor's center.

Old buildings and rock foundations near the park entrance are the remains of Sugarite Coal Camp which operated between 1910 and 1941. At its peak, the camp had a population of close to 1,000 people, most of whom were European and Far Eastern immigrants. A scenic hike and interpretive trail through the area gives you a glimpse of life in the past.

Sugarite, from the Comanche word Chicorica, means "an abundance of birds", is in frontier country. From the stately columned caprock atop the canyon walls to the shimmering lake waters that grace the valley below, Sugarite Canyon State Park is a stunning testament to the beauty of the American West.

The park offers much more than a rich history. During spring and summer, wild flowers of every imaginable color, size and shape paint the landscape. Trails wind through grassland meadows, towering ponderosa pine forests, and gnarled oak groves, which are the home to wild turkey, deer, beaver, elk, cougar, bobcat, and bears. The park lakes are stocked with rainbow trout and hardy outdoor enthusiasts can try their luck at ice-fishing in the winter.

Sugarite Canyon State Park
HCR 63, Box 386
Raton, New Mexico 87740
(505) 445-5607
E-Mail sugarite@raton.com

NM 526
Jct 72

5-G

Clifton House Site

Three-quarters of a mile west of here at the Canadian River crossing was the popular overnight stage stop on the Old Santa Fe Trail. Clifton House was built in 1867 by rancher Tom Stockton, and materials were brought here from Dodge City. For years it served as headquarters for cattle roundups. After abandonment of the Santa Fe Trail in 1879, it fell into disuse and burned.

Skilled stagecoach drivers took danger and hardship in stride. "Wild Bill" Hickock, Wyatt Earp and Buffalo Bill Cody were just some to handle the reins on the overland routes of long ago. Driving a stagecoach, with 6 to 15 passengers, loaded with baggage, mail, and a strong box full of riches, brought dangers few could appreciate. Passengers would ride for upwards of 23 days to make it across the West.

One driver, Charlie Parkhurst, was one of the earliest and best of drivers. He drove for nearly 20 years. Twice he was held up. The first time, with no gun, he had to throw down the strong box. The second time, he was prepared. When he heard the command to "halt", he fired his shotgun, wounded the would be robber, and escaped.

Parkhurst was small, about 5'6", slim, wiry, and had alert grey eyes. He rarely smiled, and kept to himself, rarely volunteering information about himself. He died in a small cabin in California in 1879.

It was when his body was being prepared for burial that he became famous. It turns out that Charlie was a woman, and that she had had a child at some point in her life. When Charlie cast a ballot in an election on November 3, 1868, she became the first woman to vote—52 years before that right was guaranteed to women by the 19th Amendment.

10 Miles West of Raton
I-25 Rest Area on Hwy 64

5-H

Points of Interest

On most of the historical markers, there is text describing geological, historical, or other interesting facts about the area you are visiting. On the back of most of these signs are Points of Interest maps. These maps lead you to other Historical Markers in the area.

New Mexico has a rich and fascinating history. Its tri-cultural influence can be seen throughout the state. Whether you're taking a break from a long car ride, or exploring, the historical markers will give you a chance to explore and learn about this great state.

I-25
South Bound Lane
MM 434.4

5-I

Santa Fe Trail

William Becknell, the first Santa Fe Trail trader, entered Santa Fe in 1821 after Mexico became independent from Spain and opened its frontiers to foreign traders. The Mountain Branch over Raton Pass divided here. One fork turned west to Cimarron, then south and joined a more direct route to Rayado.

The difficulty of bringing caravans over rocky and mountainous Raton Pass kept most wagon traffic on the Cimarron Cutoff of the Santa Fe Trail until the 1840's. Afterwards, the Mountain Branch, which here approaches Raton Pass, became more popular with traders, immigrants, gold-seekers, and government supply trains.

William Becknell left Old Franklin, Missouri, on September 1, 1821. He headed west to trade with the Indians, but didn't have much luck. In New Mexico, he encountered Spanish dragoons. Instead of taking him prisoner for having entered Spanish Colonial Territory illegally, the soldiers urged him to bring his goods to Santa Fe.

He arrived there on November 16 and quickly sold all he had brought. Mexico had declared it's independence from Spain, and American traders were now welcome in Santa Fe.

Within a few weeks, Becknell had organized another expedition. He took several wagons crammed with $3,000 worth of trade goods. His profit in Santa Fe was 2,000 percent, and the Santa Fe Trail was born.

The Santa Fe Trail was the first of America's great pathways from the Mississippi River area to the West. It preceded the Oregon and California trails by more than two decades.

B I-25 Rest Area

5-J

Black Jack's Hideout

In Turkey Creek Canyon near here, the outlaw gang of Thomas "Black Jack" Ketchum had one of its hideouts. After a train robbery in July 1899, a posse surprised the gang at the hideout. The outlaws scattered after a bloody battle, and the Ketchum gang was broken up.

Sam Ketchum, Black Jack's brother, and other members of the gang held up the Colorado Southern on July 11, 1899. It was here that the posse caught up to them. Sam was wounded and captured. He died two weeks later in the penitentiary in Santa Fe.

Black Jack, not knowing the outcome of Sam's attempt on the train, tried single handedly to hold up the Colorado Southern Railroad, near Folsom. On August 16, 1899, the conductor managed to wound Black Jack and he was captured by the train tracks the next day.

Black Jack was hung on April 26, 1901. He was the only person known to be decapitated during a hanging in the United States. Only one other known case of decapitation occurred in England. He was one of the last outlaws to "swing". His grave is located in Clayton Cemetery, in Clayton, New Mexico.

US 64
In the Middle of Cimarron

5-K

Colfax County Wars

For twenty years after the 1869 sale of the Maxwell Land Grant, homesteaders, ranchers, and miners fought the new owners for control of this enormous region. The resulting murders and general breakdown of law and order led to the removal from office, in 1878, of Territorial Governor Samuel B. Axtell.

Five years before the start of the war, the Maxwell Land Grant had been sold to a group of speculators. The Grant, embracing some 1,714,746.93 acres, (2,679 square miles, larger than the state of Delaware) had many possibilities to line the pockets of the investors. Suggestions ranged from exploiting the gold mines, to lumber cutting, to land sales, and to obtaining a railroad line.

First on the agenda, however, was the removal of all the Indians and squatters who had moved onto private Grant land during the past 30 years. Grant officials, in league with a group of lawyers, politicians and businessmen, began making false allegations against locals. A Grant supported law was passed attaching Colfax to Taos County. This meant a 50 mile trip for the accused to attend court in Taos.

As people suffered from the cost of money and time, an outspoken Methodist preacher announced that he would do what he could to break up the Grant. In a very short time, his body was discovered in Cimarron Canyon.

His murder, along with two others, has never been solved. Eventually, the law attaching Colfax to Taos County was repealed and Governor Axtell's tenure of "corruption, fraud and murder" was replaced with the honest one of Governor Lew Wallace.

Peace came to Colfax County. The United States Circuit Court upheld the validity of the Grant, and the Supreme Court confirmed this ruling, making the Maxwell Land Grant one of the largest owned by private individuals ever.

US 64
I-25
MM 310.3

5-L

Cimarron

This village on the Mountain Branch of the Santa Fe Trail was settled around 1844. In 1857 it became the home of Lucien B. Maxwell, and headquarters for the famous Maxwell Land Grant of almost 2,000,000 acres. An agency for Utes and Jicarilla Apaches was located here from 1862 to 1876. Population 888. Elevation 6,427 feet.

Once the home of Jicarilla-Apache and Ute Indians, Cimarron is located on the mountain branch of the Santa Fe Trail. The pioneer spirit which gave rise to Cimarron brought famous and infamous people like Wyatt Earp, Annie Oakley, Buffalo Bill Cody, Frank and Jesse James.

Cimarron, which means wild or unruly, dates back to the early 1800's. The Mountain Branch of the Santa Fe Trail entered on the northeast corner of the plaza. Not only a stop for the trail, it was a hangout for traders, mountain men, and desperados.

Lucien Maxell, friend of Kit Carson, inherited much of the Maxell Land Grant from his father-in-law. What he didn't inherit of the nearly 2,000,000 acres, he managed to purchase over the next few years. He became the largest single landowner in the western hemisphere.

It was Maxwell that convinced Kit Carson to join him at Rayado. Maxwell built a large house and several smaller outbuildings with Carson adding a much smaller adobe hut to the complex. By 1857, Maxwell sold his interests in Rayado and moved his family to Cimarron where he was appointed Postmaster and Indian Agent. Though his house burned many years ago, the plaza still exists.

Cimarron Chamber of Commerce
104 North Lincoln Avenue
P.O. Box 604
Cimarron, NM 87714
(505) 376-2417
1-800-700-4298
chamber@cimarron.springercoop.com

On US 64
I-25
MM 310.3

5-M

Cimarron Canyon

You are now at the Great Plains-Rocky Mountain boundary. The Cimarron Range, one of the eastern most ranges of the Sangre De Cristo Mountains in this part of New Mexico. Elevation 6,800 feet.

The tall wall of cliffs is known as a palisade, and is a challenge to avid rock climbers. Here the Cimarron River cuts through the softer rock to form these magnificent Palisades. Known as the Cimarron Cutoff, the Santa Fe Trail cut through here on its way to Santa Fe.

US 64
MM 305.0

5-N

Philmont Scout Ranch

Oklahoma oilman Waite Phillips gave this 127,000 acre property to the Boys Scouts of America in 1938 and 1941. The first national Boy Scout Camp ever established. Philmont now hosts young men from all over the world. Kit Carson, Lucien B. Maxwell, and Dick Wootten were important in the history of the area.

Lucien B. Maxwell, the largest private landowner in the Western Hemisphere, sold over 1,700,000 acres, in 1870, to the English Land Company. After several court battles with squatters and others, the English Land Company sold it to a Dutch-based company who attempted several development schemes, but eventually sold the land in tracts for farms and ranches.

Oklahoma oilman, Waite Phillips, became interested in developing a ranch out of the old land grant in 1922. He eventually amassed over 300,000 acres of mountains and plains in a ranch he named Philmont.

The Philmont Ranch became a showplace with immense herds of Hereford cows and Corriedale sheep grazing its pastures. Phillips built a large Spanish Mediterranean home for his family at the headquarters, naming it Villa Philmont.

Waite Phillips believed in sharing his wealth with others. As a result, he offered 35,857 acres of his ranch to the Boy Scouts of America in 1938 to serve as a national wilderness camping area. The area was named Philturn (after Phillips and Good Turn) Rocky Mountain Scout Camp. After observing the enthusiastic response of the first Scout Campers, Phillips augmented his original gift in 1941. The addition included the Villa Philmont and the headquarters farming and ranching operations. He also endowed the Scouts with his 23-story Philtower Building in Tulsa, Oklahoma so that the costs for maintenance and development would not be entirely derived from camper fees.

Philmont is a working cattle ranch and was the first permanent camp for Boy Scouts to enjoy.

NM 21 at Jct 21
MM 1.0

5-O

Cimarron Canyon State Park

This high mountain park is part of a state wildlife area and is managed by the New Mexico State Park Division in cooperation with the New Mexico Department of Game and Fish. Trout fishing is excellent in the Cimarron River, and the park offers fine opportunities for backcountry hiking and wildlife viewing. The crenellated rock formations known as the Palisades is popular with rock climbers.

Cimarron Canyon State Park is inside the 33,116 acre Colin Neblett Wildlife Area. This is the largest wildlife area in the state of New Mexico.

The Cimarron river traverses the canyon past the sheer cliffs of the Palisades that dominate the park's scenery. Wildlife abounds here, elk, deer, bear, turkey, songbirds, and grouse call the park home.

It has a developed picnic site, and camping is allowed in the cool, high mountain park. There is excellent trout fishing and hiking, as well as rock climbing the crenelated granite formations with special use permits available from the park.

Cimarron Canyon State Park
P.O. Box 185
Eagle Nest, NM 87718
(505) 377-6271

US 64
MM 295.9

5-P

Palisades Sill

These spectacular cliffs are cut by the Cimarron River through ingeneous rock known as sill and composed of a rock type monzonite wich was emplaced some 40 million years ago as these southern Rocky Mountains were being uplifted.

Sill, being softer than the Granite of the palisades, allowed the river to cut away the magnificent towering palisades, or wall, of rock you see here.

Popular with rock climbers, the palisades offer a good challenge to all who seek to conquer them, or to those just wishing to enjoy their beauty.

Cimarron, meaning "wild, unruly", has been the setting for novels by Zane Grey, provided inspiration to many artists, and has inspired generations of young men coming to visit the nearby Philmont Boy Scout Ranch.

US 64
MM 293.9
Colfax County

5-R

Eagle Nest Lake

This is one of the finest rainbow trout waters in New Mexico. The lake is privately owned and a permit is required to fish. Water impounded in Eagle Nest Lake provides irrigation for a farming area 50 miles east of this point. The reservoir has a capacity of 78,800 acre feet and the altitude of 8,218 feet.

Once the home to Ute Indians, the Village of Eagle Nest got it's beginning with the discovery of gold in the 1860's. A collection of ramshakle buildings, it provided a homebase for those seeking gold. Originally known as Therma, this mountain hideaway has a bawdy past and today is paradise for summer visitors.

It wasn't until around 1919 that it became a viable place for homesteading. John Springer, a local rancher, built a damn at the end of Cimarron Canyon. Within a year of winter and spring runoff, the dam provided a permanent source of water. From then on, ranching and farming in the area grew in importance.

At 8,300 feet in elevation, Eagle Nest Lake is a nature lovers paradise. For the camper, back packer, and hiker, there are bear, elk, mountain cats, beavers, and, of course, eagles, both bald and golden to glimpse as you explore this high mountain area.

The lake is privately owned, and you'll need to get a permit to fish there.

Village of Eagle Nest
P.O. Box 168
Eagle nest, NM 87718
(505) 377-2486
village@eaglenest.org

US 64
MM 287.6

5-S

Elizabethtown

The discovery of gold on Baldy Mountain in 1866 brought such a rush of fortune-seekers to the Moreno Valley that "E-town" became a roaring mining camp almost overnight. Because of water and transportation problems, and a decline in ore quality, it had become virtually a ghost town by 1875.

Elizabethtown was the first incorporated town in New Mexico. Located in Colfax County, it was also the first of the county's four county seats. Springer, Cimarron, and currently, Raton have all served as county seat.

At one time, there were at least seven saloons and three dance halls, giving the hard working miners a place to relax and spend their hard earned gold.

Now a ghost town, only a few buildings and families remain, but the dream of yesteryear, the sound of a miner calling out "Gold" can still be heard echoing through the air as the music swells and coins clink on the counter.

US 64
NM Jct 38

5-T

Wheeler Peak

Across Moreno Valley stands Wheeler Peak, 13,161 feet, highest peak in New Mexico. Rocks of Wheeler Peak and the Taos range are highly resistant granites and gneisses of Precambrain age. Moreno Valley is underlain by soft sandstones and shales which are covered by stream and glacial deposits. Placer gold was mined at Elizabethtown north of here during the 1860s.

Originally named Taos Peak, the mountain was renamed after George Montugue Wheeler. A West Point graduate, Wheeler was an ambitious officer. He craved distinction and adventure, and was anxious to explore the uncharted areas of the southwest for military and commercial purposes.

Wheeler proposed the exploration of the Sangre De Cristo Mountains of New Mexico. The survey began in 1874 and lasted 5 years. Wheeler was commanding officer, but left the actual survey duties to his men. His maps were well done, but inaccurate. Wheeler never entered the Sangre De Christo Mountains or set foot on the peak which bears his name. Instead, he explored the Colorado River. It was first lieutenant Stanhope Blunt who climbed and chartered New Mexico's highest mountain.

Jct 38
US 64

MM 281.8

5-U

Springer

Located in the old Maxwell Land Grant and near the Cimarron cutoff of the Santa Fe Trail, Springer served as Colfax County seat from 1882 to 1897. Several men were killed here in one of the late flare-ups of the Colfax County War, a disputer between land grant owners and settlers. Population 1,696. Elevation 5,857 feet.

Springer was named for Frank Springer, a brilliant lawyer from Iowa who arrived in Cimarron in 1873. He was an attorney for the Maxwell Land Grant Company where he stubbornly contested litigation by people hoping to break up the land grant.

The historic case lasted nearly 20 years, going to the U.S. Supreme Court. It is said that Mr. Springer presented one of the finest land grant arguments ever made before that tribunal.

In 1891, Mr. Springer became president of the Maxwell land Grant Company and oversaw the development of this vast area, larger than the state of Delaware. His CS Ranch brought one of the first herds of Hereford cattle to the area in 1882.

He and his brother Charles were responsible for building Eagle Nest Dam in 1916. He was the founder of both New Mexico Highlands University in Las Vegas and the New Mexico Art Museum in Santa Fe.

The town that is now Springer used to be called Maxwell in honor of Lucien B. Maxwell, sole owner of the Maxwell Land Grant.

Nearby is Springer Lake, a premier fisherman's lake and camping spot.

Springer Chamber of Commerce
P.O. Box 323
Springer, NM 87747
(505) 483-2998

5-V

New Mexico Boys School

Established in 1903 by the 35th Legislative Assembly. Original location was to have been within the counties of Rio Arriba, Taos or San Juan. Transferred to present location in 1909.

Boys, on their way to becoming men, sometimes found themselves on the wrong side of the law. Not wanting to incarcerate them with older men, knowing that some could be turned from their criminal ways, the New Mexico Legislature established the New Mexico Boys School. It was a way to both protect society and give the boys a chance to redeem themselves.

Over the years, it has helped many young men to turn their lives around, providing them with a place to live and learn and to become productive members of society.

NM 468
MM 2.1

5-W

Raton Pass

This important pass on the Mountain Branch of the Santa Fe Trail was used by Brigadier General Stephen Watts Kearny for his 1846 invasion of New Mexico, and by the Colorado Volunteers who defeated the Confederates in 1862. Richens L. "Uncle Dick" Wooten operated a toll road from 1866 to 1879, when the Santa Fe Railroad crossed the Pass.

Though treacherous and a dangerous place to cross the Rocky Mountains, it was one of the few natural passes through the rugged mountains. Early Spanish explorers and Indians for centuries used the pass as a short cut, but it was just too rough for wagons on the Santa Fe Trail

In 1866, "Uncle Dick", a mountain man and an Indian Scout, recognized a chance to serve his fellow man and make a little personal profit at the same time. He blasted his way through the mountains and a set up a toll gate.

He charged everyone, with the exception of traveling Indians, who wanted to pass through the mountains. If they didn't want to pay the toll, well, they could just turn around and take the detour 100 miles to the east.

In 1879, the Atchison, Topeka and Santa Fe Railroad bought the toll road from "Uncle Dick" and established a busy rail line.

5-X

Willow Springs

In 1861, the U.S. Army established a government forage station here by a small spring. A well was dug, and the station became a water stop for Barlow and Sanderson stagecoaches. With the arrival of the railroad in 1879 and the founding of Raton, the station was incorporated into the new town and eventually was razed.

Raton was founded at the site of Willow Springs, which was originally a stop on the Santa Fe Trail. This station was a rest stop for the stagecoaches passing through. Horses were changed out here and the well brought an important source of water to the area.

When the original 320 acres for Raton Townsite was purchased from the Maxwell Land Grant in 1880, the stop was incorporated into the new town.

In Town of Raton

5-Y

Curry County

George Curry, a Kansas native who was territorial governor of New Mexico from 1907-1910 helped to create Curry County in 1909.

County Seat: Clovis
Communities: Grady, Texaco, Melrose, Bellview

1,404 Square Miles

Windmill

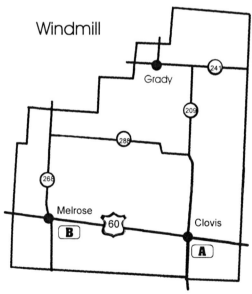

Clovis

During the 1700s and early 1800s, Comanche Indian buffalo hunters used trails that passed near here. In 1907 the Santa Fe Railroad established Clovis to serve as the eastern terminal of the Belen Cutoff, which would connect the transcontinental line at Belen. Formerly the domain of ranchers, the railroad opened the area to farmers.

The area's history goes back thousands of years before the settlers, ranchers and Indians. In 1932, A.W. Anderson of Clovis, discovered evidence of human occupation about 11,000 years ago at the Blackwater Draw site.

The Curry county seat, Clovis was incorporated in 1906–07. Like many of the cities of the West, it was the railroad that breathed life into the area. The story goes that a railroad official's daughter had been studying French history. Clovis was the name of the first Christian King of the Frankish Empire and she named the city Clovis.

Cannon Air Force Base, eight miles to the West, adds to the community's economy and available workforce. The surrounding rangeland makes it ideal for dairies and cultivating crops such as corn, wheat, sorghum, cotton, hay, potatoes and other vegetables.

It was in Clovis at the Norman Petty Studios that Buddy Holly recorded the smash hit, "Peggy Sue," as well as 18 other hits.

Clovis Chamber of Commerce
215 Main Street
Clovis, NM 88101
505-763-3435
Fax (505) 763-7266

HWY 70
Town of Clovis

6-A

Llano Estacado

Nomadic Indians and countless buffalo herds dominated this vast plain when the Vasquez de Coronado expedition explored it in 1541. Later it was the focus of Comanchero activity, and in the 19th century it became a center for cattle ranching. The name LLANO ESTACADO, or stockaded plains, refers to the fortress like appearance of its escarpment.

When the Rocky Mountains were forming in the west, sediments collected here, forming this amazingly huge, and relatively flat mesa. Water eroded deep arroyos and canyons and left this level surface.

When viewed from space, this flat land is like a huge table. It was covered with natural grasses and the pioneers had to follow stakes to navigate the "sea of grass".

The test on these two markers was misinterpreted. Llano Estacado does no refer to the escarpments, but to the stakes themselves.

US 60-84
West of Clovis, MM 357

6-B

De Baca County

Billy the Kid's Grave

DeBaca County was created in 1917 and named for Ezequiel Cabeza de Baca, New Mexico's second state governor.

County Seat: Fort Sumner
Communities: Tiaban, Yeso

2,366 Square Miles

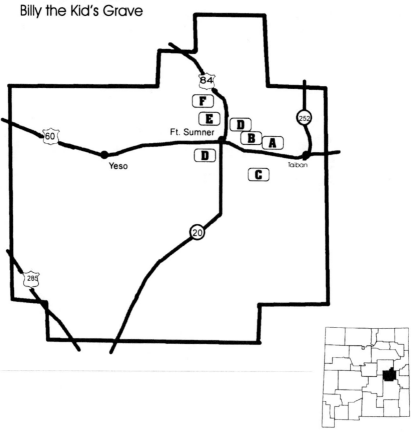

Billy the Kid's Grave
Old Fort Sumner Cemetery

Billy the Kid, whose real name was Henry McCarty, was buried here on July 15, 1881. This cemetery was established by the U.S. Army in 1863 and contained the bodies of 21 soldiers, whose remains were removed to the National Cemetery at Santa Fe in 1906. Civilians buried here include Lucien B. Maxwell, the famous frontiersman, and Charlie Bowdre and Tom O'Folliard, two of "the Kid's" friends.

Two of Billy the Kid's closest friends were Charlie Bowdre and Tom O'Folliard. Billy, Charlie and Tom were killed within months of each other and all three were buried here. They share a single headstone with the word "Pals" above their names.

Charlie Bowdre was born in 1848 in Georgia. He moved to Lincoln County around 1874 and was deeply involved with the "Regulators" of the Lincoln County war. After the war, he and Billy were still hunted by the posse. It was during a shootout with Pat Garrett on December 20th, 1880 that Charlie met his end.

Tom O'Folliard was from Texas. When his parents died of small pox, he was raised by other family members. In 1878, he and James Woodland hit the trail for New Mexico. His timing was off. He found himself in the middle of the War that would ultimately take his life. He was killed on December 19, 1980 during an ambush by Pat Garrett and his posse outside the home of Charlie Bowdre's wife, Manuela.

There has been some speculation that Pat Garrett did not shoot Billy. He and Billy were saddle pals for a number of years, and Pat knew of Billy's hideouts. There are some that say Pat and Billy arraigned for another body to be buried here.

Some say Billy then went to Mexico City, others to Texas or Arizona and still others say he just moved to a different area of New Mexico where he lived out his life as a law abiding citizen.

Hwy 60-84 West
MM 330.0

7-A

Fort Sumner State Monument
Old Fort Sumner, 1862-1869

Fort Sumner was established by the U.S. Army in 1862 as a supply and control post for the Bosque Redondo Indian Reservation. More than 8,500 Navajo were forcibly relocated here from the Four Corners region by a tragic march known as the Long Walk. About 450 Mescalero Apache were also brought here. After the reservation was closed in 1868, the fort was abandoned, and the site sold to Lucien Maxwell in 1870.

In the 1860's, some 9,000 Navajo and several hundred Mescalero Apache people were *interned* here by the U.S. Government at the site known as the Bosque Reservation. Located two miles east of the village of Fort Sumner on Billy the Kid Road, its wide open area was easier to keep track of the charges under the soldiers' care.

Fort Sumner and the Reservation was at the heart of the conflict of the Lincoln County War. Supplying beef contracts to the reservation made many men rich.

The Goodnight-Loving Trail brought many cattle in from Texas to this area, as well as such powerful ranchers as John S. Chisum, and Lucien Maxwell.

Ft. Sumner State Monument
P.O. Box 356
Ft Sumner, NM 88119
1-800-426-7856
505-355-2573

US 60/84
South of Fort Sumner

7-B

Old Fort Sumner and "Billy the Kid's" Grave

Fort Sumner was established in 1862 to guard the Navajo and Apaches on the Bosque Redondo Reservation. It was discontinued as a military post in 1868 and the buildings and site sold to Lucien B. Maxwell. William "Billy the Kid" Bonney was killed here by Sheriff Pat Garret the night of July 14, 1881. Bonney is buried in the nearby cemetery.

Pat Garrett was born on June 5, 1850 in Chambers County, Alabama. During the 1870's he was a buffalo hunter in Texas and moved to Fort Sumner in 1878 when buffalo hunting became no longer profitable.

Garret was elected sheriff of Lincoln County in November of 1880. Within days, a warrant was issued for Billy the Kid's arrest. On December 12th, Garrett and his possee captured Billy the Kid at Stinking Springs near Fort Sumner. Charlie Bowdre was killed during the incident.

On July 13, 1881, Sheriff Garrett arrived at the home of Lucien B. Maxell in search of Billy the Kid. At midnight, as the sheriff knelt beside the bed of Pete Maxwell, Billy the Kid entered and was shot dead by Sheriff Garrett.

Pat Garrett lived until February 29th, 1908, when he was shot in the back by Wayne Brazil during a dispute over the use of land that Wayne Brazil leased from him.

NM 272 at
Old Fort Sumner

7-C

Fort Sumner

Named for the fort built in 1862 to guard the Bosque Redondo Indian Reservation, the town of Fort Sumner grew out of settlements clustering around the Maxwell family properties. It moved to its present site with the construction of the Belen Cutoff of the Santa Fe Railroad around 1907.

The Belen Cutoff was built by the Atchison, Topeka and Santa Fe Railroad in 1907 to alleviate traveling over Raton Pass. Travel through the Pass required two or three large engines, due to its high elevation (approximately 7,600 feet above sea level).

The Belen Cutoff traveled through Kansas and Oklahoma, then westward into the plains of Texas and New Mexico. It turned the town of Fort Sumner into an important shipping point for the Pecos Valley. Likewise, Belen became an important shipping point for the productive Rio Grande Valley.

Fort Sumner Chamber of Commerce
P.O. Box 28
Fort Sumner, NM 88119
1-505-355-7705

North of Ft Sumner
US 60/84

US 60 MM 326.8
West of Fort Sumner

7-D

Early Spanish Route

In 1582, Antonio de Espejo and his exploring party left New Mexico to return to Mexico by way of the Pecos River. Eight years later, Gaspar de Sosa led another group into New Mexico along side the same river, a route little used again until the Territorial period.

In 1563 an expedition was led into New Mexico by Francisco de Ibarra: it is worth mentioning only for the reason that de Ibarra returned in 1565 with the boast that he had discovered "a new Mexico", which was, probably, the origin of the name.

Gaspar Castano de Sosa was the lieutenant-governor of Nuevo Leon in northeastern Spain who thought that great riches were to be discovered in New Mexico. He found some Indians who carried tales of riches in the undiscovered area. While doing a test on some of their ore, he took a silver cup and threw it in with the test ore. The result was that the rocks had a high silver content. Castano de Sosa was able to convince his followers that the journey would be profitable. He took 170 people from Almaden and left for New Mexico in 1590. Two and one half months later, 50 soldiers found the group, arrested Castano de Sosa, and took him back to New Spain. The expedition was a failure.

Gaspar Castano de Sosa is important to New Mexico history because he was the first pioneer to lead an expedition into the area that was not government sanctioned. Gaspar Castano de Sosa's party crossed into the Pecos River Valley into southern Texas and then wandered along the Rio Grande. The expedition's journey was important because it marked the first excursion of wagons on land destined to become part of the United States.

US 84
MM 1.1

7-E

Sunnyside Springs

Nearby is a "sweet water" spring which has been used through the centuries by Plains Indians, Spanish Explorers, and most recently, ranchers and settlers. A Stagecoach station was located at the spring, which was a popular stopping place for travelers. The spring was named after Sunnyside, the nearby settlement whose name was changed to Fort Sumner in 1910.

The term sweet water refers to the fact that the water is drinkable. There are many springs in the desert which are poisonous. The stagecoach station was located here to insure a supply of fresh water for the travelers and their horses.

Sunnyside was first recognized by the U.S. Government with a post office in 1878. In 1910, the town was renamed Fort Sumner after the military fort by the same name.

The military Fort Sumner was named after General Edwin Vose Sumner who served in the Union Army during the American Civil War.

US 84 N. of Ft Sumner
MM 1.1

7-F

Dona Ana County

Dona Ana County is reputed to be named for a legendary Dona Ana who was renowned for her charitable acts in the 17th century. It was created on January 9, 1852.

County Seat: Las Cruces
Communities: Anthony, La Mesa, Mesilla, Organ, Radium Springs, Leasburg, Hatch

3,804 Square Miles

Ft. Selden State Monument

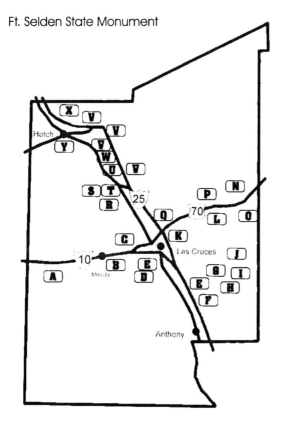

Fort Cummings— 1863-1886

This small and isolated post was built on the Mesilla-Tucson road to protect the Butterfield Trail against Apaches. Notorious Cooke's Canyon, located nearby, was a particularly dangerous point on the trail. Only ruins now remain of the ten-foot adobe walls which once surrounded it.

Cooke's Canyon was one of Chiricahua Apache Chief Cochise's strategic places of attack. Here, during the summer of 1861, he would ambush passersby, trying to force the white settlers out of his native homeland, and retaliating for the murder of his brother and two of his nephews.

In his day Cochise embodied the essence of Apache warfare. He was an Indian who so loved his family, his people, and the mountains in which he was reared, that he would fight to protect and preserve all that was Apache.

When it became inevitable that he would have to make peace with the Americans, he revealed his contempt for reservation life by declaring his people's desire to "run around like a coyote; they don't want to be put in a corral." The idea of a reservation was completely alien to an Apache warrior's view of his world.

While there can be no question that he was capable of unspeakable cruelties and violent acts of revenge on whites, Cochise was forced to witness the disappearance of his homeland, and his people. He will be forever a giant in the history of the American Southwest.

I-10 West of Las Cruces
MM 120

8-A

Las Cruces on the Camino Real

In 1849, following the Mexican War, fields were first broken in Las Cruces. The town became a flourishing stop on the Camino Real, deriving its name, "The Crosses," from the marking of graves of victims of an Apache attack. Las Cruces since 1881 has been the county seat of Doña Ana County. Population 75,000. Elevation 3,909 feet.

The first settlement in this area was Dona Ana, just north of Las Cruces. The area was part of Mexico until 1848 when the Mexican War ended. The Treaty of Guadalupe-Hidalgo gave Dona Ana and the lands east of the Rio Grande to the United States. The United States sent in Army troops to protect the area and settlers began to arrive.

The troops were under the command of Lt. Delos Bennett Sackett. The leader in Dona Ana asked Sackett to plan a new town to take the pressure off of Dona Ana. Sackett cooperated and using rawhide ropes and stakes, laid out the beginnings of present-day Las Cruces.

Sackett laid out 84 blocks, each containing four lots. People gathered at the plaza and drew numbers from a hat to determine who got what site. However, Sackett did not take into account the lack of wood for building. The streets were crooked, and the houses crowded. The lack of wood made adobe bricks the building material of choice. People dug holes in the street to get the dirt they needed, and before the streets could be paved, they were full of potholes. Finally, a Judge ordered the townspeople to stop digging up Main Street and to fill in the holes.

When the Railroad entered into Las Cruces, it quickly outgrew it's neighbors.

Las Cruces Convention & Visitors Bureau
211 N. Water
Las Cruces, NM 88001

I 10 East Exit 135 in East Bound Rest Area
MM 135

8-B

Dona Ana County Courthouse
County Seat
Las Cruces, New Mexico
Built 1937

At one time, Dona Ana County extended from the Colorado River to include most of the Arizona Territory and westward to include most of what is today, Otero county. Today, the Rio Grande is the only river in Dona Ana. Once wild and threatening with floods, it has since been tamed by reservoirs such as Caballo and Elephant Butte. Very little water from this area ever reaches the Gulf of Mexico. Most is diverted for agricultural purposes along the Mesilla Valley, past El Paso, and for use by Mexico.

Before the dam was built, the mighty Rio Grande was as much as a mile and a half wide in some places.

Dona Ana County is noted for its rich, fertile valley. One of the world's largest pecan groves, Stahmann Farms, Inc., is in the valley south of Las Cruces.

In Las Cruces
West on Amador Ave.

8-C

La Mesilla

After the Treaty of Guadalupe-Hidalgo, which concluded the Mexican War in 1848, the Mexican government commissioned Cura Ramón Ortiz to settle Mesilla. He brought families from New Mexico and from Paso del Norte (modern Ciudad Juárez) to populate the Mesilla Civil Colony Grant, which by 1850 had over 800 inhabitants.

In November 16,1854, a detachment from nearby Fort Fillmore raised the United States flag confirming the Gadsden Purchase; thus the Gadsden territory was officially recognized as part of the United States. In 1858, Butterfield stage began its run through Mesilla. During the Civil War, Mesilla was the capital of the Confederate Arizona Territory.

La Mesilla has changed little over the past 100 years. The time when citizens settled matters with a gun are gone. The Republican and Democrat "Battle of the Bands" which ended with 10 dead and nearly 50 wounded has quieted. The tree where Kit Carson carved his name while passing time, has long since been cut for firewood.

Billy the Kid is no longer swaggering down the streets of La Mesilla laughing and joking with the residents. It was here the trial for the murder of Sheriff Brady took place and the town was overflowing with curiosity seekers.

While many old towns of the Wild West have been reduced to foundations and shapeless piles of stone and bricks, La Mesilla quietly continues.

In Las Cruces West Calle De Parian
MM 29.5

In Las Cruces MM 28
(Missing)

8-D

Butterfield Trail

Stagecoaches of the Butterfield Overland Mail Co. began carrying passengers and mail from St. Louis to San Francisco, across southern New Mexico, in 1858. The 2,795-mile journey took 21-22 days. In 1861 the service was re-routed through Salt Lake City. From La Mesilla west, the trail paralleled I-10.

Before 1857, there was no organized, commercial system of transportation west of the Mississippi River. New York business man, John Butterfield obtained a $600,000 government contract to establish and run an overland mail company from St. Louis, Missouri to San Francisco, California.

John Butterfield had already managed to prove his ability to organize and administer such an undertaking. He had erected the first telegraph line between New York City and Buffalo, built and managed several passenger stagecoach lines and constructed the first steam railroad and first street horse railway system in Utica, New York. He also helped with the formation of the American Express Company.

The Butterfield Overland Mail Company was to be the first transcontinental stage line stretching some 2, 800 miles from the Mississippi River to the Pacific Coast. Because it was to be used year around, it was decided to use the southern route as much as possible to avoid winter storms. During its two and a half years of service, the stage arrived within its 25 day contract, occasionally reducing it to 21 days.

John Butterfield had to build about 150 stations and corrals, dig wells and cisterns, grade fording sites, purchase and distribute 1200 horses and 600 mules, as well as build hundreds of coaches and hire between 750 to 800 men. In the arid terrain of southern New Mexico, the stops were spaced further apart, either at existing springs or where wells were successfully dug. Once the Stage hit the Gila River, which the route followed to California, it had water and the stations returned to the 15 to 20 miles apart, as it did from Mississippi through Texas.

The stage was only in service for two and a half years. The Civil War brought an early demise to the stage that managed to stitch together the growing country.

US 10 N of Anthony (Missing)

MM 29.5 On US 70 (Replaced)

8-E

Franklin Mountains

Franklin Mountains to east are tilted uplifted block of Paleozoic limestones. Spectacular Organ Mountains to north are mainly igneous rocks, mineralized in places. Paleozoic rocks encountered in oil tests to northwest in the Rio Grande trench are 5 miles lower than in mountains, illustrating the Basin and Range geologic structure. Elevation 3,950 feet.

Overlooking the Rio Grande, the Franklin Mountains, located in Texas, are the northern ramparts of the Paso del Norte (Pass of the North), leading from Mexico into what is now the United States.

For thousands of years, Native Americans, and for the last four centuries, soldiers, priests, traders, adventurers, gold-seekers, entrepreneurs, and just plain folk have passed through the gap in both directions in an endless procession of expansion, settlement, raiding, and conquest.

Native American groups made the area home, using the plant and animal resources of the Franklins for more than 12,000 years, until their forced removal during the late 19th century. These people left their marks upon the rocks of the Franklins—colorful pictographs on boulders, on rock shelters and deep mortar pits (used to grind seeds), and on rock outcrops near scattered water sources.

Beginning in the 1580's, Spanish conquistadors and priests passed beneath the peaks of the Franklins on their mission to conquer and colonize the Puebloan villages in present-day New Mexico.

I-10 By Anthony NM
(Marker Missing)

8-F

Espejo's Espedition on the Camino Real

In 1582 and 1583, Antonio de Espejo and his party paralleled the Rio Grande north to the Bernalillo area. He was trying to learn the fate of two Franciscan friars who had stayed with the Pueblo Indians after the Rodriguez-Sánchez Chamuscado expedition returned to Mexico in 1581.

Mesa Del Contadero

The Chihuahua Trail passed by the large volcanic mesa on the east bank of the Rió Grande, marking the northern end of the Jornada del Muerto (Journey of the Dead Man). "Cantadero" means "the counting place," or a narrow place where people and animals must pass through one- by- one.

On June 5, 1581, three Franciscans-Agustín Rodríguez, Francisco López, and Juan de Santa María-left Santa Bárbara, Mexico, to explore missionary possibilities in the country to the north. They were accompanied by an armed escort of eight soldiers under the command of Francisco Sánchez (also called Chamuscado), nineteen Indian servants, ninety horses, and 600 head of stock.

The Rodríguez-Sánchez expedition continued along the west bank of the Rio Grande through the area of present El Paso and in August 1581 arrived at the Piro and Tigua pueblos of New Spain. On August 21 the party took formal possession of the land for the king of Spain. For the remainder of the year the party explored extensively in all directions, covering much of the same territory viewed by Francisco Vásquez de Coronado forty years before. In the meantime, Fray Santa María had ill-advisedly set out on his own to report to the viceroy and was killed by Indians in September 1581, though his companions did not learn of his fate until sometime later.

In early 1582, Sánchez and his men discussed returning to Santa Bárbara to report to the viceroy, but the two Franciscans announced their intention of pursuing further their missionary endeavors in New Spain. They did not heed Sánchez's warnings of the great dangers involved and on January 31, 1582, stayed behind when the rest of the explorers returned to Santa Bárbara, Mexico. Glowing accounts of great wealth in New Spain, together with the concern about the safety of the friars, led to preparations for an expedition led by Espejo to the new land.

US Hwy 10 South of Las
Cruces (Marker Missing)

8-G

El Camino Real (The King's Highway)

The oldest historical road in the United States, running over 2000 miles from Mexico City to Taos. Parts of the Camino Real were used by Spanish explorers in the 1580s, but it was formally established in 1598 by Juan de Oñate, New Mexico's first colonizer and governor. It was later referred to as the Chihuahua Trail.

The Camino Real was the only link between New Mexico and the rest of the world for many years. The 2,000 mile route sometimes followed ancient paths created by native Americans. Sometimes it crossed new territory the natives considered too hostile. Caravan after caravan, some miles long, followed the same route, stopping at the same camping sites.

It took six months to travel from Parral, Mexico to Santa Fe. It took six months to rest and restock for the trip South, and another six months to return. From Mexico, they brought trade goods, religious articles, government communications and new colonists.

The return trip took blankets, extracts from mining and whatever New Mexicans could offer in trade to the southern provinces of Spain's colony.

The arrival of the Spanish with their horses, sheep, and religion created profound changes in the cultures of the natives and the new comers. Some, like horses, were readily adapted. Others were not welcomed as warmly.

The Camino Real helped to develop and influence much of the culture that is present today.

On US 10
by Anthony NM (Marker Missing)

8-H

Onate's Route—On the Camino Real

Juan de Oñate, first governor of New Mexico, passed near here with his colonizing expedition in May 1598. Traveling north, he designated official campsites (called parajes) on the Camino Real, used by expeditions that followed, In Oñate's caravan were 129 men, many with their families and servants.

Don Juan de Onate set forth from Mexico in January of 1598. His caravan consisted of eighty-three wagons which carried munitions, supplies and food. There were over seven thousand head of livestock, grapevine cuttings, seeds and tools to help the settlers survive and colonize their new homes.

The column of soldiers and colonists were accompanied by eight priests and two lay brothers and the caravan stretched out four miles in length as it marched north.

It took them four months to reach the Rio Grande. There, Onate called for a rest and they celebrated Easter, giving thanks for having made it so far. This first Thanksgiving included a dramatic presentation and a formal speech by Onate claiming all lands watered by the Rio Grande for Spain and King Phillip.

On US 10 by Anthony, NM
(Marker Missing)

8-I

Brazito Battlefield

One of the few battles of the Mexican War to be fought in New Mexico occurred near here on Christmas Day, 1846. U.S. troops under Colonel Alexander W. Doniphan defeated a Mexican army commanded by General Antonio Ponce de León. Two days later, Doniphan entered El Paso without opposition.

General Stephen Kearny took possession of Santa Fe, setting up an American Government. Kearny then headed to California. He was the superior officer of Colonel Alexander W. Doniphan. Two months after Kearny left, Col. Doniphan headed south to meet General Wood at Chihuahua, Old Mexico.

The troops were in bad shape. They were footsore and hungry after marching across the desert. They stopped in the town of Dona Ana where they found not only food and water, but also Lieut. Colonel Jackson and Major Gilipin with their detachments. Christmas Eve morning, they all were headed for El Paso. Though in bad condition, they were happy, singing and joking.

When they sighted the Organ Mountains, they called a halt at Brazito, "Little Arm". While setting up camp, a great cloud of dust was seen. Advance patrols galloped back to camp, "The enemy is advancing upon us!" The Mexican objective was to prevent the Americans from marching to Chihuahua to enforce the American troops under General Wood.

Officers sprang up and began to snap out orders. Soon thirteen hundred Dragoons and volunteers flanked them on the left and right. Colonel Doniphan used a bit of strategy that worked like a charm. He acted uncertain about the next move and held his men back. Thinking the Americans were afraid, the Mexicans charged with full force. The battle waxed hot and furious for about thirty minutes, but the Mexicans were soon routed and retreating towards El Paso. In the end, 71 of the Mexicans were killed and 50 wounded. The Americans had eight wounded, but none killed.

Following the battle, the American soldiers tossed their hats above their head and shouted, "On to Chihuahua!"

US 10 North of El Paso
(Marker Missing)

8-J

Pat Garrett Murder Site

Pat Garrett, the Lincoln County Sheriff who shot and killed William "Billy the Kid" Bonney at Fort Sumner in 1881, was himself murdered at a remote site nearby on February 29, 1908. Wayne Brazel, a local cowboy, confessed to shooting Garrett but was acquitted of all charges. The motive and circumstances surrounding Garrett's death are still being debated.

Pat Garrett was one of New Mexico's famous lawman. His rise to fame occurred during the Lincoln County War when he killed New Mexico's most famous outlaw, Billy the Kid. The circumstances surrounding Garrett's death are still being looked at and wondered over.

Garrett owned the Bear Canyon Ranch and had leased it to Wayne Brazel, who was using the ranch for a goat raising scheme. Garrett did not like the fact that there were goats on his ranch. Garrett was also having money problems and had an opportunity to sell the ranch, ending those problems. The goats and the lease had to be dealt with before he could sell the land.

Garrett and Carl Adamson, one of the prospective buyers of the ranch, were riding in a buggy to Las Cruces when Brazel came upon them. Brazel and Garrett were arguing about the goats as they continued along the road. At one point, Adamson stopped the buggy and stepped down to visit with nature. Garrett joined him. It was then that the first bullet smashed into the back of Garrett's skull. A second shot hit his stomach while he was on the ground. The famed lawman died without uttering a word. He was 57 years old.

Adamson turned to see Brazel astride his horse, a smoking revolver in his hand. Brazel handed the gun to Adamson, and the two continued to Las Cruces. At his trial, Brazel was defended by Albert B. Fall. Brazel claimed he had been threatened with a shotgun and fired in self defense. He was acquitted.

Without funds for a lengthy investigation, two men, Attorney General James M. Hervey and Captain Fred Fernoff of the New Mexico Mounted Police, decided to pursue the murder on their own. One man was told, "I know that outfit around the Organ Mountains, and Garret got killed for trying to find out who killed Fountain and you will get killed for trying to find out who killed Garrett. I would advise you to let it alone."

In 1961, 8 years after his death, at his request, Hervey's story was published, but the mystery is still debated.

71 62On US 70 East of Las Cruces MM 153.6 **8-K**

Organ Mountains

Spectacular Organ Mountains to east tower over water-rich Rio Grande Valley. High sharp peaks and massive cliffs of igneous rocks are part of ancient volcanoes. Copper, silver, gold, lead and zinc were mined from Organ Mining District at north end of mountains. Basin and Range country is to west. Elevation 4,190 feet.

The beautiful Organ Mountains rise just 11 miles east of Las Cruces. The tallest peak, Organ Needle, reaches 9,012 feet high.

The Organ Mountains were named for their appearance. From the distance, the spiraling peaks resemble a pipe organ, but in fact, are the eroded remains of volcanic activity.

Several millions of dollars worth of copper, silver and gold have been taken from mines carved deep into the Organ Mountains. The Maggy G, a large gold mine located on the missile range, and off limits to prospectors and visitors, produced approximately $850,999 gold ore concentrate and about half again that much in high grade ore.

Near Baylor Gap, an archaeologist discovered the bones of homosapiens in a cave with remains of several extinct animals which strongly suggest this may be the earliest record of Man on the American continent.

The arid climate and natural springs support a tremendous variety of vegetation and wildlife. The Bureau of Land Management operates a number of camping sites and biking, camping, hiking, horseback riding are just some of the activities available.

There is also a visitor's center with exhibits and restroom facilities available.

BLM-Mimbres Field Office
1800 Marquess Street
Las Cruces NM 88005
505-525-430

US 70 East of Las Cruces
MM 164.2

8-L

San Agustin Pass

Divide between Tularosa Basin to east and Jornanda del Muerto to west, cut between Organ Mountains to south and San Agustín-San Andrés Mountains to north. White gypsum sands glisten to northeast. Roadcuts in Tertiary monzonite. Organ mines yielded copper, lead, silver, gold, zinc and fluorite. Elevation 5,710 feet.

One of the few natural passes through the San Andres and Organ Mountains, this pass leads from the Interstate to White Sands Missile Range.

Most of what is today White Sands Missile Range was once a private ranch owned by the Cox family. The headquarters for the ranch was located by five springs which flow from the edge of the mountain. San Augustin Springs brought the necessary water to allow for development, and the pass brought a continuous stream of customers to where the San Augustine Inn, and the San Augustin Hotel once stood.

Only the ranch house and corrals remain today, but the stories of the area form a cross-section of Southwest history, and bring to life happenings of 150 years ago.

Inside the corral is a small gravestone surrounded by an iron fence. A lamb is surmounted onto the stone. The grave belongs to the daughter of one of the past owners of the San Augustine Ranch. She was their only child and died of rattlesnake poisoning. Soon afterwards, the man and his wife left the area, and time marched on.

US 70 West
MM 178

8-N

Albert J. Fountain

Albert Jennings Fountain was a Civil War veteran, New Mexico legislator and prominent lawyer. Colonel Fountain and his young son were presumed murdered near this spot while traveling between Lincoln and Las Cruces on February 1,1896. Their bodies have never been found. Oliver Lee and James Gilliland were tried for their murder in 1898. Both were acquitted.

Colonel Albert Jennings Fountain came to New Mexico with the Union Army in 1862. He had been a Republican legislator in Texas and later in New Mexico. He founded a Las Cruces newspaper, The Republican.

In August of 1871, Republicans and Democrats opened fire on each other during a candidate's forum and parade in the town square of Mesilla. Nine people died and nearly 50 were wounded.

Col. Fountain became a lawyer for the Southeastern New Mexico Stock Growers Association. He hired a detective to help seek rustlers. One of Col. Fountain's main suspects was Oliver Lee. Lee was a prominent Democrat and major landholder. The private eye turned up enough evidence that an indictment against Lee was filed. Lee and 25 other ranchers faced charges of rustling or brand altering.

Col. Fountain was the prosecuting attorney in Lincoln, NM at the trial. His wife, fearing for Col. Fountain, sent their 8 year old son, hoping that the presence of the young boy would deter any problems.

The Fountains disappeared a day after leaving Lincoln. Three riders were seen following them. Lee and another man were tried and acquitted for the murders as no bodies were ever found, only the young boy's bloody handkerchief with 15 cents change tied up in it. The boy had bought some candy the day before and had wrapped his change up.

Some believe the bodies may have been disposed of at a local saw mill, still others think the bodies are buried somewhere on White Sands.

The truth may never be known.

On US 70 East of Alamogordo
MM 178

8-O

Site of San Agustin Springs

Here on July 27, 1861, less than 300 Confederate troops intercepted 500 Union soldiers retreating from Fort Fillmore to Fort Stanton. Exhausted from the heat and famished for water, the Union troops straggled across the desert in a five-mile evacuation train. Unable to fight, Major Isaac Lynde surrendered his command without firing a single shot.

The San Andres Mountains were once the haven to many. Interestingly enough, modern technology allows complete and highly accurate recreations of battles and skirmishes that occurred.

During the Victorio War of 1879 and 1880, the Warm Springs Apache, led by Chief Victorio, eluded the military for 5 months before bringing his people to the nearby Hembrillo Basin in the San Andres Mountains. On April 6, 1880, two companies of Buffalo-Soldiers were quickly surrounded by about 150 Apache warriors. The soldiers took refuge and managed to hold them off through the long night.

As the sun rose, the Apaches moved closer and just before they could attack en mass, Cavalry reinforcements arrived from the north and west, forcing the Apaches to retreat.

In the 1990's, White Sands Missile Range archaeologists conducted extensive research on the battle. They found new documents and many artifacts which gave a more complete picture of the battle than ever before.

They mapped the positions of hundreds of rifle and pistol cartridges from the battle field. Using the Global Positioning System to precisely plot each item on a computer generated map, the artifacts were mapped to within 10 centimeters of their original location. Next, an archaeologist examined all the cartridges under a microscope to identify the unique scratches and firing pin marks every gun leaves on the cartridge. The researchers could, for instance, identify that rifle #7 was fired at these three locations.

By putting this into a data base, then electronically mapping it, the researchers were able to "See" the battle, putting things into motion over the period of the battle, recreating the past and bringing its people to life.

US 70 East of Las Cruces
MM 162.9

8-P

Bartlett-Garcia Conde
Initial Survey Point

On April 24, 1851, John Russell Bartlett, for the United States, and Pedro Garcia Conde, for the Republic of Mexico, erected near here a monument designating 3222' north latitude on the Rio Grande as the initial point for the official survey of the U.S.-Mexico boundary. After the Gadsden Purchase, the boundary was moved south.

The 1848 Treaty of Guadalupe-Hidalgo, which ended the Mexican War, caused misunderstandings. The treaty not only defined the border between Mexico and the U.S., but is also made the U.S. responsible for restraining marauding Native Americans on the frontier. When the U.S. did not enforce the article, Mexico claimed millions of dollars in damages. The situation was also complicated by the fact that a transcontinental railroad was considered the best route to the Pacific and the Southern route was in the disputed area.

When Franklin Pierce became president in 1853, he sent James Gadsden, American railroad entrepreneur and diplomat, to Mexico as a minister. Gadsden's instructions were to purchase the disputed territory and also lower California, if possible.

Mexico's administration was in financial need, and the new treaty was negotiated for $15 million. The article pertaining to the Indians was removed, and all claims for damages were canceled.

In Mexico, the sale met with great opposition and contributed to the political downfall of Santa Anna. In the US, it was bitterly debated which centered on adding more slave territory to the U.S. The U.S. Senate did ratify the treaty on April 25, 1854.

The Southern Pacific Railroad was eventually built through the region which comprised of a narrow band of today's southern New Mexico and roughly the southern quarter of Arizona. It was bound on the east by the Rio Grande, on the north by the Gila River, and on the west by the Colorado River.

On US 70 Exit 6A
(Marker Missing)

8-Q

Fort Selden Cemetery

Fort Selden was established nearby in 1865 to help protect the settlements of the Mesilla Valley and travelers along the Jornada del Muerto from Apache raids. The post cemetery was located in this field until the fort was abandoned in 1891. Military personnel were reinterred at the National Cemetery at Santa Fe. A number of unmarked graves in an adjacent potters field apparently still remain.

Built in 1865 by troops from Albuquerque, the entire post was constructed of flat, dirt roofed, one story adobe buildings. The exception was the Administration Building. The site was once an ancient Indian campground and place where Spanish caravans headed across the Jornada del Muerto.

The Fort was established to protect travelers and settlers from Apaches. However, it saw very little action. General Douglas A. MacArthur spent part of his childhood at the Fort when his father served there in 1884. It was here that the Army established heliography, a system of communication using the sun and mirrors. Messages could be sent to Fort Bliss, 50 miles away.

When Fort Selden was abandoned and troops were sent to Fort Bliss, the bodies of fallen comrades were removed from the cemetery for re-internment at Fort Bliss. It is rumored that in exchange for his labor, a contractor received the wooden portions of the buildings, thus leaving only the adobe walls to become a historic ruin.

Fort Selden was designated a State Monument in 1974. The Visitor's Center exhibits displays showing life there in the nineteenth century.

Fort Selden State Monument
Post Office Box 58
Radium Springs, New Mexico 88054
Phone: 505-526-8911

On I-25 South of Hatch Exit 19 on NM 157
MM 19

8-R

Leasburg Dam State Park

Built in 1908, the historic Leasburg Diversion Dam channels water from the Rio Grande to irrigate the vast farming area of the Upper Mesilla Valley. The dam also provides a pleasant spot for fishing, and canoes and kayaks may be used on the river. Picnicking and camping facilities are also available.

Leasburg Dam was named for Leasburg, a settlement with only a few remaining buildings. The Dam was constructed in 1908 and is one of the oldest in the state. It provides water via canal systems to irrigate an extensive area of farmlands as far south as Las Cruces.

The Park was created in 1971. It has camping facilities, electric sites, RV dumping, showers, picnicking, fishing, visitor center and trails. Nearby Fort Selden State Monument has a museum and trails at the site of a 19th century Army outpost.

The park contains 140 acres and the visitor's center is open from 7 am to sunset.

**Leaseburg Dam State Park
P.O. Box 6
Radium Springs, NM 88054
505-524-4068**

On I-25 South of Hatch, Exit 19
MM 19

8-S

Paraje De Robledo

This site was named for Pedro Robledo a member of the Juan de Onate expedition who was buried nearby on May 21, 1598. This paraje, or stopping place, was a welcome sight for caravans entering or exiting the dreaded Jornada del Muerto to the north. Its strategic location along the Camino Real made it an ideal site for the establishment of Fort Selden in 1864.

400 years ago, there were not many gray haired officers. Pedro Robledo was one of the oldest members of the Onate expedition at 60 years old. His four sons, aged eighteen to twenty-seven, also were on the journey and would be available to help with his duties. Pedro figured with their help, that the journey would not be too much for him. He was the first one on the expedition to pass away. Most of the colonists mourned Pedro's loss.

After his death, he was buried near here. The mountain overlooking the site of his burial was named after him as was the camping site on the Camino Real.

On I-25 South Exit 19 on NM 157 at
Fort Selden State Monument MM 19

8-T

Fort Selden State Monument
1865-1891

Fort Selden was established to protect settlers and railroad construction crews in the Mesilla Valley and the Jornada del Muerto from Apaches. The first regular army troops to garrison it were four companies of the black 125th Infantry. General Douglas MacArthur spent two years of his childhood here. The fort was finally abandoned in 1891.

Fort Selden was built in 1865 by troops from Albuquerque. The post was constructed of flat, dirt roofed, one story adobe buildings, with the exception of the Administration Building. Once, the location of an ancient Indian campground, and later a place where Spanish caravans headed across the Jornada del Muerto, the Fort was established primairly to protect travelers and settlers from the Apaches.

It saw very little action, and was evidently not successful as far as military installations were concerned.

In 1974, Fort Selden became a State Monument. The visitor's center exhibits displays showing life in the nineteenth century.

Fort Selden State Monument
505-526-8911

On I-25 South of Hatch

8-U

Jornada Del Muerto on the Camino Real

This stretch of the Camino Real leaves the Rio Grande and cuts across 90 miles of desert with little water or shelter . Despite its difficulty, the dreaded "Journey of the Deadman" was heavily used by Spanish, Mexican, and Anglo travelers between El Paso and the northern New Mexico settlements.

The stretch between Las Cruces and Socorro was the roughest and deadliest part of the Camino Real. The broad, flat valley with no water, grazing or firewood offered nothing but hardship for 90 miles. It would not be until Socorro, where friendly Pueblo dwellers would offer food and succor, would there be relief. Oñate promptly changed the village name to Socorro, meaning help.

The relative safety and convenience of the river became too difficult to follow. For 100 miles huge canyons led from mountains, creating gigantic ridges to climb and descend one after another. Also, the river often changed its course leaving quicksand in its wake. What had been safe just a few months before could now be a death trap or completely washed away.

Despite the hardships of lack of water, travelers made better time on the flat, dry valley.

Here, the caravans left the comparative ease of the Rio Grande and prepared for a brutal three day march. There would be little rest and no water. The trail was first blazed by Oñate in 1598. His notes say the group suffered terribly for lack of water until someone's dog appeared with muddy paws. The travelers followed the dog to temporary water where the animals and people relieved their thirst. Known from then on as Los Charcos del Perillo, "the puddles of the little dog", it became a paraje, or camping place, where caravans prepared for the harsh trip ahead.

The desert route earned its name in 1680. During that year, the Pueblo Indians revolted against Spanish rule, killing many and driving the rest out. Of the two thousand Colonists and loyal natives who attempted to make it back to El Paso, the Jornada del Muerto claimed almost six hundred.

On I-25 N of Las Cruces
MM 22.8

On I-25 North of Las Cruces   On I-25 S of Hatch
MM 27.5   MM 24

8-V

Paraje San Diego

This paraje, or stopping place, provided travelers along the Camino Real with a final opportunity to water their stock and prepare their caravans before leaving the Rio Grande Valley and entering the desolate Jornada del Muerto. Caravans on their way to Santa Fe started in the evening and traveled non-stop until they reached the Paraje de Fra Cristobal 100 miles to the north.

North from Robledo lay paraje San Diego, where the trail departed east of the river, and entered the Jornada del Muerto. For many fearful miles of mostly forced night march, through parajes Perillo, Laguna del Muerto, and Tusas, to paraje Fra Cristobal, there was no reliable water, escape from the dusty winds, or protection from hostile Indians.

The caravans would rest here for a day or two. After averaging 15 miles per day, then suddenly traveling the 100 miles in only 3 or 4 days, this was one of the worst stretches of Camino Real and a remarkable achievement.

on I-25 North of Las Cruces
MM 22.8

on I-25 South At Rest Area
MM 23

8-W

Mormon Battalion

The Mormon Battalion, composed of 500 volunteers, left Council Bluffs, Iowa, June 5, 1846, as part of the expeditionary force of Brigadier General Kearny. The battalion followed the Santa Fe Trail to Santa Fe and down the Rio Grande near here, where it turned west. The 2000 mile march ended in San Diego, California, January 30, 1847.

The U.S. Army was in urgent need of assisting their forces against the Mexican military during the war in 1846. President James K. Polk instructed the Secretary of War to authorize Col. (later General) Stephen W. Kearney, Commander of the Army of the West, to enlist a battalion of Mormons to go to California to aid the army there.

Many of the Mormons were at first, reluctant to enlist. They had received no protection from persecution and mob action in Missouri and Illinois; they had hundreds of miles of hostile Indian territory to cross; and were concerned about protection for their families located on the western frontier.

The President of the Church of the Latter Day Saints, Brigham Young, urged the men to enlist, telling them it was their patriotic duty to join. Over 500 men were mustered in at Council Bluffs, Iowa on July 16, 1846. Some brought their families as well.

The Mormon Battalion made the longest march in military history consisting of 2,000 miles from Council Bluffs, Iowa to San Diego, California arriving in just under 7 months.

On I-25 South of Hatch
Marker Missing

8-X

Hatch

Originally established as Santa Barbara in 1851, Apache raids drove the settlers away until 1853 when nearby Fort Thorn was established. Abandoned again in 1860 after the fort closed, it was re-occupied in 1875 and re-named for General Edward Hatch, then Commander of the New Mexico Military District. Population 1,028. Elevation 4,055 feet.

Hatch's fertile valley has become well known to New Mexicans as the Chile Capitol of New Mexico. Local residents of Hatch might say "Chile Capital of the World." They would be the first to point out that they spell Chili with an "e".

After the Elephant Butte and Caballo dams were built, Hatch worried less about floods, and the rich bottomland farming enabled it to prosper.

New Mexico has 12 chile producing counties, with Dona Ana leading. Chiles are the state's top cash crop and ranks first in the amount produced, double it's closest competitor, California.

The annual Chile Festival brings hundreds of visitors to sample the tastiest or hottest varieties found. Be sure and drink milk, not water, to put out the fire!

Chile thrives under the New Mexico sun and Hatch is the place to buy quality, newly harvested chiles during the fall season.

Hatch Valley Chamber of Commerce
P.O. Box 38
Hatch NM 87937
505-267-5050

At Jct of Hwy 26 and 187
Marker Missing

8-Y

Eddy County

Created in 1889, Eddy County was named for the developer who brought the railroad to the area, Charles B. Eddy

County Seat: Carlsbad
Communities: Artesia, Loving, Malaga, White City

4,180 Square Miles

Carlsbad Caverns

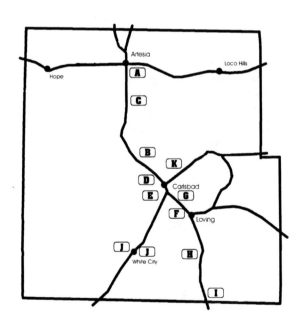

Artesia

Artesia, named for the area's many artesian wells, lies on the route of the Pecos Valley cattle trails used by Charles Goodnight, Oliver Loving, and John S. Chisum. The town, established in 1903, is located in what was once part of Chisum's vast cattle empire.

Water is scarce and very necessary for survival in the Desert Southwest. Early explorers used rivers to help explore what would later become the United States.

Originally named Miller for a railroad worker, then changed to Stegman after the local postmistress, who was none other than Sallie Chisum Robert Stegman, John Chisum's niece. It was when she changed her name that the city was renamed Artesia in 1903 after the discovery of the artesian wells in the area.

Artesia became an agricultural oasis until the early 1920's when many of the area's artesian wells began to dwindle. Fortunately, in 1924 another kind of well was discovered when the Illinois #3 oil well came in, opening up the Artesia oil fields locally and the Permian Basin regionally.

Today, the oil & gas industry continues to flourish in the Artesia area along with farming, ranching, dairies, small businesses and the Federal Law Enforcement Training Center. At the Federal Law Enforcement Training Center, people from all over the United States come for specialized training.

Artesia Chamber of Commerce
408 West Texas
Artesia, NM 88210
1-800-658-6251

US 285
South of Artesia

9-A

Guadalupe Mountains

Guadalupe Mountains to southwest rise from Pecos River Valley, with higher southern peaks at 8,750 feet. Bold escarpment is famous Capitan limestone, an ancient reef similar to Great Barrier Reef of Australia, and host to Carlsbad Caverns as well as deep petroleum and underground water. Elevation 3,270 feet.

Driving south from Artesia, you see some hills on the horizon of the Chihuahuan Desert. These are not just any hills. What you are looking at is The Great Reef. That's right. It is a reef just like the Great Barrier Reef. Technically called the Capitan Reef, geologists from all over the world come to see this giant, exposed formation composed of ancient fossils and riddled with caves.

If you were to see a cross-section of the hills, it would look like Swiss cheese. It is the home to two national parks, Carlsbad Caverns in New Mexico and The Guadalupe Mountains National Park in Texas. A ten mile section of the Lincoln National Forest separates the two parks.

The reef slowly rises in southeastern New Mexico and extends southward into northwestern Texas where it abruptly ends with the venerable El Capitan. There is an incredible diversity of desert flora and fauna as well as the caves to explore.

Rattlesnake Canyon is one of the most scenic and accessible trails in Carlsbad Caverns, but you're most likely to have the trail all to yourself. Rattlesnake Canyon is a large, open valley where you can quietly soak in the true essence of the Chihuahuan Desert and the ruggedness of its plant and animal life. You might want to consider hiking the trail early, while it is cool, and then going to the caverns during the heat of the day.

Hwy 285
South of Seven Rivers

9-B

Castano De Sosa's Route

In 1590-91 Gaspar Castaño de Sosa, a Portuguese by birth, took an expedition up the Pecos River in an attempt to establish a colony in New Mexico. His venture was a failure, but it led to a permanent settlement under Don Juan de Oñate in 1598. Castaño de Sosa passed near here in the winter of 1590.

History tells us that the expansion by the Spanish into New Spain was filled with hardships. There were unfriendly Indians, hot, dry weather, and even their own government wanted to have a strong control on who did and did not colonize New Spain.

One of the ones who attempted to thwart the government and colonize what was to become New Mexico was Gaspar Castaño de Sosa. He led an unauthorized expedition through this area in the early 1590s. There were 170 people, their carts and stock. This first attempt was tracked down by royal agents. Castaño was arrested and his party was disbanded.

Castaño's party opened up routes that made it easier for those that followed to establish and colonize this area.

US Hwy 285 North
MM 67

9-C

Carlsbad Irrigation Flume

The massive concrete flume in the distance carries water from the Pecos River to irrigate much of the farmland in this area. It is a vital link in an extensive irrigation system which made possible development of the region's agricultural resources. A wooden flume constructed in 1890 washed away in 1902 and was replaced by the more substantial concrete structure in 1903.

Okay, what is a flume? Well, according to the dictionary, it is a narrow gorge with a stream flowing through it, usually, or an artificial channel or chute for a stream of water. The latter describes the Flume at Carlsbad.

Irrigation was a necessity for the desert Southwest. Rainfall and snow were erratic and could not be depended upon to provide the needed moisture to produce food. The Native Americans and Hispanic peoples watered small fields with canal networks, acequias, and brush diversion damns.

It was in 1889 that Ralph S. Tarr, an observer for the U.S. Geological Survey department, felt the Pecos Valley had potential for large scale agriculture. He estimated there was around 300,000 acres of fertile, irrigable land between Roswell and the Texas line. This was the starting point of the Pecos River Reclamation Project of which Pat Garret and Charles B. Eddy, founder of Carlsbad, were a part.

The Pecos River Flume was probably the most complex part of the canal network. One of two canals split and crossed the river itself. Originally made of wood, the flume is 475 feet long and 25 feet wide, carrying 8 feet of water. It was completed in 1890, but was destroyed by a flood in the early 1900's. When it was rebuilt, it was made of concrete. At that time, it was the largest concrete structure in the world.

Hwy 285
South of Carlsbad

9-D

Civilian Conservation Corps
Carlsbad Campsite

The Civilian Conservation Campsite provided employment for more than 50,000 young men in New Mexico during the Great Depression of the 1930's. Three CCC companies were located on the grounds where the Carlsbad Hospital now stands. They worked on flood control and reclamation projects along the Pecos River and the Guadalupe Mountains, and helped build the city's "President's Park."

The Civilian Conservation Corps was established by President Roosevelt to provide much needed jobs and training for young men during the depression.

At Carlsbad, they helped to develop a water source for the caverns. The spring at Rattlesnake Springs was used by prehistoric peoples and historic Indian groups, soldiers, travelers, and settlers. When Henry Harrison homesteaded the area around the spring in the 1880's, he developed the natural spring and built an irrigation system for his fields. When the National Park Service acquired the property, the area was further developed by the Corps during 1938 to 1942. The men were responsible for many area improvements including the rock wall of the spring pond, the ranger residence, and the planting of cottonwood trees.

Today, Rattlesnake Springs is on the National Register of Historic places and has been reexamined and inventoried as a potential cultural landscape.

Rattlesnake Springs has a picnic area for visitors, drinking water, and is wheelchair accessible. It is well-known to birders, being one of the better spots in New Mexico for attracting birds that are not common to the general area.

US 285
In Carlsbad

9-E

Loving's Bend

In July 1867, Oliver Loving, a partner in the Goodnight-Loving cattle concern, was seriously wounded in a fight with the Comanche. While his companion, "One-Armed" Bill Wilson, went for help, Loving stood off the attack for two days and nights. Loving died from his wounds at Fort Sumner in September.

Oliver Loving and Charles Goodnight developed a trail that would bring them a fortune from military beef contracts. It was late July and the contracts were to be let in August. Now, there was only the problem of gathering herds, but gold took care of that concern.

Indians had learned that if they stampeded the herd, they could steal the entire herd with little danger to themselves. It was dawn one morning when the Indians struck. The men and their crew managed to fight off the Indians, but the herd remained spooked and stampeded at anything.

Loving and "One-Armed"Wilson rode ahead of the herd, needing to be in Ft. Sumner to contract the herd. They rode for two nights and had not seen a sign of hostiles, so they chanced it, and set out at mid-day. Before the end of the day, they spotted a large band of Comanches charging towards them. The men hightailed it back to the banks of the Pecos River. They dove into a small wash that luckily had an over hang and a sand bar, literally protecting them from the Indians. It was a stand off. Loving had one of the new Henry repeating rifles, the forerunner of the Winchester. The Comanches settled in to wait them out.

Loving was injured when the Indians offered to parley. As soon as the men stood, a volley of arrows erupted in their direction. One shattered Loving's wrist and entered his torso.

By the time Goodnight caught up with Loving in Fort Sumner, his side had healed, but gangrene had set into his wrist. After amputation, an artery ruptured, and Loving died from his wounds. On his death bed, he asked his partner for two favors, to continue their partnership for at least 2 years in order that Loving's family be left out of debt, and that he not be "laid away in a foreign county." Goodnight agreed, though returning the body to Texas would be near impossible. Loving was good to his word, and managed the tasks.

HWY 285—South
County Road 712

9-F

Goodnight-Loving Trail

This famous old cattle trail, running 2000 miles from Texas to Wyoming was blazed in 1866 by Charles Goodnight and Oliver Loving. In New Mexico, the trail followed the Pecos River north to Fort Sumner, where the government needed beef to feed the Navajos at the Bosque Redondo Reservation.

Oliver Loving was born in frontier Kentucky in 1812. He spent his entire life living dangerously and has been called "The Dean of Texas Trail Drives". He earned the title through his fearless drives of large longhorn herds through territory where no others had gone before.

Former Texas Ranger, Col. Charles Goodnight began gathering a herd in 1866 to take on the trail. He knew that "whole of Texas would start north for the market" that year, making a jam on those routes headed North. As an alternative, he came up with a daring plan to move his herd south then west below the main Comanche territory, then across the Pecos and into New Mexico before heading to the gold fields of Denver.

As Goodnight was putting his outfit together, he happened upon Oliver Loving's Camp. The two discussed the plan. Loving told Goodnight about the horrors, hazards, and problems he would face. Goodnight, still determined to make the journey, agreed to let Loving go with him.

A handshake between two honorable men, more valuable than any paper contract, made the two men partners. They left the Texas Frontier on June 6th, 1866, with 2000 head of mixed cattle and 18 armed men to blaze a trail that went down into history as the Goodnight-Loving Trail, a very profitable venture.

Hwy 285
South of State Rd #31

9-G

Espejo's Trail

Don Antonio de Espejo, leader of the third expedition to explore New Mexico, passed near here on his return to Mexico City in 1583. After learning of the martyrdom of two Franciscan friars from an earlier expedition, he explored the Pueblo country and then followed the Pecos River Valley south.

The history of the Pueblo Indians begins in 1539 with the expedition of the Franciscan monk, Marcos di Niza, who, lured by rumors of great cities in the North, set out from Mexico, accompanied by some Indian guides and by a negro survivor of the ill-fated Pánfilo de Narváez expedition. The Indians were friendly at first, but the arbitrary conduct of the Spaniards soon provoked hostility and resistance.

After another winter in Tiguex, which remained hostile, with explorations along the Jemez, Piros, and other tribes, the expedition returned to Mexico in the spring of 1542. Three Franciscan monks remained behind, Fr. Padilla in Wichita, Fr. Lius de Escalona remained behind at Pecos ("Cicuye") and Brother Juan de la Cruz at Puaray. All three were killed by the Indians they were trying to convert to Christianity. They were the first missionary martyrs.

In 1581, Fr. Augusto Rodriguez asked and received permission for the undertaking of trying to colonize the area. Accompanied by two other priests, Frs. Santa Maria and Lopez, with an escort of about twenty Indians and soldiers under Francisco Chamuscado, he reached Tiguex late in the year. The escort was apparently frightened by the hostile attitudes of the natives, but the priests remained, and all three soon afterwards met the fate of the predecessors, being killed by the Tigua.

In an attempt to obtain the details of their death, and possibly recover their remains, a volunteer explorer, Don Antonio Espejo, accompanied by Father Bernadino Beltran, led a small expedition over the same route up the Rio Grande the next year. Having accomplished this purpose, he went on, visiting almost every Pueblo tribe from the Pecos to the Hopi, finally reaching Mexico in the fall of 1583.

County Rd 719
South of 285

9-H

Welcome to New Mexico

on 285 S on NM State Line

9-I

Carlsbad Caverns National Park

These vast and magnificent caverns contain over 21 miles of explored corridors. The chambers contain countless stalactites and stalagmites unrivaled in size and beauty. The caverns are within a reef that formed in an ancient sea 240 million years ago. Millions of years later, the reef was fractured, allowing ground water to begin work fashioning the caverns.

This 46,766 acre National Park contains over 85 known caves, including the nations deepest and third longest limestone cave. Comprised of a Permian-age fossil reef, Carlsbad Caverns has the world's largest underground chamber and countless formations. It is highly accessible with a variety of tours offered.

Your encounter with Carlsbad Caverns National Park begins in the Chihuahuan Desert of the Guadalupe Mountains. But beyond the somewhat familiar surroundings of rugged mountains and broad plains is another world. Away from the sunlight, away from the flowering cactus, away from the songs of the desert birds and the howl of the coyote, lies the celebrated underground world of Carlsbad Cavern. It is an incomparable realm of gigantic subterranean chambers, fantastic cave formations and extraordinary features. The first adventurers entering Carlsbad Cavern had no idea what to expect as they walked, crawled, and climbed down into the darkness. Today many of the wonders of Carlsbad Cavern are well known, yet the experience of exploring its chambers is every bit as exciting.

All trails in the cave are paved and adequately lighted. Visitors should wear comfortable, closed toe shoes with rubber soles for maximum safety and traction. The cave temperature varies little from the annual 56 F average, making a sweater or light jacket appropriate year round. Visitors may also wish to bring a camera and a flashlight. Strollers are not allowed in any underground cave areas, but infant backpacks are permitted. A pre-tour restroom stop is advisable because restrooms are only available in the visitor center and underground rest area. All tours are preceded by a mandatory cavern orientation briefing to promote resource protection and cavern safety. Visitors on all tours exit the cave by elevator.

Carlsbad Caverns National Park
3225 National Park Highway
Carlsbad, NM 88220
Phone: 505-785-2232

US 62 West
North of White's City

US 62 West
West of White's CitY

9-J

Carlsbad

Carlsbad was originally named Eddy after Charles B. Eddy, pioneer cattleman and promoter, but was later renamed for the famous European resort. In 1590 the expedition of Gaspar Castano de Sosa followed this part of the Pecos River which in the 19th century had become the center of a vast cattle empire.

Christened with a bottle of champagne in 1888, the community of "Eddy" on the Pecos River was found to be a wonderful spot for pioneer ranchers. The Goodnight/Loving Trail crossed the river before there was a city, and it was the drovers of those cattle drives that first recognized the potential.

It was in 1889 that Eddy was made the county seat, moving the local government from Seven Rivers. In 1899, by a vote of 83 to 43, the city residents voted to rename their community Carlsbad. In what is now the Czech Republic, Karlsbad was a famous European health resort. The mineral content and related healing properties of the water in the two cities, continents apart, were virtually identical.

Carlsbad offers many recreations, with Lake Carlsbad located in the heart of the city, and biking trails along the banks of the canal in the city, there are many things to do and see.

Carlsbad Chamber of Commerce
P.O. Box 99
Carlsbad, NM 88220
1-800-221-1224

Hwy US 180/62
Outside of Carlsbad

9-K

Grant County

The name "Grant" honors the great General and President of the United States, Ulysses S. Grant. Grant County came into being on January 30, 1868.

County Seat: Silver City
Communities: Bayard, Hurley, Gila, Pinos Altos, Hachita, Cliff, Santa Rita

3,970 Square Miles

Land of Minerals

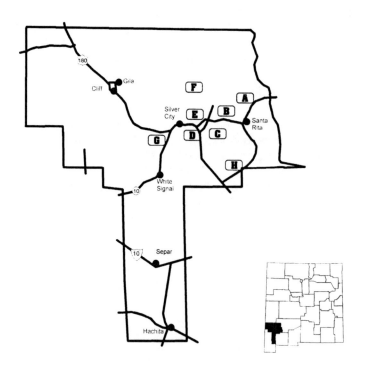

Emory Pass

Crest of Black Range, at elevation 8,828 feet; uplifted range of Tertiary volcanic and Paleozoic sedimentary rocks bordering Rio Grande graben, in which rock layers are about 4 miles lower than at pass. Same rocks cap Caballo Mountains, seen 35 miles to east, on east side of Rio Grande trough.

Slipping between Hillsboro Peak and Sawyer Peak is Emory Pass. You are on the Southeastern section of the Gila National Forest.

It was in the autumn of 1919, in a wild and scenic area of New Mexico's Gila Forest, that a young assistant district forester named Aldo Leopold was on horseback, trying to imagine what his surroundings would be like if a proposed road system was to go through the area.

Not here, he decided. Something must be done to save it so future generations would be able to enjoy the purity and beauty of this untouched wilderness.

Leopold, with the aid of a few like-minded U.S. Forest Service colleagues, and strongly supported by the local community, eventually persuaded his employer that the area should remain free of roads and be preserved for wilderness recreation.

On June 3, 1924, 755,000 acres were set aside by the Forest Service, as the Gila Wilderness. It was the world's first designated wilderness lands.

The Gila Forest is our largest national forest, with 3.3 million acres. Located in the center is the half million acre Gila Wilderness. Set aside in 1924, it was the nation's first experiment to see if humans would appreciate the gift of pristine wilderness. Thankfully, they did. The mountains are rugged, the canyons deep. The forests have never known the sound of an ax and are home to elk, bear, wolves and much more.

On US Hwy 90
West of Kingston MM 32.2

10-A

Kneeling Nun

Most famous of the many historic landmarks in the Black Range country is the Kneeling Nun, so named for its resemblance to a nun kneeling in prayer before a great altar. Many legends have grown up around the giant monolith which rests near the summit of the Santa Rita Range.

Throughout the ages, Spanish legends centering around the rock formation which resembles a convent nun, have grown and been passed down from generation to generation, likely beginning around 1800.

Apache Indians surely had legends of their own. The Apache refused to camp in the vicinity of the rock formation that uncannily resembled a veiled woman despite the excellent vantage point into the valley below.

Though no Apache stories of the Kneeling Nun seem to exist today, there are two centuries of speculation surrounding an Indian prophecy regarding a sacred messenger who would appear in the form of a female spirit. For reasons lost in the shadows of long-ago events, the Spaniards linked this prophecy with "Cibola."

Cibola, in Spanish, means female buffalo. At one time explorers called the Kneeling Nun by that name. They thought the fabled Seven Cities of Cibola lay somewhere in the region in caves, and, according to theory, they were probably buried during an earthquake.

East of Silver city on NM Hwy 152
MM 2.2

10-B

Bayard

Sites in the surrounding hills indicate that Indians of the Mogollon culture (A.D. 300–1450) lived here long before the Europeans. In the late 19th century, this was a stronghold of Apaches led by Victorio and Geronimo. Today Bayard, which was incorporated in 1925, lies in a great commercial mining region. Population 3,036. Elevation 6,152 feet.

Two miles east of Santa Clara, Bayard, now the center of the mining district, began its history as a railroad station serving as a supply terminal for Fort Bayard.

Bayard gained prominence when the company town of Santa Rita was literally consumed by the expansion of the open pit mine.

Bayard's status was again enhanced when the Cobre Consolidated School District was formed and the administrative offices, the district high school, a middle- school, and an elementary school were located in Bayard.

On US Hwy 180 In Bayard
MM 122.3

10-C

Santa Rita Copper Mines

Copper has been mined here since 1804. For five years, development by Francisco Manuel Elguea resulted in some 6,000,000 pounds of copper being transported annually to Mexico City by mule train. Brief periods of activity were halted by Apache opposition until the coming of the railroad in the 1880's, when the area became a major copper producer.

The Santa Rita Mine is the oldest active mine in the Southwest and now one of the world's largest open pit mines. Mule trains of ore were sent to Chihuahua City, Mexico, as early as 1800 and prior to the 1800's the copper was utilized by the Indians. Today the copper from the Santa Rita and Tyrone open pit mines provide the economic base of the region and employ about 2,000 men and women.

There was only a period of about 16 years that the mine was not in operation. This had to do with the Apache. 400 citizens staged a mass evacuation of the area. As they traveled down towards Chihuahua, the evacuees realized that the Apache were following. The Apache were out for blood in revenge for a massacre staged by some of the Santa Rita people. Only 6 survived the trip to Chihuahua.

It would be 16 years before the mine would be reopened. It has been continuously worked since then.

South of Silver City on NM 152
MM 120.7

10-D

Fort Bayard—1866–1900

One of the several posts created on the Apache frontier, Fort Bayard protected the Pinos Altos mining district. Company B of the black 125th Infantry served here, as did Lt. John J. Pershing. In 1900 the fort became a military hospital, and today serves as Fort Bayard Medical Center.

Fort Bayard National Cemetery

Originally established in 1866 as the military cemetery for Fort Bayard, many troopers, veterans, and civilians are buried here. It became a national cemetery, one of two in New Mexico, in 1973.

With the surrender of Geronimo in September of 1886, the Indian wars came to an end. The Indians no longer presented a threat to the area. Fort Bayard continued as an active Army post until 1899, when it was proposed that the Fort be abandoned. However, Surgeon General Sternberg of the U.S. Army noticed the general well-being of the troops posted at the fort. He suspected the area's mild climate and gentle seasons were making a difference in the health of the troops. He began posting troops sick with tuberculosis.

Surgeon General Sternberg conceived the idea of transferring the post to the Medical Department for treatment and research. During World War One there were as many as 1,700 patients at the hospital.

Today, it continues to be used by the State of New Mexico as a public nursing home for long term care. This hospital takes great pride in placing the needs of the patient first.

On US 180 North of Bayard   **10-E**

Pinos Altos

Once the Grant County seat, the town survived early Apache attacks to produce over $8,000,000 of gold, silver, copper, lead, and zinc before the mines played out in the 20th century. In this area are extensive gold, silver and copper deposits mined as early as 1803. A new gold discovery in 1860 by three 49ers from California stimulated a boom that led to the establishment of the mining camp of Pinos Altos.

Pinos Altos, "Tall Pines", has been occupied off and on for over 150 years. One of the first buildings was a horseshoe shaped fortified area to protect horses and miners from Indian attacks.

The Indians tried to drive out the Spaniards, Mexicans and Americans that continued to encroach upon their territory. As the Indians would successfully drive out one group, another would come, seeking riches.

When three Americans first stumbled upon the golden land, they contemplated what to do. They snuck back down the hill to get supplies, entrusting two brothers and a friend to secure the necessary supplies and equipment. Under the cover of darkness, they returned to their claim. The next morning, however, there were several new claims beside them when the men awoke.

Within 6 months, the area had swelled with 700 miners searching for gold.

Today, the gold and the tall pines are gone, long since hauled away. This district was estimated to have produced over $850,000,000 in ore.

So much for keeping a secret.

North of Silver City at Pinos Altos
MM 6.3

10-F

Silver City

Silver City is located in the midst of rich mineral deposits. The Santa Rita Copper Mines, opened in 1805, were the second such mines operating in what is now the U.S. A silver strike in 1870 began the commercial mining for which the area is still known. The Apache chiefs Victorio, Geronimo, and Mangas Coloradas figure in its history.

Silver City offers a mild climate, Victorian charm, friendly people from its tucked away location in rolling mountain foothills. This area once nourished the prehistoric Mogollon and Mimbres Indian cultures who farmed the rich soil.

The Apache Indians roamed through their native hunting grounds, fighting hard to stop the encroachment of Spanish and American settlers.

The discovery of silver brought a continuous stream of settlers to the area. Finally, the Army forced the Indians to the reservations and the tent city became more permanent as clay was made into bricks for homes.

As the county seat, Silver City found it's economy enhanced with mining and ranching. The mild climate attracts many retirees.

Silver City is known for its galleries, museums, historical, and natural attractions. A visit to the award winning Toy Town, located at 107 West Broadway, can add a few smiles to your day and make your vacation even more memorable.

Silver City Chamber of Commerce
1103 N. Hudson
Silver City, NM 88061
505-538-3785

On US 180 West of Silver City

10-G

City of Rocks State Park

Wind and water gradually sculpted the volcanic tuff at City Of Rocks, creating the rows of monolithic blocks that gave this park its name. Camping/picnicking sites are tucked away among these Stonehenge-like formations and the park also features a cactus garden, hiking trails and a playground.

Formed of volcanic ash 30 million years ago and sculpted by wind and water into rows of huge blocks, City of Rocks State Park takes it's name from the unique rock formations. The rock formations are so unique that they are only known to exist in six other places in the world. Imaginative visitors may see the rock formations as a small city, complete with houses, chimneys, courtyards, and streets.

Mimbres Indians roamed this area until 1200 A.D. and left behind arrowheads and pottery shards. Spanish conquistadors spent time in the area. They carved crosses into the rocks.

City of Rocks
P.O. Box 50
Faywood, NM 88034
505-536-2800

US 180 North 2 Mi at Jct 61
MM 3.2

10-H

Guadalupe County

Guadalupe County was created by the territorial legislature of 1891. The name honors Our Lady of Guadalupe, the vision of the Virgin Mary, who appeared to Juan Diego near Mexico City in 1531.

County Seat: Santa Rosa
Communities: Cuervo, Newkirk, Colonias, Dilia, Anton Chico, Milagro, Puerto de Luna, Pastura, Vaughn

2,999 Square Miles

Black Jack Ketchum

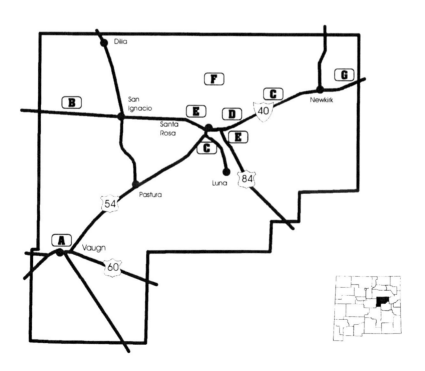

Vaughn

Vaughn, a division point in the transcontinental railway system, is located along the route of the Stinson cattle trail. In 1882, Jim Stinson, manager of the New Mexico Land and Livestock Co., drove 20,000 cattle in eight separate herds along this important trail from Texas to the Estancia Valley. Population 737. Elevation 5,965 feet.

Vaughn, 37 miles south of Santa Rosa, finds itself at the junction of three highways and two railroads. It was named for a civil engineer who worked for the AT&SF Railroad, Major G.W. Vaughn.

Vaughn was an important rest stop for large herds of cattle being driven from Texas to New Mexico under the management of Jim Stinson, an employee of the New Mexico Land and Livestock Company.

It was when the EP&RI Railroad spurred off the AT&SF railroad that Vaughn got a boost helping the small town to flourish. Transportation has always been a major factor in Vaughn's development.

Today, Vaughn is a good place to stop and catch your breath before continuing on your journey to explore this great state.

Town of Vaughn
P.O. Box 278
803 E. Highway 54
Vaughn, NM 88353
1-505-2301

Located in Vaughn New Mexico

11-A

Trail of the Forty-Niners

To give gold-seekers another route to California, Capt. Randolph B. Marcy and Lt. James H. Simpson opened a wagon road from Arkansas to New Mexico in 1849. Marcy's Road, although very popular with the Forty-Niners, still was never as well-traveled as the Santa Fe Trail. Here the route parallels I-40 to Albuquerque.

Captain Marcy spent much of his military career on the frontier. In 1859, he was recalled to Washington, where the Department of State asked him to produce "The Prairie Traveler: A hand-book for Overland Expeditions." The book was a bestseller in it's day and was considered essential to those traveling west.

In the book, Captain Marcy described the route he helped to discover as an alternate route for the Gold Seekers heading for California, "This route is set down upon most of the maps of the present day as having been discovered and explored by various persons, but my own name seems to have been carefully excluded from the list. Whether this omission has been intentional or not, I leave for the authors to determine. I shall merely remark that I had the command and entire direction of an expedition which, in 1849, discovered, explored, located and marked out this identical wagon road from Fort Smith, Arkansas, to Santa Fe, New Mexico,"

In 1848, gold was discovered at Sutter's Mill in California. Word spread like wild fire and people from the East packed up their belongings and headed West. By 1849, the Forty-Niners had many routes to California. Towns sprang up over night as Gold Fever struck the nation. John A. Sutter, the owner of the Mill could only say, "By this sudden discovery of the gold, all my great plans were destroyed."

Interstate 40, West Bound Lane
MM 252.

11-B

Santa Rosa

The Spanish explorer Antonio de Espejo passed through this area in 1583, as did Gaspar Castañ de Sosa in 1590. Santa Rosa, the Guadalupe County seat, was laid out on the ranch of Celso Baca Y Baca, a politician and rancher in the late 1800's. It was named for his wife, Doña Rosa. Population 2,469. Elevation 4,620 feet.

Founded in 1865 and located near the Pecos River on US Interstate 40, Santa Rosa is an interesting combination of tradition, natural attractions, and a growing business community.

There are 15 natural lakes and streams in the area, including The Blue Hole, one of the most unique geological phenomenons in the Southwest. The clear, bell shaped blue pool, delivers up to 3,000 gallons of water per minute at a constant 64 degree temperature. Its thermally heated waters come from the same system that flows in Carlsbad Caverns. It is 81 feet deep, and 60 feet in diameter at the surface. It widens to 130 feet in diameter at the bottom. Its amazing clarity and constant temperature have made it a favorite for scuba divers, photographers, and sightseers.

This charming city's pleasant climate, rich history, and natural beauty are well worth the visit.

Santa Rosa Chamber of Commerce
486 Parker Avenue
Santa Rosa, NM 88435
cocsantarosa@plateautel.net
1-800-450-7084

Interstate 40 East Bound lane,
MM 273
Exit 0.6 Miles to Right

11-C

Vasquez De Coronado's Route

In 1540, Francisco Vasquez de Coronado and a small army set out from Mexico to search for the fabled Quivera and its cities of gold. In the spring of 1541, the expedition halted near here for four days while they built a long bridge across the Pecos River. From here they continued their exploration deep into present-day Kansas.

Francisco Vasquez de Coronado was born into a noble family in Salamanca, Spain in 1510. At the age of 25, he came to the Americas as an assistant to New Spain's first viceroy.

An ambitious man, he married the daughter of the colonial treasurer, put down a major slave rebellion, and became the governor of a Mexican province within three years of his arrival, but he wanted more. Rumors of earlier explorations by Cabeza de Vaca about seven cites of gold inspired him to lead a royal expedition to explore the north into what is now the American West.

When they did not find the "Seven Cities of Cibola", parties were sent out, some traveling to the border between Arizona and California where they explored the Grand Canyon. Coronado himself led a party into what is now Kansas.

Returning to Mexico without locating a single golden city, the Viceroy branded Coronado's expedition an abject failure. His career quickly declined and in 1544 he was removed from office as a governor and moved to Mexico City where he worked in a modest position for the city. He died in 1554, though his legacy is seen throughout the west.

US 54
Santa Rosa

11-D

Louis and Joe D. Page Highway

This highway was named after Louis and Joe D. Page and leads from Santa Rosa up to the Santa Rosa Lake State Park. It follows the Pecos River, leading through colorful landscape where Indians once roamed free.

For more information contact

Santa Rosa Chamber of Commerce
486 Parker Avenue
Santa Rosa, NM 88435
1-800-450-7084
cocsantarosa@plateautel.net

NM 91
I-40 East Bound Lane
MM 273

11-E

Santa Rosa Lake State Park

Pronghorn antelope may be seen grazing near this reservoir on the Pecos River, at the edge of the Llano Estacado - the famed "Staked Plains." The park offers water sports; fishing for catfish, bass, and walleyes; camping/picnicking sites, a visitor center, and a boat ramp.

Just 7 miles north of Santa Rosa is Santa Rosa Lake State Park. The park is a recreational paradise, offering waterskiing, wind surfing and excellent fishing. There is a fully equipped campground, nature trails, and wildlife viewing. The countryside is dotted with Juniper and Piñon trees. Eagles roost on snags at water's edge or small islands on the lake.

Santa Rosa Dam and Lake was authorized by the Flood Control Act of 1954. It serves for conservation of irrigation water, sedimentation, and flood control. However, there is no permanent pool. When the water is needed for irrigation, it is used.

The main embankment was completed in 1981. During the development, the U.S. Army Corps of Engineers provided funding for exploration of more than 250 archeological sites located in the project area. Exhibits concerning these sites and local flora and fauna can be seen at the solar-heated Information Center.

Santa Rosa State Park
P.O. Box 384
Santa Rosa, NM 88433
(505) 472-3110

2nd Street
Santa Rosa
MM 0.7

11-F

Comanche Country

By 1700 the Comanches had acquired the horse and began moving into this area. They drove out the Jicarilla Apaches, and their raids on New Mexico's eastern frontier posed a threat to Indian, Spanish, and Anglo settlements for over a century. The Comanches were finally defeated by the U.S. Army in 1874.

The Comanches were a fierce nomadic tribe whose skills upon horseback were unmatched.

It is in part, thanks to the Comanche, that the early Spanish settlers did not roam further North than they did. After defeating many tribes of Indians, the Comanches were unstoppable.

They lived nomadic lives, roaming the plains, following the buffalo and other game.

The Comanches did not play favorites when it came to raiding. They raided Anglos, Spanish, and other tribes, stealing horses, goods, kidnapping women and children, occasionally ransoming them back to their families.

Located in the Rest Area off Interstate,
West Bound Lane
Near MM 301

11-G

Harding County

A Long horn along the
Good-Night Loving Trail

The County was created by the state
legislature on March 4, 1921, the same day
Warren G. Harding was inaugurated 29th
President of the United States.

County Seat: Mosquero
Communities: Roy

2,125 Square Miles

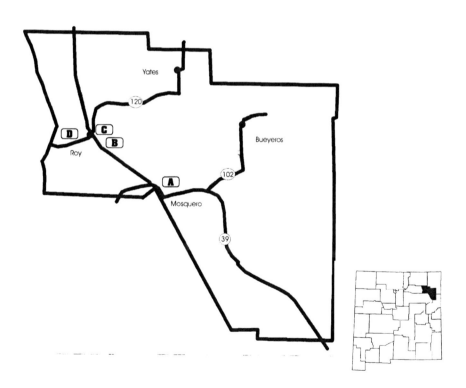

Canadian Escarpment

Prominent landform of northeastern New Mexico that extends for almost 100 miles between Las Vegas and Clayton. From this point, the grasslands of the High Plains reach northwestward to the foot of the Southern Rocky Mountains which rise to elevations of more than 13,000 feet. Elevation here 6,300 feet.

In geology, an escarpment is a steep face of a cliff usually caused by erosion or by prehistoric changes in the water line. Here, the Canadian River cut through the softer soils, leaving this 100 mile land form.

The Canadian River flows out of the Rocky Mountains and meanders its way through Texas and into Oklahoma where it joins up with the Arkansas River before emptying into the Gulf of Mexico.

Water is one of the most important natural resources of New Mexico. To protect the area and to save water for years of drought, Conchas Dam and Ute Dam were built. These reservoirs provide not only recreation, but life giving water when needed.

NM 104
MM 46.7

12-A

Goodnight-Loving Trail

After leaving Fort Sumner, the Goodnight-Loving Trail forked in two directions. This branch, developed by Oliver Loving in 1866, followed the Pecos River to Las Vegas, and the Santa Fe Trail to Raton Pass. The great Texas Cattle drives followed this and other routes to Colorado and Wyoming until 1880.

Oliver Loving was born in frontier Kentucky in 1812. He spent his entire life living dangerously and has been called "The Dean of Texas Trail Drives". He won the title through his fearless drives of large longhorn herds through territory where no others had gone before.

Former Texas Ranger, Col. Charles Goodnight began gathering a herd in 1866 to take on the trail. He knew that "whole of Texas would start north for the market" that year, making a jam on those routes headed North. As an alternative, he came up with a daring plan to move his herd south then west below the main Comanche territory, then across the Pecos and into New Mexico before heading to the gold fields of Denver.

As Goodnight was putting his outfit together, he happened upon Oliver Loving's Camp. The two discussed the plan. Loving told Goodnight about the horrors, hazards and problems he would face. Goodnight, still determined to make the journey, agreed to let Loving go with him.

A handshake between two honorable men, more valuable than any paper contract, made the two men partners. They left the Texas Frontier on June 6th, 1866 with 2000 head of mixed cattle and 18 armed men to blaze a trail that went down into history as the Goodnight-Loving Trail, a very profitable venture.

* Note: They made $24,000 on their first trip.

NM 39 at City Hall in Town of Mosquero
MM 49.4

12-B

Mills Canyon

This site of one of New Mexico's most spectacular horticultural enterprises, the Orchard Ranch, established by Melvin W. Mills of Springer and notable for its skillfully engineered irrigation system. The ranch cultivated 12 miles of land along the Canadian river. Vegetable gardens and several thousand fruit trees flourished in the 1880's and later. A destructive flood wiped out orchards, irrigation system, buildings, and other improvements in 1904. They were never replaced.

Looks can be deceiving. During most years, the Canadian river meanders its course, and it was here that Melvin Mills, an entrepreneur, planted 14,000 apple, peach, pear, cherry, plum, walnut, almond and chestnut trees. He also cultivated melons, tomatoes, grapes and cabbage. The 10 mile long canyon was crisscrossed with irrigation channels and cisterns that fed hundreds of acres of cultivated fields.

He also built Mills Canyon Hotel, a very popular vacation spot that serviced the stagecoach lines. He had a mansion in Springer, and a law partner, Thomas B. Catron.

The Canadian River flooded in 1904, wiping out everything in a matter of minutes.

Mills died in 1925, a broken man. According to the local legends, he had to beg to be allowed to die on a cot in his old home, the mansion in Springer that his ex-partner then owned.

The nearby Village of Roy was named for its founders, the Roy Brothers and was incorporated in 1916. Today, ranching is the main industry and Chicosa Lake State Park is an excellent get away spot.

On NM 39 Route
Town of Roy
MM 67.0

12-C

Canadian River Canyon

Flowing out of the Rockies, the Canadian River has cut a gorge 600 feet deep through sedimentary strata of the High Plains. Rim elevation is 5,400 feet.

Like a miniature Grand Canyon, hikers can trek down and back up the Canadian River Canyon road. Be sure and take plenty of water. As you walk along the river and admire the colors that contrast with the red canyon walls, you will see among the scattered grape vines and fruit trees, the ruins of a hotel, the sad legacy of Melvin Mills' fruit and vegetable empire that was destroyed in a flood in 1904, never to be rebuilt.

The canyon forms a wildlife island in the prairie for mountain lion, wild turkey, bald and golden eagles, antelope, bear, and Barbary sheep.

Early settlers in the area removed most of the game. In the 1940's mule deer were reintroduced to the canyon and a small resident herd is now present. African Barbary sheep were introduced in 1950 and have thrived here.

Warm water stream fishing is an added attraction. Highway 39 travels from Roy to Mills and the Canadian River Canyon and travels through the Kiowa National Grasslands. The federal government purchased them during the depression years and they were returned to grassland agriculture.

West on NM 120 Rt.
MM 62.5

12-D

Hidalgo County

Geronimo Surrenders
At Skeleton Canyon

Hidalgo County was named for the Mexican town of Guadalupe Hidalgo, where the treaty of Guadalupe-Hildago was signed in 1848. The County was created on February 25,1919.

County Seat: Lordsburg
Communities: Antelope Wells, Rodeo, Animas,
Cotton City, Virden

3,447 Square Miles

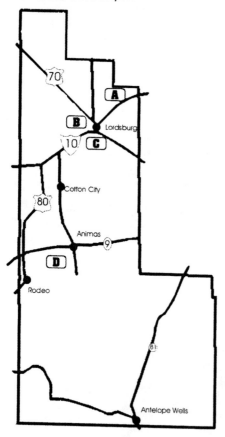

McComas Incident

In March 1883, Judge and Mrs. H.C. McComas were killed in this vicinity by a group of Chiricahua Apaches led by Chatto. An extensive manhunt failed to rescue their six-year-old son, who had been taken captive. This incident was part of a violent outbreak toward the end of the Apache wars.

Hamilton C. McComas served two terms as county judge in Monticello, Illinois. It became his lifelong habit of using the title, "Judge" in front of his name. The father of three, two older daughters by another marriage, and Charlie born in 1876, he was a lawyer engaged by a St. Louis company to travel to New Mexico to represent their interests in various mine ventures.

Judge McComas left his family in Fort Scott while he traveled to Silver City. Soon the judge was thoroughly enchanted with New Mexico and decided to make Silver City his home. In 1882, he opened a law office with a partner, sent for his family, and became a well liked member of the community.

In March of 1883, Judge McComas had mining business in the vicinity of Lordsburg. He decided to take his wife and young son with him, leaving his daughters with friends. The family spent the night on the road with friends and departed the next morning. Around noon, they stopped for lunch.

The encounter with the Indians was pure chance. The grizzly details of the Judge and his wife's deaths made national headlines, and the country searched and prayed for the missing boy. He was never found. Some believe he was killed or died of exposure. Still others feel he stayed with the Apaches down in Mexico. A picture of the surrender of some of the Apaches shows a blond haired boy among the other youth. Some believe the boy was Charlie, but the truth may never be known.

Curiously, Chatto, the Apache War Chief, surrendered within two months of the McComas Incident. Ironically, Chatto, after surviving bitter frontier warfare, died in an automobile accident in 1934.

On US Hwy 90 south of Silver City
MM 19.2 (Marker Missing)

13-A

Lordsburg

Lordsburg was founded in 1880 on the route of the Southern Pacific Railroad, near that used by the Butterfield Overland Mail Co., 1858-1861. It eventually absorbed most of the population of Shakespeare, a now-deserted mining town three miles south. Population 3,195. Elevation 4,245 feet.

Compared to it's earlier shoot-em-up days, Lordsburg is today, a quiet community. Before Lordsburg had a name, railroad freight handlers needed a way to label merchandise destined for the town. Located in New Mexico's bootheel, just 24 miles from the Arizona border, the freight was shipped by Dr. Charles H. Lord of Tucson. He owned a distribution company that served New Mexico. Soon the tag "Lords" caught on and the town became known as Lordsburg

Lordsburg is the County Seat of Hidalgo county and prides itself on its low crime rate. Base industries are cattle, cotton and copper. A considerable portion of activity has expanded in growing and processing green chili.

Lordsburg boasts year-round sunshine, and high desert and mountain scenery.

Lordsburg-Hidalgo County Chamber of Commerce
208 E. Motel Drive
Lordsburg, NM 88045
505-542-9864

US Hwy 90
Just north of Lordsburg MM 27.4

13-B

Shakespeare

After a silver strike in 1869, a townsite was laid out at the old stage stop of Mexican Springs. Named Ralston City, a diamond swindle caused its collapse in 1874. The town was revived as Shakespeare in 1879, but the depression of 1893 closed the mines and made it a ghost town.

The buildings in Shakespeare, like many across the country, were built of adobe. The walls were thick to withstand Indian attacks, the windows small so that they could be boarded up in a hurry.

The town was unique among mining towns of New Mexico. It boasted no plumbing, no club, no church, no school, no bank. Even the dance hall girls who came in from Deming and Lordsburg were permitted neither residence nor home in Shakespeare. The same carriage that brought them also took them back the same night.

When the town reached its peak of about 3,000 people, some of the extreme restrictions on the girls' activities was relaxed. Roxy Jay's Saloon opened. Its bar ran the length of the building, the longest adobe in the area. The bar was made from mahogany and was brought part way by an eighteen mule freight wagon. The wonder of the town was an enormous mirror for the back of the bar. It was respected by residents, and even though the doors were full of bullet holes, the mirror was never hit by flying lead.

Today, Shakespeare is a privately owned town where the owners have begun to rebuild, as things were damaged in a fire in the early 1990's. They are striving to give people a glimpse into what life was like during the early 1900's.

I 10 West to Lordsburg
On 494 County Road

13-C

Smugglers' Trail

Smugglers once crossed this area with mule trains of contraband from Mexico, to be traded for merchandise in Arizona. In the summer of 1881, a group of Mexican smugglers were killed in Skeleton Canyon by members of the Clanton gang, including Old Man Clanton, Ike and Billy Clanton, and Curly Bill.

Clanton Hideout

The infamous Clanton Gang had two crude dugouts here in the 1880's that served as hideouts and a base for wide-ranging outlaw activities, particularly in connection with the Curly Bill Gang's depredations along the Smuggler's Trail that passed by here. Old Man Clanton was ambushed below the border in revenge for a Skeleton Canyon massacre.

Ike and Billy Clanton were part of the most famous gunfight in the history of the Old West. The names of Wyatt Earp and Doc Holliday and the fight of the OK Corral, were legends born that day in Tombstone, Arizona.

The Clanton gang ranged over this area, with "Old Man" Clanton leading the charge. The Clantons had a ranch by Tombstone and provided beef for contracts. Some cattle might have had a different brand. The family often hired colorful characters, such as Curly Bill.

Billy Clanton along with the two McLaury brothers were casualties of the OK Corral. He was buried at Boothill by Tombstone. His father, "Old Man" Clanton was later exhumed from where he was buried near here and laid to rest beside his young son. Billy Clanton was 19 at the time of the gunfight at the OK Corral.

While Billy died from wounds from the gunfight, Ike survived. He pressed charges against the Earps and Doc Holliday. The charges were dismissed.

On NM 338
Miles South of Animas

13-D

Lea County

Land of Oil and Ranches

Capt. Joseph Calloway Lea, a prominent leader in Chavez County and founder of the New Mexico Military Academy, was honored by having Lea County named after him in 1917.

County Seat: Lovington
Communities: Caprock, Tatum McDonald, Jal, Buckeye, Oil Center, Eunice, Maljama, Bennett

4,394 Square Miles

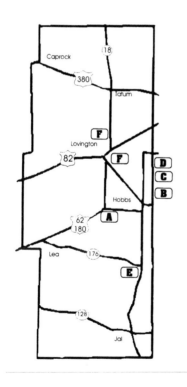

Hobbs

Named for the family of James Hobbs which homesteaded here in 1907, Hobbs became first a trading village for ranchers and then a major oil town after the discovery of oil by the Midwest Oil Company in 1928.

It was January 28th of 1910 when Hobbs was officially opened. The James Hobbs family opened a post office. For nearly two decades, the town remained isolated and inconvenient. It was a difficult place for people to reach and make a living from.

On October of 1927, everything began to change. Oil would bring an influx of Model T's, airplanes, trucks, and people on foot. The great depression saw a brief decline in population, but it did not last long. Located on both the Llano Estacado and the Permian Basin, the elevation is about 3,615 feet and just three miles from the Texas Border. It has a mild, dry climate, abundant sun and low humidity.

In addition to the oil and gas industry, dairy and ostrich farming is wide spread. It is home to the Lea County Cowboy Hall of Fame and Western Heritage Center. The city also boasts numerous parks, a golf course, swimming pool, and several jogging and bicycle trails.

Hobbs
400 North Marland
Hobbs, NM 88240
Phone: (505) 397-3202
(800) 658-6291
Fax: (505) 397-1689

US 180/62 East
Hobbs

14-A

Points of Interest

These maps located on the backs of the historical markers, lead you to other interesting sites in the area, as well as give you a good idea of your present location.

on US 180/62
West of Hobbs

14-B

Oil and Gas

A completion of the Discovery Well of the Hobbs Pool six miles south, April 12, 1929, focuses attention upon the potential of New Mexico as a major source of oil and natural Gas. Steady development under the state conservation program gradually moved New Mexico into sixth nationwide in oil production and fourth in gas production.

While Lea County attained first place in the value of oil and gas production, these positions achieved during the 1950's and 60's were maintained as the decade of the 1970's opened.

The country is high plains desert and offers magnificent, uninterrupted horizons as far as you can see. It has been said that the skies of New Mexico are bluer than anywhere else in the world. In Lea County, you can see for yourself. Dotted across this vast horizon are numerous pumpjacks, slowly bobbing up and down, and lifting the black gold secreted beneath the landscape.

From here, the oil and gas is piped to refineries where is it turned into much needed products for modern society.

The communities were initially agriculturally-based, but the discovery of oil and gas in the mid 1920's had a significant impact on the area. Today, the county's agricultural heritage continues to have underlying influences on a county's development with an active dairy industry as well as farming and ranching. The oil and gas industry still has a strong effect on the local economy, and doubtless, will, as long as there is a demand for the fossil fuels.

US 180/62 West
Rest Area

14-C

Ken Towle Park

Dedicated to Highway Commissioner Kenneth Towle, whose efforts made possible this rest area for visitors to New Mexico.

All across New Mexico, highways criss-cross and take you past different landscapes and scenery. The State Highway Department has set up small facilities where tired drivers can get out and stretch their legs before continuing on their journeys.

Lea County, at the time it was established, had essentially nothing to offer except the vision of a handful of hardy settlers. The scattered sparse settlements were connected with wagon roads and cattle trails. There was neither telegraph nor daily newspaper, and mail traveled by horse. There were no railroads, no running streams, and no major cities. Politicians in Santa Fe considered the area to be an immense, semi-arid pastureland on the southeastern corner of the state. They had no reason to justify the creation of a county from such an arid, windswept place.

It was the discovery of a great wealth of gas, oil, and potash that changed history for Lea County.

US 180/62 West
Rest Area

14-D

Llano Estacado and Oil

Llano Estacado, Staked Plain, is southern part of High Plains province, a high plateau of 32,000 square miles in east New Mexico and west Texas. Crops are irrigated by "fossil" water pumped from underground sandstones. Deeper are prolific oil and gas pools, the liquid black gold of southeast New Mexico. Elevation 3,655 feet.

Eunice and Jal are two small towns that developed around the discovery of the oil and gas pools. Eunice has had difficult times. It wasn't until 1929 that the first producing oil well came in. Carbon black, a byproduct of natural gas, which is used in ink, paints, fertilizer, carbon paper, cement, and dark chocolate, spawned several companies. Oil drilling services provide most of the employment.

With pumpjacks, resembling giant grasshoppers, constantly bringing the black gold to the surface, Eunice is less than quiet.

Further South is the small town of Jal, New Mexico. Three brothers arrived in the area, their cattle branded JAL and thus gave birth to the small community.

Recently, a local artist decided to create something that would bring people from all around. He worked with the town and created four huge 20 foot tall cowboys on horses as well as a herd of 13 huge cows. These were set on the horizon heading towards JAL Springs. These sculptures can be seen for 5 miles in any direction.

Jct of 18 North and 176 East

14-E

Lovington

Lovington is named after Robert Florence Love, who founded the town on his homestead in 1908. It was a farming and ranching community until the discovery of the Denton pool after World War II turned it into an oil town. It is the county seat of Lea County.

When Robert Florence Love filed for a post office permit, it was denied. There was already a post office permit under the name of Loving south of Carlsbad. Mr. Love changed the application name to Lovington and the Post office was established on September 12, 1908.

As with most of the area communites, the first few years were lean. Drought and isolation made it hard to attract settlers to the area. Then in the late 1920's oil was discovered and the town boomed.

Agriculture had always been Lovington's economic mainstay. More acres were tilled as irrigation was advanced. Cattle herds grew in size. The discovery of "black gold" gave the city increased wealth. More recently, the local dairy industry has branched into cheese processing.

Just 18 miles from the Texas border, it is a friendly, uncrowded and progressive place to live. With an elevation of 3,934 feet, Lovington has warm days and cool nights.

Community spirit is readily apparent with its five city parks, swimming pool, nine baseball fields and eleven acre fishing lake.

Lovington Chamber of Commerce
201 S. Main
Lovington, NM 88260
(505) 396-5311
Fax: (505) 396-2823

HWY 18 North
of Lovington

Hwy 82 East
to 18 North Tatum

14-F

Lincoln County

Lincoln County was created by the territorial legislature of 1869. Named in honor of President Abraham Lincoln, it is one of five named for him.

County Seat: Carrizozo
Communities: Ruidoso, Ruidoso Downs, Alto, Glencoe, San Patricio, Hondo, Tinnie, Piccacho, Angus, Nogal, White Oaks, Corona

4,859 Square Miles

Valley of Fires

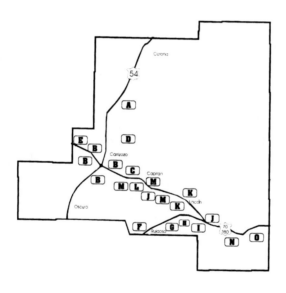

Salinas National Monument
38 Miles Northwest

This unique regional complex of prehistoric Indian Pueblos and associated 17th century Franciscan mission ruins constitutes a "capsule in time" in which the first century of Native American-European contact in what is now the United States is preserved. The complex includes Abo, Quarai, and Gran Quivira ruins. The central visitor center is in Mountainair's historic Shaffer Hotel.

Salinas, or salt, was very necessary to the early Indians as a preservative and trade good. The Estancia Valley is an enclosed valley with no natural drainage to any river. The salt lakes on the southeast side of the valley gives the valley its name.

The Salinas Pueblo Missions National Monument encompasses three 17th Century Franciscan churches and the remains of the apartment-like dwellings of the Native Americans. At one time, as many as 10,000 people may have lived in the area as it was a major trade center between the plains Indians to the East and the Rio Grande Villages to the West. The Indians of Los Salinas were both producers and middlemen of trade goods. They traded maize, pinon nuts, beans, squash, salt and cotton goods for dried buffalo meat, hides, flint and shells.

The Shaffer Hotel, located in Mountainair, is an amazing architectural feat designed and built by local craftsman "Pop" Shaffer. The front of the building has "swastikas", placed long before Adolph Hitler, they were a symbol for peace.

The central Visitor's Center is now located just off Highway 60, one block East of Highway 55 in Mountainair.

Salinas Pueblo Missions National Monument
Broadway & Ripley
P.O. Box 517
Mountainair, NM 87036
(505) 847-2585

Highway 54 North

15-A

Carrizozo

Carrizozo, county seat of Lincoln county, was established in 1899, a new town on the El Paso and Northeastern Railroad. The ghost town of White Oaks, once a booming mining camp, is nearby. Billy the Kid, Sheriff Pat Garret, Governor Lew Wallace, and Albert Bacon Fall all figure prominently in the history of the area. Population 1,222. Elevation 5,438 feet.

At the dawn of the 20th Century, the railroads were marching north from El Paso. The booming mining town of White Oaks, 12 miles to the north, was bypassed by the raidroad.

With a spur needed to reach the coal fields near present day Capitan, the location of Carrizozo was established. As Carrizozo began to flourish, White Oaks began to decline. Many of White Oaks residents relocated their homes and businesses.

According to local legend, the town received it's name from the tall reedy grasses that grew here, called by the Spanish, "Carrizo". Carrizozo was a word coined to mean "an abundance of Carrizo"

In 1909, Lincoln County voted to move the county seat from Lincoln to Carrizozo because of its proximity to the railroad. A four year court battle finally decided by the U.S. Supreme Court in 1913 in Carrizozo's favor, took place.

Lew Wallace served as governor of the New Mexico Territory and won worldwide fame with his novel "Ben Hur". Albert Bacon Fall was a wealthy New Mexico Attorney and U.S. State Senator before becoming US Secretary of the Interior under President Warren G. Harding. It was Sheriff Pat Garret that captured the notorious Billy the Kid, an outlaw who killed his first man at the age of 14.

Carrizozo Chamber of Commerce
US Hwy 54 & Airport Rd.
P.O. Box 567
Carrizozo, NM 88301
505-648-2732

On Highway 54 North   On HWY 380 MM 65
South Hwy 54
MM 22 on South HWY 54
South of Carrizozo   MM 22 on S Hwy 54   **15-B**

Lincoln

Lincoln was the focal point of the notorious Lincoln County War of 1876-79, a complex struggle for political and economic power. Sheriff William Brady, outlaw Billy the Kid, Governor Samuel B. Axtell and cattle baron John S. Chisum were some of the people involved in this violent episode.

In the 1870's, John S. Chisum was one of the West's most prosperous cattlemen. It took a special breed of man to flourish where government was rudimentary or nonexistent. John Chisum, John Henry Turnstall and attorney Alexander McSween saw an opportunity to make a sizeable fortune.

There was a lot of money to be made in supplying beef to the Government, The crooked, influential officials known as the Santa Fe Ring kept profits on the contracts sky-high to feather their own nests. The Tunstall-Chisum-McSween faction objected to the idea that mere merchants should have control of supplying the beef.

This set the stage to murders, retaliation, and set the backdrop to help Billy the Kid and Pat Garret to become famous.

On Hwy 380 in town of Lincoln

15-C

White Oaks

White Oaks grew rapidly after the discovery of gold in 1869. From tent city to bustling mining town, it was the largest town in Lincoln County with cultural events and an occasional bandit. Gold depletion and failure to grant railroad right-of-way caused its demise.

Cedarvale cemetery—resting place of many White Oaks citizens.

Named for nearby White Oaks Spring, a post office was established in 1880, a year after gold was discovered. Soon permanent buildings of stone and brick replaced tents and shacks and the town began it's rapid population growth to 4,000 people. Four newspapers, two hotels, three churches, a planing mill, a bank, an opera house, saloons and gambling houses were established.

There are stories told of a casino ran by Belle La Mar, known as Madam Varnish, because she was reputed to have slick ways. Another saloon, it is said, sold three grades of whiskey at three different prices. The saloon owner obviously did his marketing well, yet all three grades came from the same barrel.

Some of the buildings dating from the 1890's are being renovated and occupied. The well-known Hoyle Castle has a legend surrounding it. This Victorian mansion was built in 1893 by mine superintendent Andy Hoyle for his Massachusetts fiancée, a mail order bride. The story is, she came as far as Texas, then turned back, apparently disenchanted with the desert landscape. What happened after that seems to be obscured by history.

HWY 349
Town of White Oaks

15-D

Malpais—Valley of Fires

Spanish explorers called this extensive lava flow malpais, or badlands. The river of lava that flowed down this "Valley of Fires" erupted from a volcano some 7 miles south of here about 1000 years ago. Extending through the valley for 44 miles, the malpais averages 3 miles in width. This ropey type of lava is called "pahoehoe."

The harsh but beautiful landscape was developed from lava that flowed from vents in the valley floor. The exact age of the flow is undetermined. However, it can be estimated to be recent due to the lack of erosion.

The tongue of molten rock is one of the longest balistic flows created by a tube-fed method. As the lava flowed along the Tularosa Valley, it buried everything in its path except the older sandstone hills. The Dakota Sandstone which was deposited along the shores of an ancient sea, acted as confining structures that determined flow direction. Surface lava was cooling and hardening while the still molten lava beneath was continuing to flow down valley. The cooled lava was pushed up against the sandstone causing upward bending.

The Spanish called this lava flow "El Malpais" meaning "badlands". As Indian legend has it the area was a valley of fire, as expected from such a rare and spectacular event.

Today, this location supports more species and plant life than the surrounding area.

There is a public campground and an interpretive trail for exploring the interesting plant and geological terrain.

Carrizozo Travel InformationalCenter
(505) 648-2241

Hwy 380 West

15-E

Ruidoso

Originally known as Dowlin's Mill, the town was located on the Chisum Trail which ran from the Pecos River in Arizona. By 1885 it had attracted a store, a blacksmith shop, and a post office which was named Ruidoso after the local stream. Several incidents of the Lincoln County War occurred here, including the murder of Paul Dowlin in May 1877.

Ruidoso and the nearby town of Ruidoso Downs are nestled in the Southern Rocky Mountains beneath towering Sierra Blanca and are all but surrounded by the Lincoln National Forest.

Ruidoso has some of the finest artists and galleries in the Soutwest. It is also home to the world's richest quarter horse race purse, the All American Futurity. During racing season, the community population swells to an estimated 35,000 people. In 1994, attendance at the Downs was 236,225.

Early tourists were attracted to the Ruidoso area because it offered a place to escape the desert heat. Incorporated in 1946, it still offers a cool summer retreat from the heat of the summer's sun.

**Ruidoso Chamber of Commerce
720 Sudderth Drive
P.O. Box 698
Ruidoso, NM 88355
1-800 253-2255
(505) 257-7395**

East Hwy 70
in Ruidoso

15-F

Old Dowlin Mill

Famous New Mexico Landmark for nearly 100 years. Original building still stands and water turns massive water wheel during the summer. Billy the Kid, Pat Garrett and General Pershing visited here.

Paul Dowlin was an officer in the NM volunteers during the Civil War in New Mexico Territory. He moved to Fort Stanton and set up a trading post. Because he sold liquor, it caused problems with the Mescolera Indians. The post commander ordered Dowlin to move his operations.

He relocated to Ruidoso, "the noisy river", and prospered, acquiring not only a mill but also a store and other property.

In 1877, he was killed. The murder was attributed to a man known as Jerry Dillion, a former employee of Dowlin's, who disappeared at the same time.

Ruidoso was originally called Dowlin's Mill and was later changed to Ruidoso. Today, the Mill is an area landmark.

West Hwy 70
North of Ruidoso Downs

15-G

John H. Tunstall Murder Site

In one of the Lincoln County War's earliest violent encounters, John H. Tunstall was shot and killed at a nearby site on February 18, 1878. Tunstall's death set off a series of violent reprisals between his friends, among whom was William "Billy the Kid" Bonney, and forces of the Murphy/Dolan faction of this tragic conflict. Tunstall, an English businessman came to New Mexico in 1876.

John S. Chisum's closest ally in Lincoln was an Englishman named J.H. Tunstall, who had come to America with the goal of becoming rich before his 30th birthday. He was well on his way at 24, the owner of a working ranch, the Lincoln County Bank, and a dry-goods store that competed with Murphy's. Tunstall found a friend in Alexander A. McSween, a Scottish-born lawyer whom J. J. Dolan accused of embezzling funds. Briefly jailed, McSween made common cause with Chisum and Tunstall against the Ring. Tunstall made another friend when young William Bonney, "Billy the Kid", signed on with him as a ranch hand.

When he entered Tunstall's employ, Bonney took on a new air of seriousness, working hard. Events would swiftly catch up with him. Back in Lincoln, the Dolan-Murphy and Tunstall-McSween factions filed one lawsuit after another. One continuing to charge embezzlement, the other tax fraud. The Ring, in the meanwhile, bought the town's sheriff, William Brady. Tunstall arrived in Lincoln with Billy Bonney to challenge Brady in court. At the same time, a sheriff's posse went out to round up Tunstall's cattle. The young Englishman ordered Billy to return to the ranch and await instructions.

The next day, Tunstall himself set out for his ranch. On the way, members of the posse, led by Dolan, ambushed and murdered him. Billy Bonney first went to Lincoln constable Atanacio Martínez and swore out a complaint against members of the posse. Martínez deputized Billy, and they went to serve Dolan's arrest warrant at Murphy's store. When they arrived, Sheriff Brady, reinforced by soldiers from Fort Stanton, arrested the two. Martinez was released, but Billy Bonney spent the night in jail, while, in another part of Lincoln, John Tunstall was buried.

On gaining his freedom, Billy Bonney joined with other Tunstall ranch hands in a 10-man vigilante force called the "Regulators," led by an older man named Dick Brewer. They began hunting down members of the sheriff's posse and killing them one by one, a vendetta that went on until midsummer and left dozens of men, including Sheriff Brady, dead.

Hwy 70, MM 273 North of Ruidoso

15-H

San Patricio

This farming and ranching community was the scene of many events associated with the Lincoln County War. In July 1878, a posse ransacked the village while searching for William "Billy the Kid" Bonney and others of the faction known as the "Regulators" who frequently visited the town or had hiding places in the vicinity. More recently, renowned artist Peter Hurd made his home here.

Originally named Ruidoso for its river, it was changed to San Patricio because the patron saint of the church's Irish priest was St. Patrick. At one time, San Patricio had the most voters in Lincoln County, but the population began to decline during World War II.

Peter Hurd (1904-1984), was born in Roswell and attended West Point for a time. He resigned his commission and went to Chadds Ford in 1922. It was there that he lived and painted under the guidance of N.C. Wyeth during the next 10 years. Henriette, Wyeth's oldest daughter and Peter were married in 1929.

He longed to return to New Mexico to live and work. Henrietta and Peter settled in San Patricio where he is best known for his watercolors, egg temperas and lithographs depicting the New Mexican landscapes.

His portrait of President Lyndon B. Johnson hangs in the Smithsonian's National Portrait Gallery in Washington, D.C.

North US 70
MM 281

15-I

Fort Stanton
1855-1896

Fort Stanton, named for Captain Henry Stanton, was established to control the Mescalero Apaches. It was burned and evacuated by Union troops in 1861, held briefly by the Confederates, and then re-occupied by Colonel Kit Carson for the Union in 1862. Since its abandonment as a military post, it has been used as a hospital.

Located in an obscure but scenic area in New Mexico, Fort Stanton is a historic site and has probably one of a few, if not the only, military cemetery that is open and unguarded. Established in 1855, when New Mexico was part of the Arizona Territory, it was a primitive military post.

During the Civil War, Union forces tried to burn the Fort as they retreated. A rain storm put out the fire. Confederate forces took control for a short time. In 1862, Colonel Kit Carson became Commander with five companies of New Mexico volunteers.

Opinions were divided over whether or not Fort Stanton was a necessary installation. The Secretary of War in 1869–1870 felt the Fort was totally unnecessary, but the settlers needed protection from marauding Indians. It continued to exist as a military establishment until the 1890's.

In 1899, President William McKinley established it as a Marine Hospital exclusively for the treatment of tuberculosis, where the climate proved to aid those suffering from the disease. During World War II, it also served as an internment camp for the crew of a German luxury liner, who were guarded by the Border Patrol.

By 1953, drugs for the treatment of tuberculosis were available and brought a decline in the number of patients. Fort Stanton then became a state Hospital and training school for the mentally disadvantaged. This program ended in 1995 and since then the facility has been used as a minimum security location for women prisoners.

Hwy 70
Town of Hondo
Jct of US 380 and US 220

15-J

Lincoln

Spanish-speaking settlers established a town here in the 1850's, after the U.S. Army began to control the Mescalero Apaches. First known as Las Placitas del Rio Bonito, the name of the community was changed to Lincoln when Lincoln County was created in 1869.

Renamed in honor of President Lincoln, Lincoln County and the town of Lincoln was the site of many of the events of the Lincoln County War. Money was to be made, and lots of it, providing beef to the reservations scattered throughout the area.

One of the most famous people to rise out of the events of the Lincoln County War was Henry "Billy the Kid" McCarty. While awaiting execution for the murder of Sheriff William Brady, Billy was incarcerated in the Lincoln County Jail, which also happened to serve as the Court House.

Ironically, the courthouse was in the old Murphy-Dolan store and the jail cell where he was chained was the bedroom of his old enemy, Lawrence Murphy.

J.W. Bell and Bob Orlinger were left to guard Billy while the Sheriff was attending to duties in nearby White Oaks. Bell was respectful to the prisoners as was the Sheriff, Pat Garret. Orlinger, on the other hand, had supported the opposite faction during the war, and he and Billy had a "reciprocal hatred" according to Pat Garret. Orlinger took every opportunity he could to taunt the Kid, while Billy awaited execution, scheduled for May 13, 1881. While Bob escorted the five other prisoners to supper across the street at Sam Whortely's hotel on April 28, 1881, Billy stayed in his cell with Bell as his guard.

Billy asked Bell to take him to the outhouse in the back of the courthouse. The men went outside, Billy was in leg-irons, chains and handcuffs. Once they arrived back at the jail, Billy made his move. He managed to wrestle Bell's gun away from him and shot Bell. Ollinger came running from the Hotel. From the second story window, he heard his name. Olinger looked up and saw his own double-barreled shot gun pointed at him. Billy let him have it with both barrels. Olinger died instantly, and Billy went on to become one of the most well known figures of the Old West.

Hwy 380, MM 98.4
Just West of Lincoln
On Hwy 380
MM 97.4

15-K

Smokey Bear Historical Park

This park commemorates Smokey Bear and describes the history and development of this national symbol of forest fire prevention. The original Smokey is buried here within sight of the mountain where he was found orphaned by a fire raging in the Lincoln National Forest. The park offers extensive historical exhibits as well as a trail that identifies native plants.

In 1944, the National Forest Service, in conjunction with the Advertising Council, authorized and originated a poster of Smokey Bear as the symbol for fire prevention. In May of 1950, a living legend of that symbol came to be.

A human caused fire ravaged 17,000 acres of forest in the Capitan Gap. It was during this fire that a tiny bear cub was found clinging to a smoldering tree trunk. With badly burned feet and buttocks, the cub was briefly named "Hotfoot" but was soon called Smokey Bear and became the living symbol for the poster.

Little Smokey was flown to a veterinary hospital in Santa Fe. After he healed, he was flown to the National Zoo in Washington. Smokey the Bear was so popular with school children, he had to be given his own zip code because of his fan mail.

When Smokey died in 1976, his body was returned to his birthplace. He is buried in a small park which bears his name, in the heart of the village of Capitan.

The park offers a nature trail, visitor's center, as well as a place to stop and pay your respects to the legend.

Smokey Bear Historical State Park
P.O. Box 591
118 Smokey Bear Blvd
Capitan, NM 88316
1-505-354-2748

US HWY 380
Town of Capitan

15-L

Capitan

Many incidents in the Lincoln County War, 1876–79, occurred in the area around Capitan. The promoters Charles B. and John A. Eddy platted the town site in 1900, after building a spur of the El Paso & Northeastern Railroad from Carrizozo in order to open the Salado coal fields. The mines were abandoned in 1901. Population 1400. Elevation 6350 feet.

Seaborn T. Gray homesteaded the area in 1884, so the small town was known as Gray until 1900 when it was renamed Capitan. The village is home to 1400 people and located between two mountain ranges, The Sacramento and the Capitan. With an elevation of 6,350 feet, it offers a cool summer retreat.

The El Paso and Northeastern Railroad built a coal line from Carrizozo to the Phelps-Dodge coal mines, one mile west of Capitan. By 1905, the coal mines had played out and were abandoned. Therefore ranching, fishing and hunting became the basis for the local economy.

Capitan gained national recognition due to a 4 pound bear cub orphaned during a man caused fire. The small cub was found clinging to a smoldering pine tree, badly burned. The cub became the living symbol for the Forest Service's Fire Prevention Series. Smokey the Bear was buried in the town of Capitan when he died in 1976.

Capitan Chamber of Commerce
Box 441
Capitan, NM 88316
505-354-2273

Hwy 380 East of Capitan
MM 85.7
Hwy 380 West of Capitan   Hwy 48
MM 83.6   MM 20.8

15-K

High Plains

You are on the west edge of High Plains, here sloping eastward to Pecos Valley. Foothills of Capitan Mountains are to northwest and Sierra Blanca to west, and ancient 12,003-foot complex volcano, Canyon of Rio Hondo to southwest exposes Permian limestone aquifers that nourish Pecos Valley crops. Elevation 5,100 feet.

Just before the Jurassic and Triassic time frame in the formation of the earth, there was the Permian period. It was nearly 225 million years ago that a system of marine limestones and sandstones 4,000 to 6,000 feet thick formed. 225 million years ago, the limestone would more closely resemble Australia's Great Barrier Reef.

Today, this area shows some of the beauty and diversity of New Mexico. From fertile river valleys and arid desert, to high mountain splendor, New Mexico offers something for everyone.

Hwy 380
East of Hondo

15-N

Chisum Trail

Sometimes confused with the Chisholm Trail from Texas to Kansas, the Chisum Trail was used by New Mexico rancher John S. Chisum to supply cattle to the Indian agencies in Arizona. In 1875, Chisum sent 11,000 head over this route, which winds from Roswell to Las Cruces, then roughly follows modern I-10 west to Arizona.

A man could become rich providing beef for the government to feed the Indians relocated to reservations. John S. Chisum developed this route from Texas to Arizona, for a ready market of the huge cattle ranch he was developing in Southeastern New Mexico.

After Oliver Loving was killed by Indians, Chisum and Goodnight formed a partnership. In the next 5 years, Chisum earned enough capital to move permanently to New Mexico.

Though he never was directly involved in the Lincoln County War, he was known as a supporter and occasionally gave sanctuary to the "Regulators" including Henry "Billy the Kid" McCarty.* He was one who believed in free enterprise and wanted to set his own contracts with the government, bypassing the middleman.

* Henry McCarty, an alias of William (Billy the Kid) Bonney.

on Hwy 380
East of Roswell

15-O

Los Alamos County

Road to Secrets

The smallest of New Mexico's counties, Los Alamos was created in 1949 and was named for the town which became its county seat. The national laboratory located in Los Alamos was once a secret facility whose work helped to bring the end of World War II.

County Seat : Los Alamos
Communities:

111 Square Miles

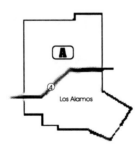

Los Alamos

Located near the ancient Indian sites of the Pajarito Plateau, Los Alamos is one of New Mexico's newest towns. In 1942 a boys' ranch school became the headquarters of the Manhattan Project, which led to the development of the atomic bomb. Los Alamos National Laboratories continue to be a center for nuclear and other scientific research. Population 17,599. Elevation 7324 feet.

In 1942, the government was looking for a place that would be easy to guard, hard to find, very remote, and so the mesa was singled out as the ideal location for the Los Alamos Scientific Laboratories.

The once remote mountain city is where the nuclear age was born with the Manhattan project. The world's first nuclear device, the atom bomb was developed here. The event changed the world and altered the face of remote Los Alamos County forever.

Today's residents are involved almost exclusively in work for Los Alamos National Laboratory and related support enterprises. There is also a thriving community of artists who represent the full spectrum of artistic styles.

A complete tour of Los Alamos should include a visit to the Bradbury Science Museum, the Los Alamos Historical Museum and the Fuller Lodge Art Center.

Los Alamos County Chamber of Commerce
P.O. Box 460
Los Alamos, NM 87544
505-662-8105

NM 502 East of Los Alamos
(Marker Missing)

16-A

Luna County

City of Rocks

Luna County was named for Don Solomon Luna, a prominent political figure during the Territorial days of New Mexico. It was created on March 16, 1901.

County Seat: Deming
Communities: Gage, Columbus, Hermanas

2,957 Square Miles

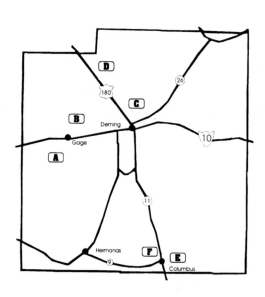

Yucca—New Mexico's State Flower

The Yucca is a member of the lily family. Its spring blossoms are pearly white. Early Indians used its tender shoots for food. Soap was made from its roots, sandals and basketry from the leaf fiber. A single variety of moth produces pollination.

Yucca Plains

Wide alluvial plains of southwestern New Mexico are feature of Basin and Range province with isolated fault block mountains scattered like islands from a sandy sea. Volcanic rocks form most of Cedar Mountains to south and Pyramid Mountains to west but Burro Mountains to northwest are mainly ancient granites. Elevation 4,560 feet.

New Mexico's State Flower is the Yucca. The Yucca is a stiff-leaved, evergreen shrub, which contains about 30 different species. All species of the yucca are native to North America and the West Indies.

The wild growing plants provided many things to early native American tribes. They were used for food and medicine. The fibers from the leaves held up well when made into shoes, and other items. Soap and shampoo were made from them as well.

Today, open rangeland can be devastated by overgrowth of yucca, and it becomes necessary to control huge infestations. Fields are sometimes burned or razed to allow for better growth of grass for foraging animals.

On I-10 West of Deming
Rest Area   MM 53

17-A

Basin and Range Country

Basin and range province of southwest New Mexico is of broad alluvial plains from which isolated fault block mountains rise like islands from a sandy sea. Victorio Mountains to south have yielded zinc, silver, gold, copper, lead, and tungsten to early miners and limestone for highway construction. Elevation 4,500 feet.

Cooke's Wagon Road

In 1846, while leading the Mormon Battalion to California during the Mexican War, Lt. Col. Philip St. George Cooke blazed the first wagon road from New Mexico to the West Coast. The potential of the route for railroad construction was one of the reasons for the Gadsden Purchase in 1854. Cooke entered Arizona through Guadalupe Pass.

The Mormon Battalion marched for over 2,000 miles, making the longest march in military history, to aide in the settling of California. This southern route was one of common sense for the Railroad as weather further north would be unbearable.

After the treaty with Mexico was signed to end the Mexican War in 1848, railroaders pushed to have the lower part of New Mexico and Arizona transferred from Old Mexico to the United States. The purchase of this land, known as the 1853 Gadsden Purchase, brought the needed rights for the railroad and further stimulated expansion of the United States.

On I-10 West of Deming at Rest Area
MM 61

17-B

Deming

In 1780, Governor Juan Bautista de Anza passed near here while searching for a trade route between Santa Fe and the mines of Sonora, Mexico. Deming was founded in 1881 when the Santa Fe and Southern Pacific Railroads were connected, giving New Mexico its first railway access to both the Atlantic and the Pacific. Population 9,964. Elevation 4,331 feet.

Once a stage stop along the Butterfield Stagecoach Trail, Deming was founded in 1881 at the junction of the Atchison, Topeka and Santa Fe and the Southern Pacific railroad lines. The town was named after Mary Deming Crocker, the wife of a Southern Pacific magnate.

Deming became an important military headquarters where troops trained at Camp Cody during World War I. During World War II, bombardiers were trained at Deming Army Air Base.

Deming's roots are in agriculture and trade with Mexico. Tourists in the form of people seeking relief from winter's chills flock to the area. Deming enjoys a mild climate and the sun shines about 360 days a year.

Deming is the county seat of Luna County and has a population of about 14,200 people.

Deming-Luna County Chamber of Commerce
800 E Pine St.
P.O. Box 8
Deming, NM 88031
505 546-2674

Hwy 180 Just West of Deming

17-C

Butterfield Trail

Stagecoaches of the Butterfield Overland Mail Co. began carrying passengers and mail from St. Louis to San Francisco, across southern New Mexico, in 1858. The 2,795-mile journey took 21–22 days. In 1861 the service was re-routed through Salt Lake City. From La Mesilla west, the trail paralleled I–10.

Before 1857, there was no organized, commercial system of transportation west of the Mississippi River. New York business man, John Butterfield obtained a $600,000 government contract to establish and run an overland mail company from St. Louis, Missouri to San Francisco, California.

John Butterfield had already managed to prove his ability to organize and administer such an undertaking. He had erected the first telegraph line between New York City and Buffalo, built and managed several passenger stagecoach lines, and constructed the first steam railroad and first street horse railway system in Utica, New York. He also helped with the formation of the American Express Company.

The Butterfield Overland Mail Company was to be the first transcontinental stage line stretching some 2, 800 miles from the Mississippi River to the Pacific Coast. Because this was to be used year around, it was decided to use the southern route as much as possible to avoid winter storms. During its two and a half years of service, the stage arrived within its 25 day contract, occasionally reducing it to 21 days.

John Butterfield had to build about 150 stations and corrals, dig wells and cisterns, grade fording sites, purchase and distribute 1200 horses and 600 mules, as well as build hundreds of coaches and hire between 750 to 800 men. In the arid terrain of southern New Mexico, the stops were spaced further apart, either at existing springs or where wells were successfully dug. Once the Stage hit the Gila River, which the route followed to California, it had water and the stations returned to the 15 to 20 miles apart, as it did from Mississippi through Texas.

The stage was only in service for two and a half years. The Civil War brought an early demise to the stage that managed to stitch together the growing country.

US 180 Rest Area
MM 144.4 (Marker Missing)

17-D

Columbus

Here revolutionary forces of Francisco (Pancho) Villa attacked on March 9th, 1916, burning much of the town and killing civilians and soldiers. From here General "Black Jack" Pershing pursued Villa into Mexico. His expedition of 10,000 men made first military use of mechanized equipment and airplanes. Founded 1691. Elevation 4,050 feet.

Columbus, New Mexico has a fascinating history, a 24-hour border crossing, unique and varied geology, Pancho Villa State Park and a mild winter climate. It attracts visitors from the US, Asia, and Europe year after year.

The village was first established in 1691, and in 1902, it was moved three miles to its present location, becoming the El Paso/Santa Fe Railroad station. It also has the dubious distinction of being the site of the last foreign invasion into the United States, prior to the Japanese invasion of Alaska during World War II.

With mountain ranges on all four sides, the population ranges from 700 during the hot dry summers to 1000+ during the winter as people from across the US come to seek warmth during winter's chill.

Be sure and check out the Pancho Villa and Railroad Depot Museum, where historians will find a film on Villa as well as facts on the First Aero Squadron.

Columbus Chamber of Commerce
P.O. Box 350
Columbus, NM 88029-0350
(505) 531-2663

.

On Hw 9
MM 4.3

17-E

Pancho Villa's Raid

On March 9,1916, Francisco "Pancho" Villa, a major figure in the Mexican Revolution, crossed the international border with a large force, attacking and looting Columbus, New Mexico. Eighteen U.S. soldiers and civilians, and approximately 100 Villistas were killed. Gen. John J. " Black Jack" Pershing led an expeditionary force into Mexico in pursuit of Villa.

Pancho Villa State Park

Pancho Villa State Park commemorates the historic Columbus Raid of 1916. Ruins of Camp Furlong, headquarters for General John Pershing's expeditionary force, still exist at the park. The old Columbus Customs Service building has been restored to house exhibits about the raid and Pershing's Punitive Expedition into Mexico in pursuit of Pancho Villa and his raiders. Camping/picnicking sites are scattered throughout a beautiful desert botanical garden.

Columbus was attacked during the early hours of March 9, 1916. Pancho Villa and his army of 500-1000 men crossed the Mexico/U.S. Border and burned the sleeping village.

Retaliation was led by General Jack Pershing. This was the first time airplanes and other mechanical vehicles were used in US warfare. A replica of one of the planes is located on a concrete tower at Hacienda del sur Air Park five miles north of Columbus. It is visible from Highway 11.

On NM 11 West of Columbus
MM 3.2

17-F

McKinley County

Named for William McKinley, twenty-fifth president of the United States. McKinley County was created February 23, 1899.

County Seat: Gallup
Communities: Churchrock, Thoreau, Zuni, White
                Horse, Mcgaffey, Zuni, Crownpoint

5,461 Square Miles

Bluewater Lake

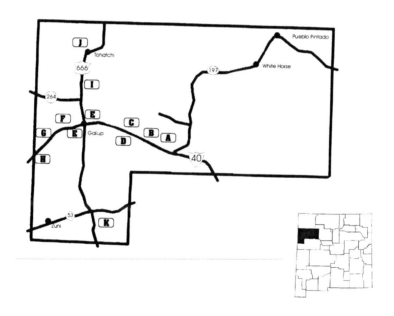

Chaco Culture National Historical Park

Chaco Canyon contains hundreds of sites documenting its Indian occupation from 5000 B.C. through the early 20th century. Most spectacular are a dozen large and excellently crafted masonry pueblos of the 11th and 12th centuries. After its abandonment around 1300, the canyon was settled by Navajos from the early 1700's until the 1940's.

Chaco Culture National Historical Park preserves the pinnacle of what is left of Anasazi civilization. These sites are some of the most highly regarded archaeological sites in the United States.

The Anasazi, or ancient ones, farmed and lived peacefully in the canyon from AD 50 to 1150.

One of the largest sites, Pueblo Bonito, has over 800 rooms, 2 large and 32 smaller kivas. There are 11 other major sites and numerous smaller ones.

The Anasazi had an advanced irrigation and road system. One of the roads leads 40 miles to the site at Aztec, NM.

There are many trails to hike to other sites, as well as ranger led tours of the central ruins.

Access to Chaco Canyon is via a 45 minute drive along a sometimes rough gravel road.

Chaco Culture
National Historical Park
PO Box 220
Nageezi, NM 87037
Phone: 505-786-7014

I-40 West of Grants, Exit 53 in Nageezi
MM 52.4

18-A

Continental Divide

Rainfall divides at this point. To the west it drains into the Pacific Ocean, to the east, into the Atlantic. Elevation 7379 feet.

Every continent has a continental divide. This is the point that determines which direction the rainfall and water shed will run.

The continental divide in the United States primarily follows the Rocky Mountain chain. This divide determines whether the water shed runs into the Atlantic or the Pacific Oceans.

This Divide begins in Alaska and runs into Central Mexico.

I-40 West of Thoreau, Exit 47
MM 48 (Marker Missing)

18-B

Chaco Cliffs

Great cliffs of red sandstone form the southern boundary of the San Juan basin. The strata exposed here are the gently upturned edge of the structural basin which contains coal, uranium, oil and gas resources. The Zuñi Mountains to the south represent the old basement rock upon which the basin strata were deposited. Elevation 6,900 feet.

It has been called America's Stonehenge. That obscure canyon in northwestern New Mexico, known as Chaco, was the site of great human activity from 950–1150 AD. Why there? Why build so many pueblos, or villages (some reaching five stories in height) in such a marginal, desert environment?

One possible explanation is that Chaco was used as a religious, rather than residential center. This theory is supported by the existence of wide, arrow-straight roads leading to Chaco Canyon from outlying areas. It is easy to imagine people, dressed for celebration, making a pilgrimage, walking several abreast, to an important yearly festival.

The Anasazi knew how to chart the seasons by observing the sky. But why did the Anasazi abandon the spiritual center they had labored so hard to build; without metal tools, without beasts of burden, and without wheels? Perhaps clues can be found buried under the desert sand or carved on the sandstone cliffs of Chaco Canyon.

I-40 West Bound
(Marker Missing)

18-C

Fort Wingate

The first Fort Wingate was established near San Rafael in 1862, to serve as the base of Col. Kit Carson's campaigns against the Navajos. In 1868 the garrison was transferred to the second Fort Wingate near Gallup. In that same year, the Navajos returned here after their imprisonment at Fort Sumner.

Situated originally where a treaty was signed with the Navajos in 1846, this post was established in 1860 to stop the plundering by both Mexican and Indian desperadoes. At first it was a tent compound called Fort Fauntleroy. Later it was renamed Fort Lyon, then Fort Wingate. The post was enlarged during the Civil War, and it supported Colonel Christopher 'Kit Carson's Navajo campaign in 1863. The post was relocated almost 40 Mlles to the northwest in 1868, to comply with another Indian treaty, where it exercised surveillance over Indian affairs until the 20th century.

From 1868 until 1911, Fort Wingate provided patrol, escort, and survey services. It also became a jumping off point for scientific expeditions. Buildings were constructed of both wood and local sandstone. In 1896 most of the wooden buildings burned. The Fort was deactivated in 1911, but during 1914-15 it was reopened to house 4000 Mexican Federalists who had fled Pancho Villa's army.

Following World War I, the Army found itself with great stores of surplus explosive devices. So, in 1918 Fort Wingate was taken over by the Ordinance Department and the world's largest munitions depot was constructed. As you drive by you can see row after row of small bunkers, dispersed so as to prevent an accidental explosion in one from setting off an explosion in the next. The old fort — grounds and barracks — were transferred to the Bureau of Indian Affairs in 1925 to become a boarding school for Navajo and Zuni students. The school has been expanded and still functions, but the military use of the area has ceased, except for the occasional test launching of a new type of missile. The Fort is now being decommisioned, probably for the last time.

I-40 West of Grants
MM 31

18-D

Gallup

Long a major trading center for the Navajo and Zuñi Indians living in communities north and south of the town, Gallup emerged in 1881 from a railroad construction camp. It is named for David Gallup, who in 1880 was paymaster for the Atlantic & Pacific (now the Santa Fe) Railroad. Population 18,161. Elevation 6,600 feet.

When Spanish Conquistadors led by Coronado first arrived in the Gallup region in 1540, they found a thriving and highly civilized Native American culture already in place. It was not the Seven Cities of Cibola they had hoped to find, but the settlements displayed building, craft, and farming methods uncommonly sophisticated, as well as a network of roads connecting them to other regions.

Modern Gallup can trace its origins to the railroad and to trading. In 1880, the railroad was pushing its way slowly westward. David Gallup, paymaster for the Railroad set up a small company headquarters. Soon, people were going to "Gallup" to receive their pay.

Gallup was originally a rough and tumble settlement with its share of saloons, and wooden sidewalks. Considered remote, the cavalry from nearby Fort Wingate helped protect the settlers from Indians.

Today Gallup is the largest Indian center in the Southwest and the ceremonial capital of Native America. The Navajo, Zuni, Hopi, Acoma and Laguna reservations are all within a close distance.

Gallup Convention & Visitors Bureau
701 Montoya Blvd.
P.O. Box 600
Gallup, NM 87305
505-863-3841

On East Side of Gallup Exit 26
MM 27
I-40 West side of Gallup, Exit 16
MM 16

18-E

Vasquez De Coronado's Route

In July 1540, Francisco Vásquez de Coronado, leader of an army of Spaniards and Indians, entered New Mexico from Arizona to the south of here. He was searching for the mythical Seven Cities of Cibola, which proved to be the six Zuñi villages then located near the present pueblo. Vásquez de Coronado was nearly killed during his attack on Hawikuh.

Francisco Vasquez de Coronado was born into a noble family in Salamanca, Spain in 1510. At the age of 25, he came to the Americas as an assistant to New Spain's first viceroy.

An ambitious man, he married the daughter of the colonial treasurer, put down a major slave rebellion, and became the governor of a Mexican province within three years of his arrival. But he wanted more. Rumors of earlier explorations by Cabeza de Vaca about 7 cites of gold inspired him to lead a royal expedition to explore the north into what is now the American West.

The expedition explored, bringing Catholic ideals to the pueblos they encountered. The Spanish influence that is still very present today.

When they did not find the "Seven Cities of Cibola", parties were sent out, some traveling all the way to the border between Arizona and California, where they explored the Grand Canyon. Coronado himself led a party into what is now Kansas.

Returning to Mexico without locating a single golden city, the Viceroy branded Coronado's expedition an abject failure. His career quickly declined and in 1544 he was removed from office as a governor and moved to Mexico City where he worked in a modest position for the City. He died in 1554, though his legacy is seen throughout the west.

I-40 West of Gallup
MM 10 (Marker Missing)

18-F

Manuelito Area

This area contained many Indian pueblos dating from about A.D. 500 to 1325, when it was abandoned. Navajos settled here by 1800. This was the home of Manuelito, one of the last of the chiefs to surrender for confinement at the Bosque Redondo Reservation near Fort Sumner. The Navajos returned here in 1868.

Standing over six foot, Manuelito became a leader and an out spoken advocate for the proud Navajo people.

Fort Defiance wanted all the Navajo livestock removed from around the military post so that their own horses and cattle would have more grazing area. Manuelito pointed out to the commander that he had horses and wagons and could harvest grasses for the army, but that the Navajos had only their feet. The commander put a deadline of midnight on the livestock being moved. Many animals were killed that night.

Manuelito was back with a vengeance, attacking the soldiers and the fort.

He and several members of his family and tribe spent the next few years hiding from soldiers, Utes, and other hunters. Facing another winter of starvation, Manuelito finally turned himself in. Reservation life was not good. The warriors had to ride out 25 miles in search of game and firewood. The dangers of attack were high.

Finally, a peace treaty allowed the proud Navajo to return to their homes. Less than 2000 lived to return from the 20,000 that had lived before the wars had started.

To see to their future, Manuelito urged education as the ladder to regaining their independence and pride. He died at the age of 75, a strong leader whose vision never completely died.

I-40 West of Gallup at Rest area
MM 3.5

18-G

Welcome to New Mexico

These signs are the first thing to greet visitors to the great state of New Mexico. Found at all major entry points, some offer special extras, such as free coffee. All give a weary traveler a place to get out and stretch their legs or get a fresh breath of air, before resuming their journey. So, whether you are passing through, planning an extended visit, or moving here permanently, welcome to New Mexico.

I-40 West of Gallup at Rest Area
MM 3.5

18-H

Fort Defiance

Now in the State of Arizona but then in the Territory of New Mexico, Fort Defiance was once described as " the most beautiful and interesting post as a whole in New Mexico." It was established in 1851 to control the Navajos, and abandoned as a military post in 1864.

Contrary to its name, Fort Defiance was built for a peaceful purpose.

In 1851 Colonel Edwin Sumner assumed command and decided on a new approach to the Navajo problem. He built a fort in the heart of Navajoland named Fort Defiance. The Army engaged in commerce with the Indians, passed out quartermaster stores during hard times and offered assistance with agriculture. Sumner's leadership and ability to fend off the civilian authorities' demands to punish the entire tribe for the actions a few resulted in nearly eight years of relative peace.

Henry Linn Dodge, appointed Agent to the Navajos in 1853, was also a notable peacemaker and seems to have spent most of his salary helping his tribal friends. But the Navajos grew restless as treaties in the late 1850's restricted their reservation lands. Incidents increased, and then, in 1860 while Fort Defiance was undermanned, Manuelito led an attack on that installation that began a new war.

US 666, North of Gallup
MM 7 (Marker Missing)

18-I

Navajo Indian Reservation

Occupants of northwest New Mexico since the 16th century, the Navajos today comprise the most populous Indian group in the United States. The 17th, 18th, and 19th centuries witnessed alternate periods of conflict and trading with their neighbors. The Navajos' economy traditionally has been based on stockraising, weaving, silversmithing, and more recently on mineral development.

Having the same roots as the Apaches and Lipanes, the Navajo were first mentioned in the writings of Zarate-Salmeron in 1626. Later explorers reported about the great farmers who lived in the area.

The Navajo call themselves Dineh, that is, people. Today they are a peaceful and pastoral people, living off their flocks of sheep and goats. Though the arid character of the country forces them to lead a nomadic life, most have one abode for their main home.

The Navajo women weave the renowned Navajo blankets, noted for their durability and beauty. The men once used Mexican silver dollars to make necklaces, belts, and bracelets of rare beauty.

They pride themselves on being self-supporting and are cheerful, friendly and industrious. One of the tribal chiefs noted how education would lead to their success. Since then, the tribe has worked hard to educate their youth.

US 666, North of Gallup
MM 7 (Marker Missing)

18-J

Pueblo of Zuni

The six original Zuni pueblos were the legendary "Seven Cities of Cibola" sought by Vásquez de Coronado in 1540. They were abandoned during the Pueblo Revolt, and the present pueblo was settled in 1699 after the Spanish reconquest. In 1970, Zuni became the first Indian community to administer its own reservation affairs.

The Zuni people love color and it is reflected everywhere in their daily lives. Most noticeable is the quality of the widely acclaimed jewelry they produce. Turqoise, shell, and jet are set in silver in intricate mosaic or inlay patterns. The Zuni are also known for fine beadwork, making belts, necklaces and even figures of beads.

One of the most famous of the Kachina dances, Shalako, is led every December in the Zuni pueblo to celebrate the end and the beginning of the new year. The ceremony also blesses all the houses of the pueblo erected during the year.

Every New Mexico pueblo holds dances for its feast day, the holiday commemorating the Catholic saint who is its patron. Other dances might be held at Christmas, New Year's Day and other times in late winter or summer. Dances commonly open to the public include the corn, deer and buffalo dances.

Every dance is a prayer, not a performance, and as such, we are privileged to observe them. The nature and timing of dances vary from village to village and proceed rain or shine. Dances usually begin mid-morning and continue until sunset with an afternoon break. Refrain from walking across the dance plaza, climbing on walls or entering the ceremonial rooms. Please keep silent during the dances and do not applaud afterwards.

Pueblo of Zuni
Zuni, NM 87327
(505) 782-4481

Hwy 602 South of Gallup
(Marker Missing)

18-K

Mora County

Mora County has the only unincorporated county seat in New Mexico. Early documents refer to " Demora," Meaning a camp or stopover, and is still a beautiful place to rest.

County Seat: Mora
Communities: Watrous, Loma Parda, Wagon Mound, Canoncito, Las Tusas, Buena Vista, Manuelitas, Guadalupita, and Golondrinas.

1,931 Square Miles

Coyote Creek

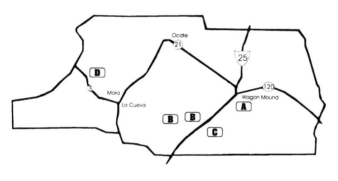

Wagon Mound

This last great landmark on the Santa Fe Trail was named for its resemblance to the top of a covered wagon. At Wagon Mound, travelers could cross from the Cimarron Cutoff to Fort Union, which is located on the Mountain branch of the Trail. The two branches joined south of here at Watrous.

As early settlers moved along the trails west, the "sea of grass" was so tall and thick that at times it was necessary to resort to navigate by means of a compass. Trail landmarks, such as the huge Wagon Mound, which looms above the prairie, would have been a very welcome sight to weary travelers.

Originally, Wagon Mound was called Santa Clara because of its association with the nearby Santa Clara Spring. Water was a very important resource to both settlers and people traveling the Santa Fe Trail. As new arrivals called both the mound and the town Wagon Mound, so it became over the years.

This important spot rests near where the Cimarron Cutoff rejoined the Mountain Branch of the Santa Fe Trail.

Exit 387 on NM 120
MM 40.3

19-A

Fort Union National Monument
1851-1891

Once the largest post in the southwest, Fort Union was established to control the Jicarilla apaches and Utes, to protect the Santa Fe Trail, and to serve as a supply depot for other New Mexico forts. The arrival of the railroad and the pacification of the region led to its abandonment in 1891.

Established by Lieutenant Colonel Edwin V. Sumner, Fort Union was established as a protector of the Santa Fe Trail. There were three different forts constructed close together during its forty year history.

At its peak this sprawling fort housed a population of 3,000 soldiers and civilians. It maintained supplies for a full year, including storehouses for two million bushels of grain, stables for 1,000 horses, yards to stack 2,000 tons of hay, and barracks for 400 soldiers.

At one time, it was the largest fort west of the Mississippi river and was a strategic military post and quartermaster deport throughout the Indian wars and the Civil Wars. It was also an important commercial center and a ready market for local produce until its abandonment in 1891.

It is open for public exploration today, with interpretive programs and living history talks and demonstrations during the summer weekends.

The visitor center has displays of military equipment and clothing, a bookstore, Santa Fe Trail information and films.

Fort Union National Monument
P.O. Box 127
Watrous, NM 87753
(505) 425-8025

I-25 South Bound Lane 65
Rest Area MM 375.5

19-B

Fort Union Arsenal

West of Fort Union near the base of the mesa are the ruins of Fort Union Arsenal. The first Fort Union was built at this location in 1851. In 1867, this wooden fort was razed and the adobe Arsenal erected. This Arsenal played a vital role in supplying armaments to military posts throughout New Mexico until 1882.

When first established, the original fort site was here, but as needs changed, the more favorable site was located. The first Fort was torn down, and the arsenal was set in its place.

With nearly 3,000 soldiers and civilians as well as the center for supply distribution to the other forts in the west, the Fort Union Arsenal played an important part in helping to settle this territory.

The largest visible network of Santa Fe Trail ruts can be seen here, where the Cimarron Cutoff from the Mountain Pass parted from the trail. Though the Cutoff was the easiest to travelers, it was also more dangerous with a long stretch of waterless territory and frequent Indian attacks.

The Mountain Pass, though longer by several days, was generally considered safer, if one had the money to pay the toll at Raton Pass.

Fort Union is open daily, only closing December 25 and January 1 each year.

Fort Union National Monument
P.O. Box 127
Watrous, NM 87753
(505) 425-8025

Exit 366 on NM 161
MM 30.2

19-C

Camp Maximiliano Luna

The 200th Coast Artillery, Anti-Aircraft, formerly the 111th Cavalry of the New Mexico National Guard trained here before going to the Philippines in World War II. About half of the men died either on the infamous Bataan Death March of 1942, or in Japanese Prison camps afterwards.

The 200th Coast Artillery was very typical of American Guard units. It was a hodgepodge of races and colors with Mexican and Native American blood running through the men's veins. There was a certain pride in this uniquely American mixture. While overseas dictators preached the dominance of a master race, they served for the freedom of all.

They had been sent to the Philippines to provide air defense for Clark Field.

At 5:00 am on December 8, 1941, the men in the 200th CA were notified that the United States was officially at war with Japan. Six and a half hours later, Japanese bombers and fighters attacked.

The men rushed to their weapons as the first bombs fell, some of them firing live ammunition for the first time. Only one of every six of the ancient shells the Guard fired exploded, yet the 200th brought down 5 enemy fighters with their fierce anti-aircraft defense.

The next four months would bring determined rearguard fighting as American and Filipino defenders retreated onto the Bataan Peninsula. On April 9, 1942, the 200th and 515th Coast Artillery, along with the rest of the Bataan defenders, began the march of death to prison camps where they would be interned for three and one half years. Of the 1841 men of the Regiment who began the March, 819 would not survive the war.

NM Jct 144
MM 0.8
MM 9

19-D

Otero County

Otero County was created in 1899 and named for Miguel Otero, the Territorial Governor of New Mexico at the time.

County Seat: Alamogordo
Communities: Oro Grande, Pinon, Sunspot,
　　　　　　　Mayhill, Cloudcroft, Tularosa,
　　　　　　　Mountain Park, Mescalero,
　　　　　　　Bent, Three Rivers

6,638 Square Miles

Oliver Lee State Park

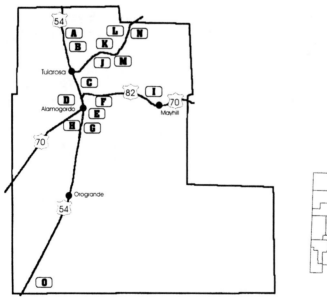

Three Rivers Petroglyphs

Three miles to the east is a mile-long array of pictures pecked into the solid rock walls of a volcanic ridge. They include both geometric and animal forms. They were likely made by prehistoric Mogollon Indians between ca. A.D. 1000 and 1400.

There are more than 21,000 glyphs of birds, humans, animals, fish, insects and plants as well as numerous geometric and abstract designs scattered over 50 acres of Three Rivers. Most of the petroglyphs here decorate a long, basalt ridge rising from the upper Tularosa Basin at the base of the Sacramento Mountains.

There is a short interpretative trail 200 yards south of the petroglyphs which leads to the remains of the Mogollon village. These people were likely the ones responsible for the petroglyphs. The foundations of three types of prehistoric buildings can be seen and were excavated in 1976. They were probably occupied for about 400 years.

The one-mile, round-trip trail along the ridge winds through thousands of petroglyphs created over a period of a few hundred years. Trail markers correspond to a trail guide provided upon admission, and indicate petroglyphs of particular interest along this somewhat rugged route.

The Mogollon lived in pithouses and adobe structures similar to their cousins the Anasazi, with whom they traded. By the time the Spanish entered New Mexico in the 1500's, the pueblos had already been mysteriously abandoned. Some believed they fled to the pueblos in northern New Mexico, while other experts think they resumed their ancestors' hunting and gathering lifestyle.

Admission fee is $3 and is open to the public 24 hours daily, year around.

US Hwy 54
MM 97

20-A

Three Rivers

Located in the Tularosa Basin east of the great lava flows known as the malpais, Three Rivers was once prominent in the cattle empires of Albert Bacon Fall, John S. Chisum, and Susie McSween Barber, "the cattle queen of New Mexico." Charles B. Eddy's El Paso & Northeastern Railroad reached here in 1899.

Three Rivers is a small community located in the Tularosa Basin. Surrounded by land where cattle roamed, it was near here that John S. Chisum grazed 80,000 head of cattle, making him the Cattle King of the New Mexico and possibly the owner of the world's largest cattle herd at the time.

Chisum was a Texas bachelor when he blazed the historic Chisum Trail from the little town of Paris, Texas, where his cattle herd first began, then North to the Pecos Valley in southeastern New Mexico. The drive began in 1867 when he headed up to Fort Sumner.

After Oliver Loving of the Goodnight-Loving Trail died, Chisum and Goodnight formed a partnership. In the next five years Chisum earned enough capital to move permanently to New Mexico.

Chisum preferred to make his contracts directly for the purchase of beef for Fort Stanton rather than go through Lawrence G. Murphy, beef contractor for a Santa Fe government contractor. This caused some problems as the "middlemen" wanted their part of the contracts.

Though he personally managed to stay neutral in the Lincoln County War, he did provide sanctuary and material support from his South Springs Ranch near Three Springs. Many of his early hands, including Billy the Kid were directly involved in the war against the Murphy faction.

John S. Chisum died of cancer on December 22, 1884. He is buried at the family cemetery in Paris, Texas. A statue of him is located in Roswell's Pioneer Plaza where his legend lives on.

South HWY 54
MM 97

20-A

Tularosa

The Tularosa Basin has been occupied by Indian groups for thousands of years. The first Hispanic settlers moved here from the Rio Grande Valley in 1862. Anglo settlers and cattlemen began moving into the region in the 1870's. The original 1862 town site has been designated a State and National Historic District. Tularosa appears as "Oasis" in the novels of Eugene Manlove Rhodes.

Though nicknamed the City of Roses, Tularosa actually derives its name from the Spanish word "tule" meaning reeds or cattails.

Original settlers in the 1860's came from washed-out villages on the Rio Grande near Mesilla. Due to frequent raids by the Apache, occupation was untenable and the site was abandoned.

Another attempt at settlement occured in 1862, and with Fort Stanton in the mountains to the east for protection, it was successful. It was not a peaceful settling though. In 1868 the settlers and Apaches battled at Round Mountain. The event was commemorated with the building of the first church, St. Francis de Paula.

Tularosa has seen the arrival of Texas cattlemen, merchants, former Union soldiers, professionals and promoters.

There is an annual Rose Festival and oldtimer's picnic and luminarias line the church plaza and highway on Christmas Eve.

Close by is La Luz Canyon and La Luz, the oldest settlement in the Tularosa Basin. The Franciscan missionaries built a chapel so well cared for it shows little signs of age.

Tularosa Chamber of Commerce
301 Central Avenue
Tularosa, NM 88352
(505) 585-9858

US 54 NBL
MM 78

20-B

Alamogordo

In 1898 the brothers of Charles B. and John A. Eddy, promoters of the El Paso and Northeastern Railroad, laid out and platted a town here. Alamogordo served as a junction with a railroad line to the lumbering operation in the Sacramento Mountains. The first atomic bomb was exploded 60 miles northwest of here on July 16, 1945. Population 24,024. Elevation 4350 feet.

Mr. Charles B. Eddy was very influential in the founding of Alamogordo. He planned a community with large wide thoroughfares and irrigation ditches lined with trees. The large cottonwoods helped the city to get its name. Alamogordo is Spanish for "fat cottonwood."

Mr. Eddy was a prohibitionist and wanted no liquor in his model community, but his attorney advised him that total prohibition would doom the city to failure. The attorney wrote an ordinance known as Block 50 Ordinance, the only block where liquor could be made and/or sold. Since Mr. Eddy sold all the lots, each deed had a provision that prohibited liquor on any lot. If there was liquor, the lot reverted to Mr. Eddy. Needless to say, homeowners were wary about drinking in their homes. The ordinance stayed on the books until 1984.

Alamogordo is the Otero County Seat, home to Holloman Air Force Base, and houses New Mexico's oldest zoo. The International Space Hall of Fame, the Tombaugh Omnimax Space Theater and Planetarium, the Astronaut Memorial Garden, Air and Space Park and a Shuttle Camp are all features at the Space Center. It is located two miles northeast of Highway 54 in Alamogordo. The phone number is 1-800-545-4021 or (505) 437-2840

Alamogordo Chamber of Commerce
1301 N White Sands Blvd
Alamogordo, NM 88310
1-800-826-0294
505-437-6120
Fax 505-437-6334
E-mail: chamber@wazoo.com

Town of Alamogordo

20-D

New Mexico Commission for the Blind Orientation Center

The Mission Statement for The SNMCB states:

"The mission of the New Mexico Commission for the Blind is to encourage and enable blind citizens of New Mexico to achieve vocational, economic and social equality.

This is accomplished by removing limitations and erasing stereotypes long imposed upon the blind by themselves and by the public at large.

The New Mexico Commission for the Blind provides career training, training in the skills of blindness and above all, promotes and conveys the belief that blindness is not a barrier to employment, and not to living a full, meaningful life."

Alamogordo Orientation Center
408 North White Sands Blvd.
Alamogordo, NM 88310
(505) 437-0401

US 54 & 5th Street
Alamogordo

20-E

New Mexico School
Visually Handicapped

The New Mexico School for the Visually Handicapped has been serving the Youth of New Mexico and their families since 1903.

Their Mission Statement states: The mission of the New Mexico School for the Visually Handicapped is to provide the training, support and resources necessary to prepare blind/visually/multiply impaired children in New Mexico to participate fully in their families, community, and work force and to lead independent, productive lives.

Their Vision Statement states: Our vision is to provide leadership that will create a comprehensive program of educational services for all blind/visually/ multiply impaired children in New Mexico that is world class and recognized nationally as the most knowledgeable, effective and efficient educational program for blind children in the United States.

**New Mexico School
for the Visually Handicapped
1900 N. White Sands Blvd.
Alamogordo, NM 88310
(800) 437-3505**

US 54
Alamogordo

20-F

Dog Canyon
(Canon del Perro)

For the Mescalero Apaches, Dog Canyon was a favorite camping area and trail through the Sacramento Mountains. It was the scene of several battles in the 19th century. In 1863 a group of Mescaleros was attacked by soldiers, and the survivors were sent to the Bosque Redondo Reservation.

Located in the rugged country between the Sacramento Mountains and White Sands, Dog Canyon is a desolate, rocky enclave in the Tularosa Basin that for centuries was a favorite Apache campsite in southern New Mexico.

With year around flowing water and abundant plants and animals, Dog Canyon attracted both prehisotric and historic inhabitants to the area. The Apache used the steep canyon as a stronghold, particularly in the 19th century conflicts with the United States Militia.

Dog Canyon was also the home to Francios-Jean Rochas, a master French woodworker turned reclusive New Mexico Rancher. Santa Fe's Loretto staircase mystery could well have been built by this man. His bullet riddled body was found in his cabin in Dog Canyon.

Oliver Lee Memorial State Park features historical exhibits and a fully restored 19th century ranch house of Oliver Milton Lee. There is also a visitor center, trails and camping facilities.

Oliver Lee Memorial State Park
409 dog Canyon
Alamogordo, NM 88310
505-437-8284

Hwy 54
South of Alamogordo

20-G

Tularosa Valley

Spectacular escarpment of Sacramento Mountains to east is of Paleozoic sedimentary rocks, well exposed along Dog Canyon. Tularosa Valley is down-dropped about 2 miles relative to Sacramentos and San Andres Mountains on west side of basin. Gypsum dunes of White Sands to west occur only in arid climates. Elevation 4,030 feet.

Where does all the gypsum come from? Well, the answers lie deep within the mountains. The mountains are striped with layers of limestone which contain gypsum. Rain washes the gypsum down to the valley floor. Because the Tularosa Basin has no river running out of it, it collects at Lake Lucero, the lowest point in the Basin. As the water evaporates, the gypsum is left behind leaving a crust on the bed lake.

Early settlers once used some of this for window glass, even though it was very soft and would scratch easily.

Wind and rain slowly break up the crust back into crystal, which the wind sweeps away. As the winds are generally from the southwest, the crystals are constantly being added to the dunes of white sand.

The park at White Sands offers camping, several trails, and special events. There is an Interdune Boardwalk which has interpretive exhibits.

White Sands National Monument
P.O. Box 1086
Holloman AFB, NM 88330
(505) 679-2599

North on Hwy 54

20-H

Cloud Climbing Railroad

In order to provide timber for the construction of his El Paso & Northeastern Railroad north of Alamogordo, Charles B. Eddy in 1898 built a spur into the Sacramento Mountains. The line operated as far as Cloudcroft until 1947. The Cloudcroft Trestle is all that remains.

Over 100 years ago, the El Paso & Northeastern Railroad was making it's way through the new town of Alamogordo. From there it would continue North. The need for timbers and railroad ties had the officials of the railroad looking to the Sacramento Mountains.

A survey crew was sent into the area to determine the feasibility of laying a railroad line up to the summit of the mountains. The report came back that not only was the project feasible, but the beauty of the area would attract visitors from all over. The name "Cloudcroft" was suggested as it was a pasture for the clouds. Soon after, the report was accepted and work on the line began.

By the end of 1898, the line had been extended as far as Toboggan Canyon and from there, people used a stage to reach the summit. It was early in the year of 1900 that the railroad finally arrived in Cloudcroft. In the beginning, three trains arrived in Cloudcroft daily, some to haul logs down the mountain and others to carry mail and passengers.

By 1938, the last passenger trained climbed the mountain. Cars and trucks became a more popular mode of transportation. By 1947, the last freight train went down the hill and the line was abandoned. Today, only the cloud climbing trestle remains.

Cloudcroft hasn't changed much over the years. The village still maintains a small-town atmosphere that is so appealing to the tourists who come from every state in the union. They appreciate the attitude of the locals and the laid-back feeling of the community as contrasted to the high-speed life in the big cities.

Cloudcroft Chamber of Commerce
P.O. Box
Cloudcroft, NM
505-682-2733

East on Hwy 54
Cloudcroft

20-I

Mescalero Apache Reservation

The Mescalero Apaches were named for their use of mescal for food. Their economy, based primarily on hunting, gathering and raiding and trading, the Mescaleros occupied much of south-central new Mexico in the 18th and 19th centuries. Since 1871, the Mescaleros have lived on a reservation about half a million acres, located on part of their ancient homeland.

The headquarters of the Mescalero Apache Indian Reservation is located in the town of Mescalero, 17 miles northeast of Tularosa. President Ulysses S. Grant originally ordered the establishment on May 27, 1873. The reservation was first located near Ft. Stanton. In 1883, it was moved to its present location and covers 463,000 acres between the Sacramento and White Mountains.

The Lipan Apaches from northwest Chihuahua, Mexico were brought to the United States about 1903 and placed on the Mescalero Reservation. In 1913 almost 200 members of the Chiricahua and Warm Springs band of Apaches were moved from Fort Sill, Oklahoma, to the reservation. The Lipan and Chiricahua bands became members of the Mescalero Apache when the tribe was organized formally in 1936 under provisions of the Indian Reorganization Act. Today, the population exceeds 3,300 enrolled members of the Tribe.

Most of the men and women today are career oriented, many with college degrees. The Tribal Council with 10 elected members, supervises the management of tribal affairs, regulates the use of tribal property and funds and, in general, functions much as does a board of county commissioners.

Activities of the tribal government are supported principally from income from timber sales. The Tribe is also striving to develop tourism potential. Other income is derived from the operation of a cattle industry. The Tribe operates Ski Apache Resort, Inn of the Mountain Gods, and the Apache Casino.

Hwy 70
East of Tularosa

20-J

Round Mountain

This cone-shaped landmark about 10 miles from Tularosa was once known as Dead Man's Hill, and has been the backdrop for several military encounters. In April 1868 a small group of soldiers and Tularosa settlers engaged in a battle with about 200 Mescalero Apaches.

When the Rio Grand flood waters destroyed their crops, Hispanic settlers wandered into the Tularosa Basin. The area around Tularosa beckons because the Rio Tularosa flows deep and cool year around. The soil is rich and needs only water to flourish.

The sun, scorpions, snakes and vultures were only some to welcome the would be settlers. The Apaches were relentless. Time after time bands of Indians raided the almost defenseless colony. Stock was driven off. Farmers were tortured and killed. The Apaches forced them off the land, yet the settlers would return and try again,

On March 11th of 1868 the Apache went on a particular vicious rampage. They killed eleven men and two women. Perhaps is was time for the settlers to abandon the village once and for all.

In April of 1868, Fort Stanton was sending a supply wagon through to Fort Seldon in Texas. Sgt. Glass selected 5 troopers to escort the wagon. Several of the young men had no previous combat experience.

Five miles outside of Tularosa, Sgt. Glass ordered the wagon to go on alone as the road ahead was considered safe. The escort turned back towards Ft. Stanton. Near the base of Round Mountain, one of the soldiers thought he heard hoofbeats. They paused. Soon all heard and knew what was coming. Two hundred Apache Warriors rounded the mountain and headed straight for them.

The soldiers found cover near an abandoned adobe wall. One soldier volunteered to try to make it to Tularosa to get help. Several hours after the solder slipped away, a contingent of twenty-six armed Hispanic settlers was riding towards them at full gallop. The Indians retreated because of superior firepower of the solders and settlers.

Round Mountain was the scene of the final battle between the settlers of Tularosa and the Apaches.

Hwy 70
East of Tularosa

20-K

St. Joseph's Mission

Father Albert Braun, who directed the construction of the remarkable mission church of St. Joseph, served as chaplain in both World Wars. He first came to Mescalero in 1916, and later built this stone church in memory of Americans killed in World War I. It took him almost twenty years to complete, and was dedicated in 1939.

When Father Albert arrived for his first assignment as an ordained priest of the Franciscan order in 1916 in Mescalero, he found a dilapidated adobe church with a leaky roof, earthen floors and no windows. The walls were crumbling and his quarters was a tiny room behind a blanket curtain in the back of the building.

Father Albert knew he was in trouble after he gave his first homily. It was customary for Franciscan priests to earn their daily bread from donations made by the faithful. The collection plate held 17 cents. Part of this was to go to his interpreter as most of the older Apaches did not speak English, and he had no idea just what his interpreter was telling his parishioners.

Father Albert stuck to his guns. He worked hard to visit all the members of his parish and to learn Apache. As time passed, the people began to accept him. Babies were baptized, the dead were buried. He was able to influence the deepest part of their lives. His own love of religion allowed him to appreciate the spiritual nature of the Apache.

During World War I, Father Albert begged to go as an Army Chaplin. While in Europe, the great stone cathedrals brought dreams which he returned with to Mescalero. When he returned in 1919, though money was hard to find, he explained his plan to the church members.

It was 1939 before the church was considered complete. It is 131 feet long, 64 feet wide, and an adjoining tower with a cross on top is 103 feet high. Passers by on U.S. 70 can't help but notice the stone monolith.

Inside is just as unique as the outside. There is an Apache Madonna in one alcove. Above the alter is a huge painting of an Apache holy man. On the Alter itself, there is a painting of twelve Apache apostles seated at a table eating traditional foods. St. Joseph's church is a rock solid tribute to Father Albert and the Apache people, and a monument to the soldiers of both world wars.

East on Hwy 70

20-L

Blazer's Mill

An early fight in the Lincoln county War occurred near this sawmill on April 3, 1878, when several men of the McSween faction, including Dick Brewer and Billy the Kid, attempted to arrest Buckshot Roberts. Roberts and Brewer were killed, and two others wounded, in the battle that followed.

Richard Brewer had been John Tunstall's chief herder. When the official county law refused to take action for Tunstall's murder, Brewer sought and won from a justice of the peace, a warrant to apprehend the murders. Billy the Kid was one of the first to sign up as a deputy to Brewer's "Regulators".

Brewer's Deputies set off in March, 1878, to seek out the men Billy had witnessed killing Tunstall, Billy's boss and a man he respected. Billy had sworn to avenge his death by bringing in those 5 men who had murdered Tunstall.

By April, two of the murderers had been laid low and the fighting had escalated. The Murphy legal faction, led by Sheriff Brady, posted a reward for the Regulators. He was offering $100 for each of them. Now, whenever the two factions crossed paths, there was sure to be bloodshed.

Andrew "Buckshot" Roberts, a former Texas Ranger, was a Murphy supporter. Charlie Bowdre, one of the Regulators riding that night, had an abiding dislike of Roberts. When the Regulators caught up with Roberts at Blazer's Mill, gunfire erupted.

When the smoke cleared, two Regulators lay dead, including Richard Brewer and John Middleton. Also dead was "Buckshot" Roberts, and the Lincoln County War continued to escalate.

East on HWY 70
MM 241

20-M

Sierra Blanca

Sierra Blanca, a complex ancient volcano, rises more than 7,300 feet above Tularosa Basin to peak at 12,000 feet. Vertical geological movement between ranges and basin is about 2 miles. San Andres Mountains on west side of Tularosa Basin are uplifted on east side and tilted westward. Elevation 4,670 feet.

Sierra Blanca, meaning White Mountain, is a sacred mountain to the Mescalero Apaches and is near the northwest center of the Reservation. For centuries, the Apaches had learned of the mountain's power to soothe the thirst of both mind and body, following the rigors of desert life long before it became a landmark for the first Spanish explorers more than 400 years ago.

It is also home to one of New Mexico's finest ski areas, Ski Apache. The Ski area is about 12 miles long and ranges from 4 to 12 miles wide. The west side of the main branch is steep and extremely rugged, while the eastern side is more gentle and broader with forested canyons and several year-around streams.

There is hiking in the summer as well as abundant wildlife. Occasionally, one may even spot a bald eagle soaring over head. The Crest Trail runs 21 miles more or less, north and south, tying the system of the White Mountain Wilderness with Ski Apache.

For more information, Contact

The Smoky Bear Ranger Station
901 Mechem Drive
Ruidoso, NM
(505) 257-4095

East Hwy 70
MM 254

20-N

Welcome to New Mexico

US 54 North on NM State Line

on 285 S on NM State Line

20-O

Quay County

Quay County and the small settlement of Quay were both named for Matthew S. Quay, a U.S. Senator from Pennsylvania who helped spearhead the effort of turning the Territory of New Mexico into the state of New Mexico.

County Seat: Tucumcari
Communities: Logan, Nara Vista, San Jon,
            Forrest, McAlister, House,
            Quay, Rayland, Montoya,
            Glenrio

Ute Lake State Park

2, 875 Square Miles

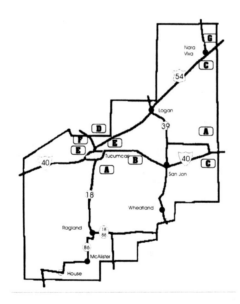

Llano Estacado

Rising above these red-earth lowlands to the south is the Llano Estacado to Stockaded Plain, a high plateau covering some 32,000 square miles in eastern New Mexico and adjacent areas in Texas. Topographically, it is one of the flattest areas in the United States, and rises to 450 feet above the surrounding Great Plains.

Sediments shed from the rising mountains to the west formed the Llano Estacado, later to be bypassed by streams such as the Pecos and Canadian Rivers and left standing in bold relief with a relatively level, uneroded caprock surface. Croplands on the plain are irrigated using "fossil" water pumped from underground aquifers.

When the Rocky Mountains were forming in the west, sediments collected here, forming this amazingly huge, and relatively flat, mesa. Water has since eroded deep arroyos and canyons and left this level surface.

Known as the Sea of Grass, navigation was made possible by following a series of stakes across the endless flat land.

On NM 54 NM 469 Junction
On Old Route 66 on I-40
MM 373.4

21-A

Black Jack Ketchum

Thomas "Black Jack" Ketchum, leader of a notorious band of train robbers, was wounded in August 1899 while trying to rob a train near Folsom. He surrendered the next day. He was tried and convicted under a law making train robbery a capital offense, and hanged at Clayton on April 26, 1901.

In the Era of Billy the Kid, Frank and Jessie James, the "Black Jack" Ketchum Gang was one of the last wild gangs to terrorize the West.

Black Jack and his brother, Sam Ketchum were outlaws in the late 1800's. Born in Texas, Tom was the younger of the two brothers. He left Texas around 1890, possibly because of a murder or a train robbery. He went to work with cow outfits in the Pecos Valley of New Mexico. By 1894, Sam had joined him, and the boys began their crime spree, including killing a merchant near Carrizozo, NM, robbing post offices, holding up stages, trains, and a railroad station.

On September 3, 1897, they held up the Colorado Southern passenger train near Folsom. In 1898, after an apparent disagreement, Sam and the other members of the gang again held up the Colorado Southern on July 11, 1899. A posse was hot on their trail. Sam was wounded and captured. He died two weeks later in the penitentiary at Santa Fe.

Not knowing the outcome of Sam's last attempt, Black Jack was determined to make one more raid. He tried, single handed, to hold up the Colorado Southern near Folsom again on August 16, 1899. The conductor managed to wound Black Jack, and he was captured by the tracks the next day.

He was hung on April 26, 1901, one of the last outlaws to "swing". He was accidentally decapitated. A doctor carefully reunited his head with his body. His grave is located in the Clayton Cemetery, in Clayton, New Mexico.

US 87 MM 8.2
Interstate 40 on NM 209
MM 71.6

21-B

Welcome to New Mexico
Land of Enchantment

This sign greets visitors and welcomes travelers home on I-40 at the New Mexico-Texas Border. There is a modern rest area with restrooms and picnic tables as well as a visitor's center and free coffee to welcome you to our Land Of Enchantment.

And what a wonderful, enchanting state it is. With high mountain country, deep river valleys, multi-colored deserts, fertile farm land, modern cities, quaint towns and villages, and arid cattle country, there is something for everyone.

If you are a lover of the great outdoors, New Mexico offers dramatic winter skiing, year around fishing and hunting, camping, swimming, and just about any type of sport you can imagine.

For art lovers, New Mexico is becoming a cultural hub with many diversified artists creating amazing works inspired by this unique state.

New Mexico also has interesting geological, biological, and paleontological regions that will expand your knowledge of how this planet came to be. Extinct volcanoes, dinosaur tracks, and deep ravines give many clues as to how time has changed the land and evolution over billions of years.

Socially, New Mexico boasts of a Tri-culture, again making it an enchanting place to visit. From Native Americans to the influence of Spanish settlers, to the coming of Anglos, each have left their own addition very visible today. Ancient pueblos and churches as well as remains of the Santa Fe Trail, are a walk through the past.

This state has also had a wide array of colorful characters. Billy the Kid, Pat Garret, Black Jack Ketchum add to the rich history.

So, enjoy your coffee, and get ready to explore and learn of this amazing state.

New Mexico, truly the Land of Enchantment.

Interstate 40 West Bound
NM 373.4

21-C

Ute Lake State Park

Offering the best walleye fishing in new Mexico, this reservoir on the Canadian River also provides good fishing for both white and largemouth bass, channel catfish, and crappie. Park facilities include camping/picknicking sites, a playground, boat ramps, and a marina.

Located 25 miles northeast of Tucumcari on Highway 540 and three miles west of Logan, this lake has numerous coves and inlets, excellent for fishing and all water sports.

Ute Lake is the second largest lake in New Mexico. Built in 1963 with the construction of the 5,750 foot-long, earth-filled Ute Dam, it is almost 13 miles long, and a slender 1 mile wide. It is fed by the Canadian River and Ute Creek.

Boasting sandy beaches, windsurfing, and holding the state record for walleye, Ute Lake State Park has something to offer everyone. There is the Cedar Valley Nature Trail which loops 1.5 miles through fairly rugged terrain offering majestic views of the lake. It also has an off-road vehicle area near Ute Creek and a small visitors' center with exhibits and information on park activities.

Ute Lake State Park
Box 52
Logan, NM 88426
(505) 487-2284

The Visitors' Center is always open.

US Highway 54
MM 326.9

21-D

Tucumcari

This area was troubled by both Comanches and Comancheros, New Mexicans who traded illegally with the Indians, until the military campaigns of 1874. With the coming of the railroad in 1898, the small community of Liberty, eight miles to the north, moved here to form the nucleus of Tucumcari, which was incorporated in 1908.

Originally called Six Shooter Siding, Tucumcari owes its beginning to a snowstorm. In 1900, two men stayed at a nearby ranch during a bad snowstorm which lasted three weeks. In return for the rancher's hospitality, the men told the rancher, Mr. A. D. Goldenberg, that the railroad would be going through the area about 4 miles from his home. Mr. Goldenberg, his brother, Max, and two other businessmen, bought up the land where they felt the railroad would have to lay tracks. Today, Tucumcari does not depend on the railroad as much as it does today's modern highways. First, Historic Route 66, and today, Interstate 40 runs through Tucumcari allowing it to thrive and prosper.

Tucumcari is the Quay County seat and the county's largest community. Tucumcari is hailed as "The Gateway to New Mexico" for the travelers on I-40 coming into New Mexico or headed for the Texas Panhandle. With many motels, two lakes, a wildlife area, and a golf course, Tucumcari is an excellent place for a traveler's stopover.

Tucumcari Chamber of Commerce
404 W. Tucumcari Blvd
P.O. Drawer E
Tucumcari, NM 88401
(505) 461-1694
FAX (505) 461-3884

Interstate 40 Business Loop
Tucumcari, 5.1 miles I-40 East
US Highway 54
MM 305.5

21-E

Tucumcari Mountain

Tucumcari Mountain has long been a landmark for travelers along the Canadian River. Pedro Vial mentioned it in 1793, while opening a trail between Santa Fe and St. Louis. In order to find the best route from Arkansas to California, Capt. Randolph B. Marcy led an expedition past here in 1849.

There is a legend about how Tucumcari got its name. Long ago, an Apache Chief was nearing the end of his time on earth. He sent for his two finest braves, Tonopah and Tocom. The two Warriors were not only rivals, but also sworn enemies. The Chief's daugter, Kari, loved Tocom. The Chief told the two Warriors, "Soon I must die and one of you must succeed me as chief. Tonight, you must take your long knives and meet in combat to settle the matter between you. He who survives shall be the Chief and have for his squaw, Kari, my daughter."

The two braves met for the mortal combat, unaware that Kari was hiding nearby. Tonopah's knife found the heart of Tocom. The young squaw rushed from her hiding place and used a knife to take Tonopah's life before taking her own life. When the Chief was shown this tragic scene, he took his daughter's knife and buried it deep within his own body, crying out in agony, "Tocom-Kari"!

Less romantic historians believe the word "Tucumcari" is a derivation from the Comanche word "tukanukaru," which means to lie in wait for something. This is historically possible as the mountain was known as a Comanche lookout many years ago.

Tucumcari Business Loop I-40
5.1 Miles East I-40

21-F

Nara Visa

This area is rich in prehistoric evidence, and was home of the buffalo and Plains Indians. Explored by the early Spanish, the area was settled when the Rock Island Railroad was built through in 1901.

The brick building, built in 1921, was home for a fine school. The adobe gym was built in 1935 by WPA laborers. The buildings are listed on the National and State Historic Registers. Now a Community Center, it is the heart of community activity. Founded in 1902. Elevation 4,200 feet.

In the 1880's a sheepherder named Narvaez lived in this area. As English speaking settlers moved into the area, they mispronounced his name and Nara Visa was born. In 1901 as the railroad was built, the first permanent settlers lived in a boxcar.

A small creek, known as Nara Vista Creek, flows through the village. The old trains could not run without water for their steam engines, thus Nara Vista was an important stop along the lines.

Not far away is the town of Logan, another town that grew around the railroads need for water. Eugene Logan, a well known Texas Ranger, came to work on the CRI&P Railroad when they were constructing a bridge over the Canadian River.

In later years, a dam creating Ute Lake was built, and the community of Logan took to calling itself, "The best little town by a dam site."

21-G

Rio Arriba County

Created in 1852, Rio Arriba means "Upper River" and was the Spanish designation for the upper Rio Grande area. The county was one of the 7 original " Partidos" under Spanish rule.

County Seat: Tierra Amarilla
Communities: El Rito, Espanola, Chama, Vallecitos,,
Ojo Caliente, Tres Piedras, San Juan,
La Madera, Abiquiu, Los Ojos

Heron Lake State Park   5,861 Square Miles

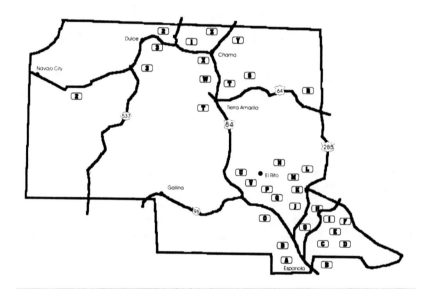

Pueblo of Santa Clara

Founded around the fourteenth century, Santa Clara traces its ancestry to Puyè, an abandoned site of cave dwellings on the Pajarito Plateau. Increasing tensions with the Spanish led to its participation in the Pueblo Revolt of 1680. The mission church, once thought to be the narrowest of its kind, has been reconstructed several times since the 17th century.

The pueblo's major attraction is Santa Clara Canyon, a deep, tree-lined retreat with several mountain-ringed fishing lakes, developed camp sights, and picnicking, all by permit. Santa Clara Pueblo has a very large land base, with a wide variety of geographic features. There is a majestic beauty to the landscapes of the Santa Clara Pueblo's homeland.

Santa Clara has emerged with a strong tribal government and prosperous economy. This is, in part, due to cultural pride and a strong sense of identity. While retaining many of their ancient traditions, they also integrate the best that the majority culture has to offer.

In June, Saint Anthony's Feast Day features Comanche Dances. In August, the Harvest Dances and the Corn Dances are performed in honor of the patron saint, Saint Clare.

The Pueblo also features many wonderful artisans creating pottery known as redware, carved black ware, melon bowls, and other artistic mediums. Wandering through the village, keep an eye out for shop signs of potters and painters.

Santa Clara Pueblo
P.O. Box 580
Espanola, NM 87532
505-753-7326

Southwest of Espanola
At Santa Clara Pueblo

22-A

Espanola Valley

When it was described by Gaspar Castaño de Sosa in 1591, the Española Valley contained about ten Tewa-speaking pueblos, several of which are still occupied today. Juan de Oñate established New Mexico's first colony here in 1598. Long on the northern frontier of Spanish settlement, the Valley has continuously reflected its Indian and Spanish heritage.

Situatued between the 12,000 foot Jemez Mountains to the west and the 13,000 foot Truchas Peaks to the east, The Espanola Valley is part of the northern Rio Grande Valley.

Three rivers, Rio Grande, Rio Chama, and Santa Cruz converge near the city of Espanola.

This valley has a deep and rich history. Once the home of dinosaurs, the remains of Coelophysis, New Mexico's State Dinosaur, are still found near Abiquiu.

The Anasazi, ancestors of the present-day Santa Clara people also settled in the Valley centuries ago, leaving only their ruins at Puye. There are eight Indian Pueblos, each with its own distinct character, but all deeply interconnected to the others by an ancient, common heritage. Several Spanish villages and lovely historic Catholic mission churches dot the valley.

Espanola is the "Low-rider capital of the U.S." In the New Mexico exhibit at the Smithsonian in Washington D.C., there is a classic low-rider from Espanola on display.

Espanola Valley Chamber of Commerce
417 Big Rock Center
Espanola, NM 87532
505-753-1746

On US Hwy 285/84 North
North of Espanola
On US Hwy 84

22-B

Dominguez Escalante Trail

On July 25, 1776, two Franciscans, Fray Francisco Atanasio Dominguez and Fray Silvestre Velez de Escalante set out on horseback on an expedition from Santa Fe, New Mexico to Monterey, California. The purpose of the expedition was two-fold; to open communications between the two missions (Santa Fe and Monterey) and to convert the Indians (Utes and Havasupais) between pueblo land and the Pacific Coast. The party did not reach Monterey, however, but only got as far as the Utah Basin. Due to the onset of winter weather, lack of provisions and frequent desertion of Indian guides, their goal was reconsidered, causing much dissension. Lots were cast to continue on or to return to Santa Fe. Thus it was decided to turn back to Santa Fe.

When the Frays passed through this area, they were headed to California. The Spaniards realized that an overland trail from Santa Fe to the recently founded Spanish missions in Alta, California, would be valuable to Spain for defensive, economic, and political reasons. Not to mention, it would give them an opportunity to explore the area and to convert the inhabitants of the region. They were well received in Utah, and promised to return within the year to claim the valley which was "so spacious with such good land and beautiful proportions that in it alone a province like New Mexico can be established and can be maintained..."

It proved impossible for the small expedition to return to Utah as promised. Conditions in New Mexico had deteriorated and missionary efforts along the frontier were declined.

From Utah Valley, the Spaniards proceeded to their original destination, traveling South and southwest towards California. On October 8, an unseasonable snow storm forced them to stop for three days. The padres decided it was impractical to continue on. Ever since Utah Valley, the two padres apparently had lost all desire to continue their original mission, as their missionary zeal rekindled, they preferred to head back to Mexico to recruit settlers.

By casting lots, as the civilians wanted to continue, and become rich for finding the route, it was determined to return to Santa Fe.

The expedition was significant and important to history because of the remarkable journal the two Franciscans kept while on their expedition.

North of Espanola on US Hwy 84   **22-C**

Santa Cruz De la Canada

In 1695, Governor Diego de Vargas founded his first town, Santa Cruz de la Cañada, designed to protect the Spanish frontier north of Santa Fe. The church, which still stands, was constructed in the 1730s. In 1837, residents revolted against Mexican authorities, resulting in the death of Governor Albino Pèrez.

Santa Cruz Plaza on the Camino Real

In 1695 Governor Diego de Vargas founded Santa Cruz de la Cañada south of the Santa Cruz river. The town was later moved to this site north of the river. The church facing the plaza dates from the 1730s. Santa Cruz was an important stop on the Camino Real between Santa Fe and Taos.

To settle and protect their interests in New Mexico, the Spaniards needed colonists. In Mexico City, they advertised for colonists to travel up the Camino Real, promising land grants and support. The stipulations were that the people be of Spanish descent only. Church records were consulted to verify that couples were indeed legitimately married.

The majority of responding families were of the tradesman class—tailors, weavers, millers.

One of the largest groups of people to traverse the entire length of the Camino Real from Mexico City to Santa Fe, consisted of 41 percent children. The 88 children and their parents must have had a memorable and challenging adventure.

It took nine months to make the journey. When they arrived in Santa Fe it was 1694. In April 1695, Santa Cruz de la Canada was founded specifically to accommodate the families recruited from Mexico City.

Many of those colonizers have descendants still in the area.

Face Missing
On State Hwy 76
Near Jct 84
West on NM Hwy 76
At Jct 583

22-D

Truchas

In 1754, Governor Tomás Vèlez Cachupìn granted land on the Rìo Truchas to families from Santa Cruz and Chimayó. Because Nuestra Señora del Rosario de Truchas was on the northern frontier, and subject to attack by Plains Indians, the governor stipulated that the houses should form a square with only one entrance.

The Rosario grant was established by petition to the Spanish king and local governor in 1754 by twelve families. They established the fortified Plaza of Truchas and today, the primarily Hispanic village has approximately 1000 people located within a 15,000 acre grant.

After choosing a defensible site on a point of land overlooking the canyon they had come to claim, the local alcade, or mayor, laid out a town plaza of 60 yards inside and 70 yards outside. The houses were then laid out 15 foot wide.

For defensive purposes, there was only one entrance to the plaza. There was also 10 yards of garden space for each family around the plaza. A well that provided drinking water was also part of the plaza.

Truchas was a subsistence agriculture community up until Los Alamos offered a local source of wages after World War II. Its population has grown slowly, but steadily through the years. It was around 1950 when electricity and running water was made available.

On NM Hwy 106
South of Truchas- MM 15.7

22-E

Truchas Peaks

Ice age glaciers carved these beautiful alpine peaks, among the highest in the New Mexico Rockies, rising to 13,101 feet. Precambrian quartzite, some of the oldest rock in New Mexico, forms the core of the Truchas ("trout") Peaks, part of the Pecos Wilderness which encompasses some of the most pristine mountain terrain in the state.

The Pecos Wilderness, designated in 1933 and containing 223,333 acres, lies at the southern end of the majestic Sangre de Cristo Mountains, at the headwaters of the Pecos River. From its origin, the Pecos flows 13.5 miles and is designated "wild" in the Wild and Scenic Rivers System. It includes some of the most beautiful and scenic country in New Mexico. Excellent fishing and hunting, magnificent scenery, and quiet solitude attract many visitors. Truchas Peak, second highest in New Mexico, provides a challenge for mountain climbers and ecologists who may observe rare species of plants and animals. Many lakes, more than 150 miles of streams, a 100-foot waterfall, and innumerable springs are in the area.

An extensive trail system provides many opportunities for both day use and camping. Camping and other uses at some lakes and other areas are regulated to prevent damage to the fragile environment.

Administered jointly by the Santa Fe and Carson National Forests, the wilderness encompasses parts of the Pecos/Las Vegas, Espanola, and Camino Real Ranger Districts.

A legislated wilderness is an area where the earth and its community of life are untrammeled or unchanged by man, where man himself is a visitor who does not remain. Some of the key elements in a wilderness setting are solitude and freedom. These essential qualities are most sensitive to visitor behavior and the degree of restrictions placed on the use of a wilderness.

North of Truchas
On NM Hwy 76-MM 17

22-F

Pueblo of Picuris

The pueblo of Picuris, first visited by Spaniards in 1591, was described as being 7 to 8 stories high. In the 18th century Picuris cooperated with the Spaniards against the raids of the Plains Indians. The church, the third at this pueblo, dates from the 1770s.

At one time, Picuris was one of the largest Tiwa pueblos in New Mexico. Today, with less than 300 inhabitants, it is one of the smallest. Like Taos Pueblo, it was influenced by Plains Indian culture, particularly the Apaches.

Camera permits are available and there are self-guided tours to excavated structures. The Pueblo's San Lorenzo Feast Day is in August and includes dances, pole climbing and a morning footrace.

The Pueblo is near Penasco. The San Lorenzo de Picuris Catholic Church is a popular sight at the Pueblo, as is the Picuris Pueblo Museum which displays and sells beadwork, weavings, and pottery crafted by local artists.

Picuris Pueblo
P.O. Box 127
Penasco, NM 87553
505-587-2519

West on NM Hwy 75
½ mile from turn-off

22-G

Embudo Stream-Gaging Station
Established in 1888

Site of the first United States Geological Survey training center for hydrographers, those trained here made some of the earliest hydrological studies in the nation, leading to stream-gaging of many streams throughout the country, and thus providing important evaluations of the nation's surface water resources.

As the population grew during the late 1800's, people moved west into more arid regions of the country where the flow of rivers and streams was much less dependable than in the humid East. The necessity of reliable water supplies led to the need for streamflow data with which to design storage and distribution facilities.

In 1889, the first stream-gaging station operated in the United States by the U.S. Geological Survey (USGS) was established on the Rio Grande near Embudo, New Mexico. The establishment of this early station was an outgrowth of efforts to train individuals to measure the flow of rivers and streams and to define standard stream-gaging procedures.

In 1994, as the need for streamflow data increased, the stream-gaging program operated by the USGS, grew to include 7,292 continuous-record stream-gaging stations in the United States, Puerto Rico, and the Trust Territory of the Pacific Islands. More than 90 percent of these stations are operated with at least partial support from other federal, state, and local agencies.

Streamflow data are needed at many sites on a daily basis for forecasting flow extremes, water-management decisions, assessing current water availability, managing water quality, and meeting legal requirements. These activities require streamflow information at a given location for a specified time or period. These needs generally are best satisfied by operating a station to produce a continuous (or daily) record of flow.

Marker Missing
On NM Hwy 68
North to Taos-MM 19

22-H

Velarde on the Camino Real

Founded in 1875, this small farming community was first named La Jolla. It was once famous for finely woven blankets. Here the Camino Real left the Rìo Grande and followed a canyon northeast to Embudo Creek where it began a climb over the mountains to Taos.

Velarde is a small, picturesque farming community that sprang up along the Rio Grande and El Camino Real, or Kings Road.

This small town has been known for its chili ristas and the Black Mesa Winery. It is a wonderful town to pass through as you travel the river route between Santa Fe and Taos.

On NM Hwy 68
North of Espanola-MM 14.9

22-I

Hacienda De Los Luceros

This complex of five adobe buildings is situated on the historic Sebastian Martin Land Grant of 1703. The main house, a fine example of 19th century territorial architecture, served as Rio Arriba County Courthouse from 1846 to about 1854. The site is listed on the New Mexico Register of Cultural Properties and National Register of Historic Places.

There are over 500 recognized Land Grants in New Mexico. In order to own property under the land grant system, a person had to "physically step on the land, run your fingers through the soil, and make a public commitment to live on it, cultivate it, and, if necessary, defend it with your life."

After the governor reviewed a petition for a land grant, he typically ordered an alcalde, or other government official to investigate whether the land was indeed vacant and as described by the petitioners.

Once this had been done, the official would lead the settlers to the site, and boundaries would be pointed out. Usually things such as hills, arroyos or mountain ranges and rivers would describe the exact boundaries. They would then walk through the area, pulling up grass and throwing stones, shouting to the four winds, "Long live the King and may God guard him." This was a very important part in the granting of land. When these grants were adjudicated by the American government, some grants were declared invalid and lost because the settlers could not prove the official had given them formal possession.

On NM Hwy 68
North of Espanola-MM 8.4

22-J

San Gabriel on the Camino Real

Governor Juan de Oñate set up his headquarters in San Juan Pueblo in 1598, but by 1601 he had moved the Spanish capital across the Rìo Grande to Yuque-Yunque Pueblo. Named San Gabriel, it served as the seat of government until 1610, when Oñate's successor founded a new capital at Sante Fe.

First came the Folsom Paleo-Indians, who left behind bison bones and fluted projectile points undiscovered until the early 1900's. The river valleys west of their hunting grounds later flooded with refugees from the declining Four Corners Anasazi cultures. Sometime between A.D. 1130 and 1180, the Anasazi drifted from their high-walled towns to evolve into today's Pueblo Indians, so named by early Spanish explorers because they lived in land-based communities much like the villages, or pueblos, of home. Culturally similar American Indians, the Mogollón, lived in today's Gila National Forest.

On this relatively placid scene from the north burst the Southwest's latest-arriving Indians, the Athapascans, dividing into two related groups: Apache and Navajo. As the tribes sorted out territorial differences through trading and raiding, a new element entered the cultural mix on a previously unknown animal, the horse. The Spanish had arrived—with soldiers and settlers accompanied by priests, the well-known Spanish combination of cross and sword. Although there were several previous attempts at exploring Mexico del Norte's wilderness, the most successful one was engineered by Don Juan de Oñate, who lost a considerable fortune outfitting his entrada.

In 1598, his soldiers, oxcarts and livestock arrived at Caypa, one of two Pueblo villages at the confluence of the Río Chama and the Río Grande, north of present-day Española. He soon moved across the river to Yungueingge (Tewa for mockingbird place), a now-ruined pueblo he renamed San Gabriel del Yunque, the first Spanish capital of New Mexico. New Mexico's third governor, Don Pedro de Peralta, founded a new capital, Santa Fe, in 1610.

On NM Hwy 68 North
MM 4.2

22-K

Pueblo of San Juan

The first church in New Mexico was dedicated here in 1598 when Juan de Oñate used the pueblo as his headquarters. Popè, leader of the Pueblo Revolt of 1680, was from San Juan. The unusual Gothic-style church was built in 1912–13 by Father Camilo Seux, a French priest.

The San Juan Pueblo has been traditionally the center of an Indian meeting ground. One of the largest of the Tewa Pueblos, its people were so powerful that only a native could declare war for the Pueblo Indians. The leader of the Pueblo Revolt that drove the Spanish out of New Mexico in the 1700's, Pope, was a native of San Juan Pueblo, although he has also been called a member of the Taos Pueblo.

Located 5 miles north of Espanola, today San Juan Pueblo is the headquarters of the Eight Northern Indian Pueblos Council and also home of the Oke-Oweenge Crafts Cooperative, which exhibits the art of the eight northern Pueblos. The main focus of this village is red ware pottery, weaving and painting.

Fishing is permitted year around, with permits. There's also a fee for taking photos or videos or sketching. The Ohkay Casino has brought many jobs and much needed revenue to the area.

The Okay Casion
P.O. Box 1099
San Juan Pueblo NM 87566
505-852-4400

Marker Missing
On NM Hwy 68
North of Espanola

22-L

Ojo Caliente

Ojo Caliente ("hot spring" in Spanish) was a strategic point for the defense of the Chama and upper Rìo Grande Valleys. Colonization began in the early 18th century, but pressure from the Utes and Comanches delayed permanent settlement until 1793. In 1807, Lt. Zebulon Pike reported a population of 500. Elevation 6,294 feet.

Lieutenant Zebulon M. Pike's expedition was sent to explore the southwestern section of the Louisiana Purchase. In 1806, he was given orders to search for the head waters of the Arkansas and Red Rivers. He led his men over the Colorado Rockies and built a fort on Spanish soil near one of the Rio Grande's tributaries in 1807. Spanish soldiers took the expedition as their prisoners.

Pike was taken to Santa Fe and viewed the town for the first time. Its appearance was not as extravagant as rumors reported it to be. Officials questioned Pike and his men. They weren't satisfied with Pike's answers so the expedition was sent to Chihuahua. In June of 1807, Pike was informed that the expedition would be taken back to American soil and released at Natchitoches, Louisiana.

The Spanish didn't want the Americans to publicize the Spanish lifestyle or the direct route leading to Santa Fe. Pike was sent back to American soil without his notes or his maps.

Pike learned that other Americans wanted to extend America's territories to the Pacific Ocean. The information Pike acquired was important to this effort. Pike wrote about his experiences in New Spain. In 1810, the publishing of his adventures gave Americans their first insight into the Hispanic lifestyle along the Rio Grande.

Marker Missing
On US Hwy 285
North to Ojo Caliente-MM 353

22-M

El Rito

This village was settled in the 1830s by residents from the Abiquiú area. The Territorial Legislature of 1909 established the Spanish-American Normal School here to train teachers for northern New Mexico schools. After several changes in name and purpose, the institution is now the Northern New Mexico Community College. Elevation 6,870 feet.

Northern New Mexico Community College is a supportive, nurturing environment where you can explore new horizons which will challenge and excite you.

Established in 1909 about a half-hour's drive from Espanola, the campus sits at an elevation of approximately 6,790 feet and is nestled in the Carson Nation Forest.

Originally established to provide training for teachers, the El Rito Campus is home to several vocational programs including Adobe Construction, Barbering, Cosmetology, Electricity, Plumbing, and Automotive Technology. It also offers traditional arts programs such as Spanish Colonial Furniture Making, weaving, and a community theater program.

El Rito is also the hometown of Phil T. Archuletta, co-author of this book, and owner of P&M Signs, Inc. and P&M Plastics, Inc.

On NM Hwy 554
in El Rito at NNMCC School

22-N

Abiquiú

Established on the site of an abandoned Indian pueblo, Abiquiú in the mid-18th century became a settlement of Spaniards and genizaros (Hispanicized Indians). In 1776, explorers Fray Francisco Atanacio Dominguez and Fray Silvestre Velez de Escalante visited here. In 1830, the settlement became one of the stops on the Spanish Trail which linked Santa Fe with Los Angeles, California.

A beautiful church built by the community in the 1930's is the Plaza centerpiece. The village was settled following a 1754 Spanish land grant to Hispanicized Indians (Genizaros) and was a frontier settlement for more than 80 years. In the 1700's, an annual trade fair was held in the autumn with neighboring Plains and Pueblo Indians, and in the 1830's and early 1840's, Abiquiú was the departure point for travel and trade along the northern Spanish Trail to Spanish settlements in California. As an intact community land grant, the village is located on private land similar to an Indian Pueblo. Therefore, please do not take pictures without obtaining permission first.

In 1946, Georgia O'Keeffe was able to acquire an old adobe hacienda located just off the Abiquiú Plaza which she restored and made her winter home for many years. The house is now the headquarters of the Georgia O'Keeffe Foundation. Tours of the house are available, but advance reservations are necessary. There is a fee for tours. The phone number is 505.685.4539.

Near Abiquiú is Ghost Ranch which was given by Arthur and Pheobe Pack to the Presbyterian Church in 1955. The 21,000 acres that comprise Ghost Ranch were part of the original land grant to Pedro Martin Serrano from the King of Spain in 1766. The grant was called Piedra Lumbre (shining rock). The name "Ghost Ranch", or the local name Rancho de los Brujos, was derived from the many tales of ghosts and legends of hangings in the Ranch's history.

In a beautiful and isolated spot not far from Abiquiu is the Monastery of Christ In The Desert: A Benedictine Monastery (now an Abbey), is located on the Chama River 18 miles from Ghost Ranch. The road is not totally maintained and is often impassable after snow or rain storms. Inquire making this trip.

On US Hwy 84
North of Espanola-MM 211.9

22-O

Red Rocks

The colorful formations exposed here are the slope forming Chinle Shale of Triassic age deposited in streams, lakes and floodplains some 250 million years ago and the cliff forming Entrada Sandstone of Jurassic age deposited as windblown sand some 160 million years ago. These are typical landforms of the Colorado Plateau province.

It was to this area of witches and ghosts, pastoral simplicity, and solitude that Georgia O'Keeffe was drawn in the early 1930's. Her artist's eye was captivated by the incredible shapes and colors of the landscape. Her Abiquiú home is near the plaza, a little to the south, but spontaneous visits are not permitted. A tour must be arranged by calling the Georgia O'Keeffe Foundation.

Continuing north on the highway about six miles, you reach a plateau. Off to your left, Cerro Pedernal ("Flint Hill") with its flat, seemingly sheared off top, can be seen in the distance. Loved and painted often by Georgia O'Keeffe, the Pedernal has become a famous symbol of the Southwest. Also close by is the Echo Amphitheater, a small, eroded sandstone that echoes back the cries of the night.

In the late 1950's, the Army Corps of Engineers began building the Abiquiuú Dam to create a flood control reservoir. Highly controversial because of its effect on ancestral lands and ecological habitats, it did, however, create the beautiful Abiquiú Lake which offers countless recreational opportunities. Surrounding the lake is some of the most breathtaking scenery in New Mexico — gigantic cliffs in layers of color, created over a 200-million year period by sandstone deposits.

On US Hwy 84
North of Abiquiu-MM 215.7

22-P

Vasquez de Coronado's Route

Under orders from Francisco Vásquez de Coronado in 1540, Captain Hernando de Alvarado explored among the pueblos and followed this route from Española to the Pueblo of Taos. Captain Francisco de Barrionuevo also passed this way the following year on his way to the same pueblo.

Francisco Vasquez de Coronado was born into a noble family in Salamanca, Spain in 1510. At the age of 25, he came to the America's as an assistant to New Spain's first viceroy.

An ambitious man, he married the daughter of the colonial treasurer, put down a major slave rebellion, and became the governor of a Mexican province within three years of his arrival. But he wanted more. Rumors of earlier explorations by Cabeza de Vaca about 7 cites of gold inspired him to lead a royal expedition to explore the north into what is now the American West.

The expedition explored, bringing Catholic ideals to the pueblos they encountered, and the Spanish influence that is still very present today.

When they did not find the "Seven Cities of Cibola", parties were sent out, some traveling all the way to the border between Arizona and California where they explored the Grand Canyon. Coronado himself led a party into what is now Kansas.

Returning to Mexico without locating a single golden city, the Viceroy branded Coronado's expedition an abject failure. His career quickly declined and in 1544 he was removed from office as a governor and moved to Mexico City where he worked in a modest position for the city. He died in 1554, though his legacy is seen throughout the west.

Marker Missing
On NM Hwy 68
North of Espanola-MM 24.1

22-Q

Rio Grande Rift

A tremendous split in the earth's crust has resulted in the Rìo Grande rift basin filled with thousands of feet of alluvium from bordering mountains and lava flows from deep within the earth. About 650 feet of this basin-fill is exposed in the Rìo Grande Gorge at the bridge crossing.

The earth's crust shifts, creating deep rifts between each crust. Fast moving water eroded sand, silt, clay, gravel and other loosened materials from the mountains. As the water slowed on the level bottom of the rift, the materials were left behind, creating the alluvium.

Volcanic flow also filled the basin.

The Rio Grande cut through these softer materials creating the deep gorge with its magnificent colors.

On US 285 North
of Tres Piedras

22-R

Brazos Cliffs

These precipitous cliffs form the western edge of the Tusas Mountains, a Rocky Mountain highland that enters New Mexico from Colorado. They are composed of some of the oldest rock known in New Mexico, the Precambrian quartzite about 1.7 billion years old. Vertical distance from summit to base is more than 2,000 feet. Elevation here is 10,000 feet.

This beautiful valley has been the back drop for many movies including Butch Cassidy and the Sundance Kid, The Cowboys, The Ballad of Gregorio Cortez, Indiana Jones and the Last Crusade, Wyatt Earp and Jericho.

With the stunning waterfall and pristine scenery, nearby lakes for fishing and boating, hiking, skiing, mountain bicycling, and three National Forests to explore, this is a truly wonderful area to explore.

On US Hwy 84 North
Off Jct. 64-MM 194.2

22-S

Tierra Amarilla

Manuel Martìnez of Abiquiú received a large land grant in this area in 1832, but opposition from the Utes interrupted colonization until the 1860's. Tierra Amarilla, first called Nutritas, became the Rìo Arriba County seat in 1880. In 1967 it was the focus of conflicts between National Guardsmen and land rights activist Reies López Tijerina.

Reies Lopez Tijerina was born in 1926 and was an evangelical minister. Many local Hispanics believed that tens of thousands of acres of land that should have been part of an 1848 Land Grant were taken by the US Federal government and set aside for national forests.

Tijerina and a group of New Mexicans from the village of Canjilon drove to Tierra Amarilla on June 5, 1967. They thought to arrest the District Attorney who had not enforced the 1848 Treaty of Guadalupe Hidalgo. The raid on the court house ended with a jailer and state policeman shot and wounded, a reporter and deputy sheriff taken hostage, and National Guardsmen swarming over northern New Mexico.

It was the biggest manhunt the state had ever known. The reporter and deputy managed to escape. Tijerina was captured and went to prison for his part in the raid.

After being released, he lived for a while in the village of Coyote before moving to Mexico early in the 1990's.

This incident brought to national focus the rights of Hispanic settlers descendants.

On US Hwy 84
North of Abiquiu-MM 175.5
On US 64 North
At Jct. 162

22-T

Old Spanish Trail

In 1829-30, Antonio Armijo traveled from Abiquiú to California to trade for mules, thus extending the Old Spanish Trail and opening it to trade between Santa Fe and Los Angeles. His route turned west, near present-day Abiquiú Dam, to Largo Canyon, which led him to the San Juan River.

The Old Spanish Trail had many branches, much like a braided stream. There were North and South branches on the eastern end, western end, and through the Mojave Desert.

It ran from Santa Fe to Los Angeles, California and was used from 1829 to 1850. New Mexican goods were carried west for sale in Los Angeles while mules and horses, some stolen, were transported to New Mexico.

Emigrants from Mexico and points east also moved westward over the trail. Most of the trails were used by mule pack trains, some did eventually see wagon trains.

Marker Missing
On US 84 North of Abiquiu

22-U

Colorado Plateau

From this point, the Colorado Plateau extends across northwestern New Mexico into northeastern Arizona, southeastern Utah, and southwestern Colorado. A colorful landscape of mesas, and canyons, it is underlain by natural mineral, oil, and gas resources locked within sedimentary strata deposited millions of years ago. Elevation 6,400 feet.

More than 100 million years ago, dinosaurs walked across a vast flood plain in what is now the Colorado Plateau. Tracks would be left in the wet mud. Thousands of centuries later, wind and water exposed the tracks, leaving glimpses of the ancient life.

Petrified wood, fossils, both invertebrate and vertebrate, and plant life abound in this wide area.

Later, the arrival of ancient man also left tantalizing glimpses into the past, as they lived and traveled across the wide expanse. Now, generations later, visitors discover and appreciate as they explore and learn of just how far we've come, and just how much is still left to be done.

There is much to learn from the remnant of history. Collecting some specimens of fossils is illegal or limited. Check with local laws to find out what is safe to remove, as the location of the find is as important as the find itself.

Marker Missing
North of Abiquiu

22-W

Fort Lowell

Fort Lowell was established in 1866 to protect the Tierra Amarilla area settlements from the Southern Utes. Originally named Camp Plummer, this post was garrisoned by a detachment of New Mexico Volunteers, some of whose descendants live in the area. The fort was abandoned in 1869 and its log, or "fuerte" buildings sold to local residents.

Settling the wild west was a dangerous business. Many of the Native American tribes fought to keep their land free. Settlers were looking for a better life. As settlers moved West, forts sprang up to protect the settlers. As the United State's hold strengthened in the area, the Forts fell into disuse and were sold off or abandoned.

The remnants of yesteryear give clues as to the way life was. In those simpler times, the soldiers of these forts were the last line of defense for the settlers. They were a very important part to the survival and growth of the United States.

On US Hwy 84 North
To Chama-MM 173.2

22-X

Chama

From a small crossroads town, Chama became an important site on the Denver & Rio Grande Western Railroad after 1880. The Cumbres & Toltec Scenic Railroad is the remnant of the San Juan Extension, a narrow-gauge line which once served the mining areas of southwestern Colorado. Population 1,090. Elevation 7,860 feet.

Beautiful Chama was a settlement long before the arrival of the railroad arrived in this mountain area. Little is known about the history before the train arrived. Records show the railroad reached here December 31, 1880.

The town thrived with the arrival of the train. Stores, bars and less reputable businesses opened. Throughout 1881 lawlessness was fought and soon the town settled.

It wasn't until 1970 that Chama became incorporated and boasted its first Mayor.

The railroad and the scenery still draw visitors today. The facilities for the narrow gauge track have changed very little over the last 75 years.

Chama Valley Chamber of Commerce
P.O. Box 306-RB
Chama, NM 87520
Call (800) 477-0149
(505) 756-2306

On US Hwy 84
Just South of Chama

22-X

Cumbres & Toltec Scenic Railroad

In 1880-82 the Denver & Rìo Grande Railroad built the San Juan Extension to serve the mines of southwestern Colorado. The Cumbres & Toltec Scenic Railroad still operates 64 miles of the narrow-gauge system between Chama, N.M. and Antonito, Colorado. Jointly owned by the two states, it is a "living museum" of railway history.

Today's railroad tracks are wider than the narrow-gauge tracks that were originally used. For many years, three sets of rails were laid, to accommodate both sizes of train cars. As the narrow-gauge fell into disuse, most tracks were abandoned, as trucks and other means of transportation were easier and more cost effective to use.

The Cumbres & Toltec Scenic Railroad was saved from being disassembled in 1970 when the states of Colorado and New Mexico purchased it in a joint effort to save a bit of history.

Since 1971, the railroad has carried over a million riders. The locomotives are the original ones that arrived in 1925 and essentially the same operating procedures are being used, letting you glimpse what life might have been like decades ago.

The train runs from late May to mid October daily. Reservations are strongly recommended.

Cumbres and Toltec Scenic Railroad
P.O. Box 789
Chama, NM 87520
888-Cumbres
800-724-5428

On US 84 North
In Chama-MM 1.3

22-Y

Cumbres Pass

A major encounter between the U.S. Army and a large group of Utes and Jicarilla Apaches occurred here in July 1848. Old Bill Williams, the famous scout and guide, was badly wounded while fighting the Utes, who had once adopted him as a tribesman.

The Cumbres Pass is the highest point on the Cumbres and Toltec Scenic Railroad, and just over the Colorado/New Mexico border. This high pass is one of the few natural passes where the train can pass through the mountains to the other small settlements and mines in the area.

Cumbres translates into "Summits". At one time, a railroad station was near here.

The Utes and Jicarcarilla Apaches were some of the most fierce Indians of the area and time. They fought long and hard against the encroachment of Spanish and Anglos into their land.

Occasionally, the Indians would adopt an outsider into their tribe. The person would have presented remarkable character and a deep honor to be formally adopted. This adoption allowed them to move freely about the Utes territory.

On US Hwy 17 North
of Chama-MM 9.4

22-Z

Continental Divide

Rainfall divides at this point. To the west it drains into the Pacific Ocean... to the east, into the Atlantic. Elevation 7379 feet.

Every Continent has a Continental Divide. This is the point that determines which direction the rainfall and watershed will run.

The Continental Divide in the United States primarily follows the Rocky Mountain Chain. This Divide determines whether the water shed runs into the Atlantic or the Pacific Oceans.

This Divide begins in Alaska and runs through Mexico and into Central Mexico.

On US Hwy 84 West
of Chama-MM 151.9

22-1

Jicarilla Apache (Tribe)

The Jicarilla Apaches, primarily a hunting and gathering group, once occupied vast portions of northeastern New Mexico and southern Colorado. Pressure from Comanche Indians and European settlers eventually pushed them from their homeland. In 1887, the Jicarillas were given a permanent reservation in north-central New Mexico, near Dulce.

Present day, (1989) size of the reservation is 842,315 acres. The northern one-half of the reservation was established by Presidential Executive Order in 1887 and the southern one-half in 1907. New additions to the reservation are the El Poso Ranch in 1982 and the Thesis Ranch in 1986.

Anthropologists say that the Jicarilla (little basketmakers) came from Canada down the eastern flanks of the Rocky Mountains about 1300-1500 AD. All tribes deny the migration theories saying they are the First People, and have always been here.

Very successful as raiders, they were not recognized as being distinctive from other Apache tribes until about 1700.

Today, there is no question of their modern identity. Money from the wool of their thousands of sheep has been supplemented handsomely by the income from their gas and oil rich lands, and more recently, from the lucrative casino. They have been able to adapt to the cultural and environmental changes over the past 200 years while still maintaining their own cultural distinctiveness.

The capital of the Jicarilla Apache Reservation is in Dulce, NM. The Jicarilla are hospitable people and their visitor's center has a museum with exhibits of beadwork and basketry.

Jicarilla Apache Tribe
P.O. Box 507
Dulce, NM 87528
(505) 759-3242

On NM Hwy 64
West of Dulce

On US Hwy 64West of Dulce-MM 115

22-2

Jicarilla Apache Reservation
Centennial Highway

The Jicarilla Apache Tribe commemorated the Centennial Anniversary of their present reservation on February 11,1987. The Centennial was also observed at the annual Little Beaver Pow-wow and Round-up in July and the Go-Jii-Ya Fiesta, September 13–15. The Jicarilla Apache Centennial Wagon Trek, a 200 mile horse and wagon journey from Cimarron to Dulce, was undertaken May 26-June 14,1987, to acknowledge earlier homelands around Cimarron, Taos, and Abiquiú.

During the 19th century, the United States government attempted to establish reservations to separate Indian tribes from settlers along the frontier. The Jicarilla Apache initially agreed to settle on a reservation in 1851, but unratified treaties and local political squabbles hampered the process of obtaining a reservation for 36 years. President Grover Cleveland finally issued the Executive Order which established a permanent home for the Jicarilla on February 11, 1887.

With almost one million acres of the most varied landscape, the Reservation sits high upon the Continental Divide. The road moves across the reservation crossing mountains, steep canyons, valleys, small lakes, and forest, to beautiful semi-desert sandstone and mesas.

On NM Hwy 64
In Dulce

On US Hwy 64
In Dulce

22-3

Roosevelt County

One of the five counties nationwide named for President Theodore Roosevelt, it was created in 1903.

County Seat: Portales
Communities: Tolar, Floyd, Elida, Dora, Causey, Kenna

2,457 Square Miles

Oasis State Park

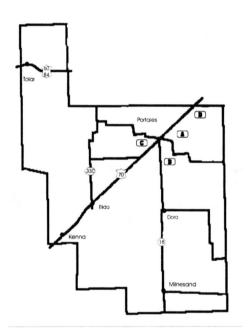

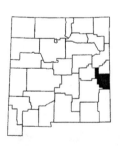

Portales

Portales derives its name for the porch-like appearance of a cave entrance at nearby Portales Springs. It developed as a major peanut producing region in the early twentieth century, after the Pecos Valley Railroad opened the area for commercial agricultural development. Eastern New Mexico University was founded here in 1934.

Originally known as "Los Portales," or "the Porches", Portales derived it's name from a series of caves and the spring waters gushing from them.

It is also a door to human history with the discovery of artifacts and skeletons of mastadons and humans dating back 11,000 years.

Established in the 1800's, agriculture has been a major industry. Peanuts, cotton, wheat, corn, hay and dairy products are some of the things grown in this area.

Cannon Air Force is located about 15 miles north of the city, and the third largest university in the state, Eastern New Mexico University is located on a 400 acre campus in Portales. With almost 4,000 students from all 50 states and 16 foreign countries, it is a diversified addition to the broad curricula of the classes.

Near by is Oasis State Park, an annual Peanut Valley Festival, and a Living History Pageant provides recreation and entertainment to residents and visitors alike.

Portales Chamber of Commerce
200 East 7th Street
Portales, NM 88130
1-505-356-8542

Hwy 70
North of Portales

23-A

The Roosevelt County Museum

Open Daily Visitors Welcome
Eastern New Mexico University
Founded 1939 History and Anthropology of
Roosevelt County.
Open weekdays 8–11:45, 1–4:00. Sat. And Sun. 1–4:00
Admission free.

Take a trip back to the days when homesteaders settled raw, untamed land where only Indians and a handful of cowboys roamed. The history is fascinating, and for those who enjoy rediscovering the past, the Roosevelt County Museum is the place to find it.

Located on the Eastern New Mexico University campus near Highway 70, it was founded by the Roosevelt County Society of Art, History and Archaeology which began meeting in 1937.

The two story brick building was completed in September of 1940. The building contained not only rooms for display, but also rooms to hold meetings and community functions.

Visitors to the campus are reminded they must get a pass from the campus police station before parking on campus.

US 70
North in Portales

23-B

Eastern New Mexico University

This University was established at Portales in 1927 by the State Legislature as the Eastern New Mexico Normal School. It opened for the 1934–35 School year with 274 students. Originally established to train teachers for rural schools, Eastern now has a wide range of undergraduate and graduate programs to serve the instructional, public service and research needs of the state and the nation.

Although it is the youngest state university in New Mexico, ENMU looks with pride upon its accomplishments since the dream of having a university in eastern New Mexico first arose many decades ago.

The Legislature of 1927 located the University in Portales, and the Legislature of 1929 approved the first appropriation for the buildings. Although the first building was constructed in 1931, its doors were not opened to students until 1934.

The institution operated as a two-year college from 1934 to 1940 when the third and fourth years of college were first offered. ENMU was accredited by the north Central Association of Colleges and Secondary Schools as a four-year liberal arts college in 1946-47. Graduate work leading to the master's degree was added in 1949, and ENMU is also accredited by the North Central Association.

Established in 1948, ENMU-Roswell moved to its present facility (formerly Walker Air Force Base) in the fall of 1967. ENMU-Roswell offers a wide variety of programs for Students of Eastern New Mexico.

The ENMU-Ruidoso Off-Campus Instruction Center opened in 1991. The Center offers both an academic and vocational curriculum.

University Relations
Station 6
Portales, New Mexico 88130

US 70-S
In Portales

23-C

Blackwater Draw

In Blackwater Draw stream gravels are famous camp sites of Folsom Man. Draw is in Portales Valley, eroded into High Plains, and headwaters of Brazos River, beheaded by lower Pecos River in Pleistocene time. Local sand dunes conceal underlying Ogalalla sandstones whose "fossil" water feeds irrigated corps. Elevation 4,070 feet.

The importance of Blackwater Draw was first recognized in 1929 as a significant site in North American archaeology. Early investigations at Blackwater Draw recovered evidence of human occupation in association with Late Pleistocene fauna, including Columbian mammoth, camel, horse, bison, sabertooth cat, and dire wolf.

Since its discovery, it has been a focal point for scientific investigations from across the nation. It has been incorporated into the National Register of Historic Places in 1982, and more recently been declared a National Historic Landmark.

There is a Blackwater Draw Museum which houses artifacts and displays that describe and interpret life from 13,000 years ago. The Museum is owned by the Eastern New Mexico University and is located on Highway US 70 7 miles Northeast of Portales.

Blackwater Draw Museum
Station 9, ENMU
Portales, NM 88130
505-562-2202

Hwy 70
North of Clovis

23-D

San Juan County

Named for the River and the nearby San Juan Mountains, San Juan county was once the home of Diverse ancient cultures including Chaco and Anasazi. It was created in 1887.

County Seat: Aztec
Communities: Farmington, Bloomfield, Shiprock, Kirtland, ,La Plata

5,516 Square Miles

San Juan River

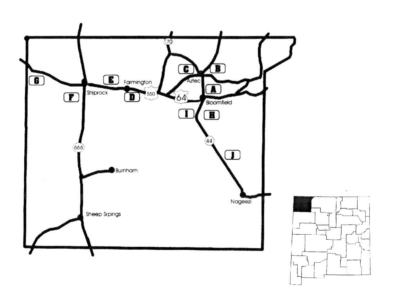

259

City of Bloomfield

Prehistoric farmers established major communities along the rivers of this region in the eleventh century. Eight hundred years later, historic settlement was also made possible by abundant water. Bloomfield was established in 1879 near a site which afforded a safe crossing of the San Juan River. The hard lives of the early settlers gradually gave way to increasing prosperity made possible by irrigation farming and horticulture.

The San Juan River runs directly through the city bringing water from the Navajo Lake Reservoir. The Lake is 25 miles upstream and was built in the 1960's to provide water for the Navajo Nation and the downstream communities.

The Navajo Lake State Park and the San Juan River area below the dam are world renowned for excellent trout fishing and is New Mexico's second largest lake. Evidence of some of the earliest known villages in the Southwest are found in the area.

Bloomfield Chamber of Commerce
224 West Broadway
Bloomfield, N.M. 87413
505-632-0880

On US Hwy 64
East of Bloomfield-MM 66

24-A

Aztec

Aztec, named for the nearby National Monument, was founded in 1876 when portions of the Jicarilla Apache Reservation were opened for non-Indian settlement. It is the seat of San Juan County, which was created in 1887 partially as a response to the desire of the residents to be free from the political forces of Rìo Arriba County. Population 5,512. Elevation 5,460 feet.

The new county of San Juan needed a county seat, and Aztec was selected to fit the bill. First settled over a thousand years ago, this valley has long been the home to farmers who tended the land. The Animas River provided the necessary water to flourish. Established as a town in the late 1800's, it was unlike the rest of the Wild West. The early Anglo settlers of Aztec had agriculture and horticulture backgrounds.

Later years brought cattle ranching to the area. This "backwards" settlement developed a unique flavor that is very different from the rest of the Southwest.

The oil and gas industry, as well as coal, uranium mines and power plants allowed Aztec to develop into a thriving community, where jobs are plentiful and life is good.

Aztec Visitor/Welcome Center
110 N. Ash
Aztec, NM 87410
505-334-9551

Historical Replaced By Rotary of San Juan
On NM Hwy 550 in Aztec

24-B

Aztec Ruins National Monument

Despite its name, this magnificent site reflects 11th century influence from nearby Chaco Canyon rather than from the later Aztecs of Mexico. The striking masonry pueblos illustrate the classic Chaco architectural style with later Mesa Verde additions. Aztec was finally abandoned by 1300.

Originally thought to be related to the Aztecs, this site was mistakenly named Aztec. The rise and fall of this culture occurred centuries before the Central American peoples. While Chaco is considered to be the center of this cultural area, both Aztec Ruins and Salmon Ruins are called outliners.

Located about halfway between Chaco and Mesa Verde, Aztec was occupied by both cultures during different times. It was occupied from 1050 to 1150 by the Chaco Canyon culture, and the Mesa Verde occupied between 1200 and 1275.

The great Kiva was reconstructed in the 1930's and is the largest fully reconstructed kiva in North America. Aztec Ruins was made a national monument in 1923, and became a world Heritage Site in 1987.

Aztec Ruins National Monument
P.O. Box 640
Aztec, NM 87410-0640
505-334-6174, ext. 30

On NM Hwy 550
West of Aztec96

24-C

Farmington

Until 1876 this area comprised part of the Jicarilla Apache Reservation. Anglo settlement quickly began at the confluence of the San Juan, Animas, and La Plata Rivers. Farmington became a ranching and farming area and, later, an important producer of oil, gas, coal, and uranium. Population 30,729. Elevation 5,395 feet.

Fertile river valleys surrounded by high desert, rolling plateaus, mesas, and mountain ranges, make Farmington a beautiful city. Three rivers flow through Farmington, the Animas, La Plata, and San Juan, accounting for two-thirds of the surface water in New Mexico, make this an oasis.

The River Trail System stretches for 2 miles along the Animas River from Berg Park on the west to Animas Park on the east. Diverse trails wind through the woods, follow the river and pass through plazas and over arching bridges. You'll find unlimited opportunities to walk, bike, ride a horse, go for a jog, and observe wildlife. Or come for a picnic, and a quiet place to watch the Animas. This peaceful riverside canopy lends the chance to enjoy the outdoors anytime. It's only minutes away from downtown Farmington, and the trails are accessible year-round.

The trail is designed to introduce you to a few of the wildlife habitats along its banks.

Farmington Chamber of Commerce
203 Main Street
Farmington, NM 87401
505-325-0279

On NM Hwy 64
West of Farmington- MM 46.2

24-D

Hogback

Steeply dipping strata define the western edge of the San Juan basin. To the west older geologic formations are exposed toward the Defiance uplift whereas basinward they are downwarped thousands of feet beneath younger rock units. Vast coal, uranium, oil and gas resouces occur in the strata buried within the basin. Elevation 5,050 feet.

There are many layers of different rocks and soils that make up the crust of the earth. As the Rocky mountains were being formed, the layers, or stratas were pushed up, and in some places, left exposed by erosion. These layers of very old earth form ridges or Hogbacks that are actually part of the plates from the Great Plains turned upwards by the formation of the Rocky Mountains.

On NM Hwy 64
West of Farmington-MM 31.6

24-E

Shiprock

This huge volcanic neck was formed in Pliocene times, over 3,000,000 years ago. It rises 1700 feet above the surrounding plain and is famed in the legends of the Navajo as "Sa-bit-tai-e" (the rock with the wings). They hold that it was the great bird that brought them from the north.

Known today most commonly by the name Shiprock, the 1700-foot eroded volcanic plume is sacred to the Navajos as Tse Bi dahi, or the Rock with Wings. This name comes from an ancient folk myth that tells how the rock was once a great bird that transported the ancestral people of the Navajos to their lands in what is now northwestern New Mexico.

The Navajo ancestors had crossed a narrow sea far to the northwest and were fleeing from a warlike tribe. Tribal shamans prayed to the great spirit for help. Suddenly the ground rose from beneath their feet to become an enormous bird.

For an entire day and night the bird flew south, finally settling at sundown where Shiprock now stands.

Geologists tell us the rock was formed 12 million years ago during the Pliocene. The legend of the rock seems more likely to be a metaphor hinting of the site's magical power to lift the human soul above the problems of daily existence into an awareness of the great spirit.

From ancient times to the more recent past, Tse Bi dahi was indeed a pilgrimage place of major importance, the destination of young men engaged in the rigors of solitary vision quests.

The rock was climbed in 1939. Since 1970, Shiprock has been off limits to climbers, accorded once again the respect due a Navajo sacred place.

On NM Hwy 666 South
MM 85.2

24-F

Beclabito Dome

Colorful red rocks of Entrada Sandstone are domed up by deep seated igneous intrusions to be exposed by erosion. The same igneous activity created the Carrizo Mountains to the west. Uranium deposits in the Morrison Formation just above the Entrada created New Mexico's first uranium boom in the East Carrizos south of here in the 1950's. Elevation 5,600 feet.

Deep arroyos, colorful mesas eroded by wind, rain, and time. This is the land of enchantment. Drawing your eye with its vividness, and pure sweet air, shaped through eons of time, and awe inspiring in its intensity, is its landscape.

Driving through New Mexico, you pass through dry deserts, emerald mountains, lush fields. Everywhere you look it's different.

This area here is no exception. As contrasting to the flat lands of Llano Estacado, these windswept towers are a vision for the imagination.

You can almost see the Coyote and Roadrunner racing across. Only this time, it won't be a cartoon.

On NM Hwy 64
At Beclabito-MM 3.4

24-G

Salmon Ruin

In the late 11th century, influence from Chaco Canyon, 45 miles south of here, began to be felt at this site and at nearby Aztec Ruins National Monument. The Chacoans abandoned this large and well-built masonry pueblo by 1150, and shortly thereafter, Mesa Verde people reoccupied it for approximately fifty years.

The Salmon family were the first to recognize the cultural importance of this site and strove to protect it for many years. In honor of their good deed, this site was named after them.

Both Salmon and Aztec Ruins were built by the Anasazi in the architectural style of Chaco Canyon. Tree ring dates from roof beams tell us that most of the Salmon Pueblo was built between 1088 and 1095 A.D., which is a very short time considering the huge dimensions of the structure.

After 40 years of occupation in the mid-1100's, the site was abandoned and then reoccupied in the late 1100s. Take a step back in time at Heritage Park, which is comprised of eight habitation units representing human occupation of the San Juan Valley through thousands of years. Sites include the ice age pond, an archaic sand dune hunting site, a basketmaker pithouse, Ute and Jicarilla Apache wickiups and teepees, Navajo forked-stick and cribbed-log hogans, and the original Salmon family homestead.

Self-guided and guided tours of the grounds are available. Salmon Ruins also sponsors guided tours of Chaco Canyon and the Dinetah area. Call (505) 632-2013 for information.

Salmon Ruin
Hwy 64
Bloomfield, NM 87413
505-632-2013

On NM Hwy 54
West of Bloomfield-MM 59.8

24-H

Chaco Culture National Historical Park

Chaco Canyon contains hundreds of sites documenting its Indian occupation from 5000 B.C. through the early 20th century. Most spectacular are a dozen large and excellently crafted masonry pueblos of the 11th and 12th centuries. After its abandonment around 1300, the canyon was settled by Navajos from the early 1700's until the 1940's.

Chaco Culture National Historical Park preserves the pinnacle of what is left of Anasazi civilization. These sites are some of the most highly regarded archaeological sites in the United States.

The Anasazi, or ancient ones, farmed and lived peacefully in the canyon from 50 to 1150 A.D.

One of the largest sites, Pueblo Bonito, has over 800 rooms, 2 large and 32 smaller kivas. There are 11 other major sites and numerous smaller ones.

The Anasazi had an advanced irrigation and road system. One of the roads leads 40 miles to the Aztec site.

There are many trails to hike to other sites, as well as ranger led tours of the central ruins.

Access to Chaco Canyon is via a 45 minute drive along a sometimes rough gravel road.

**Chaco Culture
National Historical Park
PO Box 220
Nageezi, NM 87037
Phone: 505-786-7014**

On NM Hwy 550
South to Cuba-MM 150

24-I

Blanco Trading Post

The hard work of summer is over. Fall brings summer's labor in for safety. Produce is preserved, safe and sound, for the long winter. Extras are carted off to the local trading post for things you can't make or grow at home. Winter finds time for crafting, weaving baskets, and making jewelry and blankets. These could be exchanged for sugar, salt, and other necessities.

This was the way of life for the people living far from city routes for numerous years. Money didn't mean much, when there wasn't a place to spend it. Trading was a way of life, and nothing is more satisfying than walking away with a bargain.

Often travelers in wagons would roll up to settlers' homes. They'd show new copper kettles, or a bolt of cotton, and then the haggling would begin. "I've got three new blankets to trade."

"No madam. It will take 3 blankets and a sack of corn."

Thus they would 'haggle' back and forth until both walked away either empty handed, or having accomplished the trade.

On NM Hwy 550
South of Bloomfield-MM 23.5

24-J

San Miguel County

San Miguel County was created by the territorial legislature of 1891. San Miguel derives it's name from San Miguel del Vado, once a principal crossing of the Pecos River and the area's largest community. San Miguel del Vado translates into Saint Michael of the Ford.

County Seat: Las Vegas
Communities: Montezuma, Sapello, Ledoux, Rociada, Pecos, Trujillo, San Miguel del Vado, Villanueva, Trementina

Conchas Lake

4,717 Square Miles

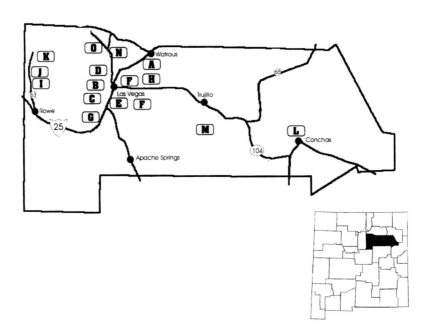

Watrous

The Mountain Branch and the Cimarron Cutoff of the Santa Fe Trail meet at Watrous. This important spot on the Trail was first known as La Junta, "junction" in Spanish. In 1879, with the coming of the railroad, it was named for Samuel B. Watrous, a prominent local rancher.

Located on the confluences of the Mora and Sapello Rivers, early travelers called Watrous, "La Junta". From Watrous to Wagon Mound, some of the finest Santa Fe Trail ruts are visible from the access road north east of the 1-25 exit 366.

Samuel B. Watrous traded with the travelers of the Santa Fe Trail, before they began the final leg of their journey that would take them to Santa Fe.

Today, Watrous is a small farming community, enjoying the peaceful life of rural New Mexico

Mora Valley Chamber of Commerce
P.O. Box 800
Route 518
Mora, NM 87732
(505) 387-6072

NM 161-I-25
MM 21.4

25-A

La Cueva National Historic District

This ranching community was established by Vicente Romero in the early 1850's. The grist mill was built in the 1870's. Its proximity to Fort Union and the Santa Fe Trail helped the ranch develop into one of the regions most important commercial centers. The mill, mercantile buildings, two-story residence and San Rafael church was designated a national historic district in 1973.

Today, Las Vegas has 900 buildings in nine historic districts on the National Registry, more than any other city in the United States. The well preserved, late 1800s architectural styles are an array of Victorian, Greek Revival, Queen Anne, Italianate, and Romanesque.

There are many self-guided walking tours of the historic districts, allowing visitors to roam and enjoy the history and culture of the city. It was on the plaza of Las Vegas that General Stephen Kearney raised the United States Flag and took possession of the territory in 1846.

Doc Holliday operated a dental office and a saloon and gambling hall in Las Vegas before moving on to Tombstone. There were some that said Las Vegas rivaled Tombstone and Dodge City for its unsavory characters prior to the turn of the century. Names like Billy the Kid, Pat Garret, Vicente Silva, Big Nose Kate, and Jesse James are just a few of the infamous people who visited Las Vegas for a time.

Pamphlets for the self-guided tours can be found at numerous businesses around the town.

Las Vegas Chamber of Commerce
P.O. Box 128
Las Vegas, NM 87701
(505) 425-8631
lvscmcc@nmhu.campus.mci.net

US 518
North to Las Vegas70
MM 23.8

25-B

Storrie Lake State Park

Long a popular spot for rainbow trout fishing, Storrie lake also features boating, swimming, and water-skiing. Facilities include camping/picnicking sites, a boat ramp, a playground, and a visitor information center.

With the arrival of the Santa Fe Railway in 1879, Las Vegas and the surrounding area became a hangout of some of the shadiest characters of the Old West, including Wyatt Earp, Doc Holliday, and Billy the Kid.

Just a few miles from Las Vegas, Storrie Lake draws avid fisherman year around. Its favorable summer breezes attract colorful wind-surfing boards and water-skiing.

There are camping/picnicking sites, and wildlife to enjoy. The gate hours are from 6 a.m. to sunset and a small visitors' center is located there.

Storrie Lake State Park
HC33 Box 109#2
Las Vegas, NM 87701
(505) 425-7278

US 518 North
MM 4.1

25-C

Camp Maximiliano Luna

The 200th Coast Artillery, Anti-Aircraft, formerly the 111th Cavalry of the New Mexico National Guard trained here before going to the Philippines in World War II. About half of the men died either on the infamous Bataan Death March of 1942, or in Japanese Prison camps afterwards.

The 200th Coast Artillery was very typical of American Guard units. It was a hodgepodge of races and colors with Mexican and Native American blood running through the men's veins. There was a certain pride in this uniquely American mixture. While overseas dictators preached the dominance of a master race, they served for the freedom of all.

They had been sent to the Philippines to provide air defense for Clark Field.

At 5:00 am on December 8, 1941, the men in the 200th CA were notified that the United States was officially at war with Japan. Six and a half hours later, Japanese bombers and fighters attacked.

The men rushed to their weapons as the first bombs fell, some of them firing live ammunition for the first time. Only one of every six of the ancient shells the Guard fired exploded, yet the 200th brought down 5 enemy fighters with their fierce anti-aircraft defense.

The next four months would bring determined rearguard fighting as American and Filipino defenders retreated onto the Bataan Peninsula. On April 9, 1942, the 200th and 515th Coast Artillery, along with the rest of the Bataan defenders, began the march of death to prison camps where they would be interned for three and one half years. Of the 1841 men of the Regiment who began the March, 819 would not survive the war.

New Mexico Highlands University
Established 1893

One of New Mexico's oldest colleges and once the state's largest university, New Mexico Highlands University is the perfect place to start out or start over.

Highlands is known for its small classes, personalized education, student achievement and excellent faculty.

There are both undergraduate and graduate programs in arts and sciences, business, education, and social work at the main campus in the heart of Las Vegas, or at any of the outreach sites.

Campus visits are encouraged and welcome. Student ambassadors are available for informal tours.

One of the buildings on the tour is the Felix Martinez Building. Built in 1983 and named for the man who sponsored legislation establishing New Mexico Normal University (Highlands) in 1893. This building houses the majority of offices relating to student services.

Contact the Office of admissions at least a week in advance of the planned visit.

New Mexico Highlands University
Office of Admissions
Las Vegas, NM 87701
(505) 545-3595
1-800-338-NMHU

In Las Vegas
on 8thStreet

25-E

Las Vegas

Las Vegas served as an important stop on the Santa Fe Trail and later as a major railroad center. Here General Kearny announced the annexation of New Mexico by the U.S. in 1846. In 1862, during the Confederate occupation of Santa Fe, Las Vegas served as a Territorial capital. New Mexico Highlands University was established here in 1893.

The fertile valley of Las Vegas, also known as "The Meadows," was occupied as early as 8000 BC by Paleo-Indians. Sedentary Pueblo Indians were present in the area during the 1100's and 1200's until forced out either by drought or the pressure of Apache Indian attack.

The community was founded in 1835, as a major center on the Santa Fe Trail. As exporters sent their wares west, enterprising Las Vegans traded east. A large influence in the growth and development of Las Vegas was Fort Union, built in 1851 to protect the trail, the fort helped to stimulate the economy.

When General Stephen W. Kearney took possession of New Mexico for the United States in 1846, he found Las Vegas to be a thriving community of 1,500 Spanish settlers. Their presence can be traced back to 15 Spanish families who petitioned the Mexican Government for a grant to establish Las Vegas in 1835. It was at the Plaza in Las Vegas that General Kearney raised the flag and claimed New Mexico as a territory for the Untited States.

Theodore Roosevelt and the Rough Riders held reunions in Las Vegas. 21 of the Rough Riders were from the area and most were at his side during the famed charge up San Juan Hill.

Las Vegas has over 900 buildings in nine historic districts on the National Registry, more than any city in the United States. The late 1800's architectural styles are an array of Victorian, Greek Revival, Queen Anne, Italianate, and Romanesque. Trail guides are available at many of the local businesses for a self-guided walking tour.

Las Vegas Chamber of Commerce
P.O. Box 128
Las Vegas, NM 87701
(505) 425-8631
1-200-832-5947
lvsmcc@nmhu.campus.mci.net

25-F

Hogbacks

Interstate 25 cuts through dipping strate that form hogback ridges between the Great Plains and the south end of the Rocky Mountains. The Santa Fe Trail, from here to Santa Fe, followed a natural valley eroded in less resistant strate between the mountains to the north and Glorieta Mesa to the south. Elevation 6,200 feet.

There are many layers of different rocks and soils that make up the crust of the earth. As the Rocky Mountains were being formed, the layers, or strates were pushed up, and in some places, left exposed by erosion. These layers of very old earth form ridges, or Hogbacks, that are actually part of the plates from the Great Plains turned upwards by the formation of the Rocky Mountains.

On I-25 US 84
Exit 339

25-G

Villanueva State Park

Couched between high sandstone bluffs in the beautiful valley of the Pecos River, this park is located near the picturesque Spanish colonial village of Villanueva. The park offers hiking trails with historical markers and camping/picnicking sites.

Located 31 miles southwest of Las Vegas, this small park offers two exceptional hiking trails: Canyon Trail takes hikers across the Pecos River and features interpretative signs of 19th century life along with a spectacular view from the top of the canyon. El Cerro Trail challenges the hiker with its steep, rocky, moderately-difficult path to the top of the canyon. The length out and back is about one mile.

The small settlement of Villanueva is situated on a bluff overlooking the Pecos River, just outside of the state park. The village was founded in 1808 and was originally called La Cuesta "the hill". The location was chosen because it was easy to defend against attacks by Plains Indians. In 1890, the villagers petitioned to rename the village Villanueva, after a family whose members still live there today.

The park has full facility camping sites, a picnic area, visitor center, fishing, and an abundance of wildflower and wildlife viewing.

Villanueva State Park
P.O. Box 40
Villanueva, NM 87583
(505) 421-2957

On 15 Rt. Off of NM 3
MM 60.3

25-H

Pecos

The upper Pecos River Valley was on the frontier of Pueblo Indian civilization from at least the 13th to the 19th centuries, when the nearby Pueblo of Pecos was abandoned. Despite raids by various Plains Indian groups, Spanish-speaking settlers around 1825 founded what is today the village of Pecos.

At 7,000 feet in elevation, the village of Pecos has cool, refreshing summers enhanced by the tangy pine-scented dry air. Winters are mild with weeks of continuous sunshine, which add to the year around appeal.

It is situated on the Pecos River, and is a mixture of old Spanish and modern west. The village has quaint adobe buildings and narrow winding streets, a charming compliment to the community.

Historic St. Anthony's Catholic Church is a landmark providing one of the areas several places to worship. Modern shops and stores complement a growing business district. New gift shops and galleries add to existing services and provide shopping for both residents and tourists.

In the Town of Pecos
on Jct 63

25-I

Glorieta Battlefield

The decisive battle of the Civil War in New Mexico was fought at the summit of Glorieta Pass on March 28, 1862. Union troops won the battle when a party of Colorado volunteers burned the Confederate supply wagons, thus destroying Southern hopes for taking over New Mexico.

During the Civil War, Confederate and Union troops battled for control of this pass situated at the southern tip of the Sangre de Cristo Mountains along the Santa Fe Trail.

In March 1862, a Confederate force of 200-300 Texans encamped at a ranch on one end of the pass. On the other end of the pass, camped 400 soldiers for the Union. On the morning of March 26, the Union soldiers moved out to attack. The Union soldiers managed to capture some Rebel advance troops and then found the main force behind them.

The Union advanced on the Confederates, but the Confederates artillery fire forced them back. The Union regrouped and split into two forces, sending one force along each side of the pass. They caught the Rebels in a cross fire and forced them to retreat about a mile and a half to a narrow section of the pass. Here the Rebels formed a defensive line and waited for the Union Troops. The Union Troops managed to regroup and forced them to retreat further and capture the rearguard.

Both Troops retired and waited for reinforcements. They arrived the next day. The following day both groups met in the pass and attacked. The long day found attack and counter attacks. When the smoke cleared, the Confederate Troops left, thinking they had won the day, but, the Union troops had destroyed all of the Confederates supplies and animals, forcing the Confederates to retire to Santa Fe.

The Union Troops won, and thereby stopped Confederate incursions into the Southwest.

On NM 223/63

25-J

Pecos National Historic Monument

In 1540–41, this pueblo stood 5 stories high and accommodated a population of 500. Four churches and an additional pueblo were build here in the 1600's and 1700's. Disease and Comanche raids in the late 1700's significantly reduced the size of the community. In 1838, the remaining 17 people moved to the Pueblo of Jemez.

The name Pecos is derived from the name given it by its Keres Indian neighbors, though the Towa-speaking inhabitants called it Cicuye. Excavations in the early 1900's and 1940 provided much information on the history of the pueblo. It has been a National Monument since 1965.

An unknown Spanish conquistador saw the pueblo in 1584. He wrote, It sits on a "high and narrow hill, enclosed on both sides by two streams and many trees... It is the greatest and best buildings of these provinces and is most thickly settled."

At midpoint in a passage through the Sangre de Cristo Mountains, the ruins of Pecos Pueblo and a Spanish mission share a small ridge. Long before Spaniards entered this country, this town commanded the trade path between Pueblo farmers of the Rio Grande and the hunting tribes of the buffalo plains.

The Pecos Indians were middlemen in this trade, transmitters and partakers of the goods and cultures of the very different people on either side of the mountains. They became economically powerful and practiced in the arts and customs of both worlds.

It was here in 1915 that Alfred Vincent Kidder began to excavate one of the extensive trash mounds. He wanted to test his theories of dating by stratigraphy. His work laid the foundation that developed the classification system to help identify the cultural development of the Southwestern people. The system, Basket and Pueblo, is still in use today.

The park preserves 10,000 years of history including the ancient pueblo of Pecos, two Spanish Colonial Missions, Santa Fe Trail Sites and the site of the Civil War Battle of Glorieta Pass.

Pecos National Historical Park
P.O. Box 418
Pecos, NM 87552
(505) 757-6032

25-K

Conchas Lake State Park

This 25-mile long reservoir offers a full spectrum of water-based activities—boating, waterskiing, fishing—along with two modern marinas. The lake has some of the best walleye and crappie fishing in the state. As a resort facility, Conchas provides recreation for all seasons, including waterfowl hunting in water. There are also camping/picnicking areas and a nine-hole golf course.

With an overall length of 25 miles, and more than 60 miles of varied shoreline, the clear, blue-green water of Conchas Lake offers boaters and anglers a unique experience. Snorklers will find the rock formations and underwater cliffs near the dam an opportunity of adventure.

There are dozens of camping sites, many with shelters, and shallow tapering flats which make great swimming areas for all ages.

Two modern marinas, rental cabins, a trailer park, and restaurant are also located within the park.

This is one of the finest of New Mexico's lakes for wind surfing, waterskiing and all other water sports.

Conchas Lake State Park
P.O. Box 976
Conchas Dam, NM 88416
(505) 868-2270

25-L

Puertocito de la Piedra Lumbre

Near this spot on November 13, 1821, a band of six Missouri traders led by William Becknell, encountered a force of more than 400 Mexican Shielders, militia, and Pueblo Indians under the command of Captain Pedro Gallego. This peaceful meeting and the subsequent arrival of Becknell in Santa Fe, marked the beginning of the Santa Fe Trail as a commercial link between the United States and Mexico.

On September 1, 1821, William Becknell left Old Franklin, Missouri headed west to trade with the Indians. He had little luck until he chanced upon Captain Pedro Gallego and the local militia. Having just declared its independence from Spain, Mexico needed the supplies Becknell carried, and needed them desperately.

Becknell and his men were led to Santa Fe. They arrived on November 16th, and quickly sold all they had brought. Becknell hurried back to Missouri with his mules laden with silver coins.

Within weeks, Becknell had organized another expedition. This time he took wagons crammed with $3,000 worth of trade goods. His profit in Santa Fe was 2,000 percent. Thus the Santa Fe Trail was born and soon the 909 mile trek was flooded with business-men, mountain-men and adventurers.

25-M

Strike Valleys

Between Sapello and Mora, State Road 3 follows a narrow strike valley eroded into soft shale between ridges of resistant sandstone called hogbacks, both the result of uplift of the Rocky Mountains. To the east stretch the Great Plains and to the west, the Sangre De Cristo Mountains rise to elevations exceeding 13,000 feet. Elevation here is 7,000 feet.

As the Rocky mountains were being forced upwards, the underlying layers, or strata tilted upwards. Wind, water and erosion carved away the softer layers, leaving ridges, known as hogbacks.

Geologically, this is the end of the Great Plains and the beginning of the Rocky Mountains.

Hermit's Peak

From 1863 to 1867, this mountain was the home of Juan Marie Agostini, an italian penitant who lived there as a hermit, carving crucifixes and religious emblems which he traded for food. Leaving this area, he moved to the Organ Mountains in southern New Mexico, where he was found murdered in 1869.

Thought to be born in 1800 to Italian nobility and to have studied for the priesthood, Agostini refused his vows. He spent a considerable amount of time walking through Europe, Mexico, South America, and Cuba. At the age of 62, he walked with the wagon train of Euginio Romero from Kansas to Las Vegas, New Mexico, roughly 600 miles.

He lived for a while in Romeroville before winding up on Cerro Tecolote, locally known as Hermit's Peak northwest of Las Vegas.

He struck up an acquaintance with the Penitentes and got along well with them. They believed in the hermit's healing powers and sanctity, and on Easter they still make rosaries of native plants to honor his memory.

In 1867 Agostini headed to Mesilla, a distance of about 250 miles, to seek advice on a legal matter. He then walked 530 miles to San Antonio, Texas, then back to a cave near Juarez, Mexico, another 500 odd miles.

In 1869, he spent time on Old Mesilla Plaza visiting with a family there and told them of his plan to live at La Cueva, the cave. The Barela family, fearing for his safety, tried to talk him out of his plan. He answered their concerns with, "I shall make a fire in front of my cave every Friday evening while I shall be alive. If the fire fails to appear, it will be because I have been killed."

On a Friday night in the spring of 1869, the Barela's fears were realized when the fire failed to appear. Antonio Garcia led a group up the mountain to find the Hermit lying face down on his crucifix with a knife in his back. His murderer was never found.

His headstone in Mesilla Cemetery bears the following Spanish inscription. "John Mary Justiniani, Hermit of the Old and New World. He died the 17th of April, 1869, at 69 years and 49 years a hermit"

US 518
MM 9

25-O

285

Sandoval County

Jemez Cliffs

Sandoval County was created in 1903 and named for the Sandoval family who lived in the area.

County Seat: Bernalillo
Communities: Corrales, Algodones, Cochiti Lake,
Los Cerillos, La Bajada, Pena Blanca,
Placitas

3,714 Square Miles

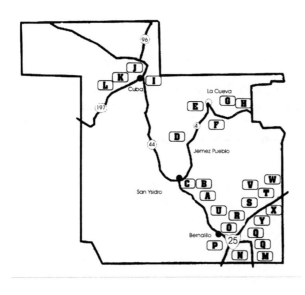

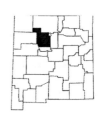

Pueblo of Zia

In 1583 Antonio de Espejo recorded this pueblo as one of five in the Province of Punamé. Following the sacking of Zía by Spanish troops in 1689, the pueblo was reestablished, but never attained its former size. The Zía ancient sun symbol is incorporated in the design of the state flag of New Mexico.

All but invisible to anyone traveling along the road northwest of Bernalillo, Zia Pueblo is situated on a rocky knoll. It blends into the landscape like a natural feature of the terrain.

The symbol of the pueblo, The Zia, means sun. The State of New Mexico interprets it in its salute, as "The Zia symbol of perfect friendship among united cultures."

Spanish records indicated that at least 5,000 Indians lived at the pueblo in 1540. During the Pueblo Revolt, many members of the Zia Pueblo were killed. Today, the pueblo has about 700 residents. Most of them work in the agricultural field, but have a strong sense of identity.

Known for their decorative pottery, unpolished redware with white slip and decorations in brown or black, the Zia crafts people are in high demand. Some Zia painters are known for their wonderful water colors.

Zia Lake on the pueblo offers excellent fishing with permits available at the Pueblo.

Zia Pueblo
135 Capitol Square Drive
Zia Pueblo, NM 87053
505-867-3304

NM Hyw 550 south of Cuba
MM 17.6

26-A

Vasquez de Coronado's Route

Francisco Vásquez de Coronado, preparing to spend his second winter in New Mexico, sent out expeditions from Tiguex, near Bernalillo, in the fall of 1541 to gather supplies. Captain Francisco de Barrionuevo went as far west as Jémez Pueblo, then visited others as far north as the Río Chama.

In July 1540, Francisco Vásquez de Coronado, leader of an army of Spaniards and Indians, entered New Mexico from Arizona to the south of here. He was searching for the mythical Seven Cities of Cibola, which proved to be the six Zuñi villages then located near the present pueblo. Vásquez de Coronado was nearly killed during his attack on Hawikuh.

Francisco Vasquez de Coronado was born into a noble family in Salamanca, Spain in 1510. At the age of 25, he came to the Americas as an assistant to New Spain's first viceroy.

An ambitious man, he married the daughter of the colonial treasurer, put down a major slave rebellion, and became the governor of a Mexican province within three years of his arrival. But he wanted more. Rumors of earlier explorations by Cabeza de Vaca for 7 cites of gold, inspired him to lead a royal expedition to explore the north into what is now the American West.

The expedition explored, bringing Catholic ideals to the pueblos they encountered, and the Spanish influence that is still very present today.

When they did not find the "Seven Cities of Cibola", parties were sent out, some traveling all the way to the border between Arizona and California where they explored the Grande Canyon. Coronado himself led a party into what is now Kansas.

Returning to Mexico without locating a single golden city, the Viceroy branded Coronado's expedition an abject failure. His career quickly declined and in 1544 he was removed from office as a governor and moved to Mexico City where he worked in a modest position for the City. He died in 1554, though his legacy is seen throughout the west.

Sandoval County
South of San Ysidro Hwy 550
MM 20

26-B

Fenton Lake State Park

Surrounded by imposing mountains and beautiful ponderosa pine woodlands, Fenton Lake has long been a popular fishing and camping retreat. This area offers both lake and stream fishing for rainbow trout, and many deer, turkey, and elk inhabit the immediate vicinity. The park area is also used for winter sports such as cross-country skiing and dogsled racing.

With summer highs not quite reaching 80 degrees, this is the perfect place to escape summer's heat. Beautiful ponderosa pines surround the 35 acre lake within the 700 acre park.

Before becoming a state park, Fenton Lake was purchased by the State Game and Fish as a resting and nesting area for migratory waterfowl. Today waterfowl, turkey, deer, muskrat, elk, and bobcat can still be observed.

"The Man Who Fell to Earth," a popular film, was shot at Fenton Lake in the mid-1970's. It tells the story of an extra-terrestrial character who came to earth when the water on his native planet dried up.

Fenton Lake State Park features a cross-country ski and biathalon trail. Only canoes, rafts, or rowboats are allowed on the lake.

Fenton Lake State Park
455 Fenton Lake
Jemez Springs, NM 87025
505-829-3630

NM Hwy 4 North of San Ysidro
MM 23.5

26-C

Pueblo of Jemez

Jémez is the sole surviving pueblo of the seven in the "provincia de los Hemes" noted by Spaniards in 1541, and the last at which the Towa language is still spoken. In 1838 the remaining inhabitants of Pecos Pueblo moved here. The mission of San Diego de Jémez was last rebuilt in the 1880's.

The Pueblo of Jemez has a closed village policy. Out of respect for the privacy of those who live at the Pueblo, please respect their wishes.

However, the Walatowa Visitor Center is open seven days a week and provides information, exhibits, and a nature walk exploring the cultural heritage of the Pueblo of Jemez.

The center also offers visitor information and brochures about the natural and scenic attractions located along the Jemez Mountain Trail Scenic By Way. The museum shop features a wide selection of arts and crafts by Jemez artisans.

Walatowa Visitor Center
040 Trading Post Road
Jemez Pueblo, NM 87024
505-834-7235

NM Hwy 4 at Jemez Pueblo
MM 5

26-D

Jemez State Monument

The village of Giusewa was occupied by ancestors of the Jémez Indians before the arrival of the Spanish in 1541. Its ruins lie close to those of the great mission church of San José de Los Jemez, which was built by the Franciscans around 1622.

The ruins of Giusewa, an ancient Towa settlement near present-day Jémez Pueblo, are in a beautiful setting shared with San Jose de los Jémez, a 17th-century Spanish mission church. It is located 43 miles north of Bernalillo and Coronado State Monument.

The Jemez State Monument Visitors Center is open April 1-September 15 annually.

Giusewa means, "place of the boiling waters." The old name comes from the naturally hot water which boils to the surface in natural hot springs. These springs are heated by lava that is near the surface, and the spring bubbles even in winter. The lava is a legacy from the volcanic past.

New Mexico State Monuments
113 Lincoln Avenue
Santa Fe, NM 87501
(505) 476-5085,
fax (505) 476-5088

NM Hwy 4 West of Los Alamos
MM 18.5

26-E

Soda Dam

This spectacular formation has built up over the centuries by deposits of calcium carbonate from a spring that bubbles to the surface at this point. The river flows under a dome that is still building. The dam is 300 feet long, 50 feet high, and 50 feet wide at the bottom.

The coppery colored natural spring and dam blocks the Jemez canyon and the Jemez River. The spring bubbles with sulfur laced water even in winter. Hot rocks fairly near the surface heat the ground water, a legacy from the area's volcanic past.

Adventurous hikers can face the challenge of Battleship Rock in the Jemez Mountains. The rock, named for its similarity to the prow of a ship, is peppered with bits of glassy smooth obsidian, a black rock created from volcanic eruptions in the area over 5 million years ago. The sheer cliff rises suddenly above the river and towers over a beautiful picnic area.

NM Hwy 4 East of Los Alamos
MM 19.1

26-F

Valle Grande

About one million years ago, the magnificent valley before you was formed by collapse, after a series of tremendous volcanic eruptions ejected a volume of material more than 500 times greater than the May 1980 eruptions of Mt. St. Helens. This event climaxed more than 13 million years of volcanism in the Jémez Mountains. Minor volumes of magma, leaking to the surface as recently as 50,000 years ago, formed the dome-like hills between you and the skyline to the north, which is the opposite wall of the enormous Valles Caldera. The heat from young volcanism makes this area attractive for geothermal energy.

Often called "the world's largest crater," Valle Grande is actually a giant caldera, formed a million years ago when a series of volcanoes collapsed, and whole mountains were engulfed forming the great valley below this highway.

A caldera was literally Spanish for cauldron, meaning a huge vessel full of boiling water. That would describe what the Spanish saw with the boiling hot springs, and the collapsed volcano which left behind this intriguing valley full of geological wonders.

One of those wonders are the Tent Rocks. Volcanos send forth tons of melted rock in the form of ash. The ash covered much of the area. It was over a hundred feet deep in some areas. The ash was light. When an explosion occurred showering heavy rocks upon the lighter ash, the rocks compacted the ash. The wind, rain and erosion washed away the lighter ash leaving amazing formations behind.

Today, though not readily apparent, this area still is effected by heated rocks just below the earth's crust. The steaming ground water laced with natural minerals is sought by many for its curing powers.

On NM Hwy 4 West of Pojoaque
MM 42.8 (Missing)
On NM 501 South of Los Alamos

26-G

Colorado Plateau

From this point, the Colorado Plateau extends across northwestern New Mexico into northeastern Arizona, southeastern Utah, and southwestern Colorado. A colorful landscape of mesas and canyons, it is underlain by natural mineral, oil, and gas resources locked within sedimentary strata deposited millions of years ago. Elevation 6,400 feet.

More than 100 million years ago, dinosaurs walked across a vast flood plain in what is now the Colorado Plateau. The dinosaurs would leave tracks in the wet mud. Thousands of centuries later, wind and water exposed the tracks, leaving glimpses of the ancient life.

Petrified wood, fossils, both invertebrate and vertebrate, and plant life abound in this wide area.

Later, the arrival of ancient man also left tantalizing glimpses into the past, as they lived and traveled across the wide expanse. Now, generations later, visitors discover and appreciate as they explore and learn of just how far we've come, and just how much is still left to be done.

There is much to learn from the remnant of history. Collecting some specimens of fossils is illegal or limited. Check with local laws to find out what is safe to remove, as the location of the find is as important as the find itself.

NM Hwy 44 South of Cuba
MM 25

26-H

Cuba

In 1769, Spanish Governor Pedro Fermin de Mendinueta made the San Joaquin del Nacimiento land grant to 35 pioneering families who had settled the headwaters of the Rio Puerco in 1766. The community was later abandoned, owing to raids by frontier Indian tribes, but was resettled in the late 1870's. Originally known as Nacimiento or La Laguna, it was renamed Cuba when the post office was established in 1887.

Originally named "La Laguna" because it was full of water, settlers drained the area. Cuba, meaning large tank, or vat, is a hub city which supports many surrounding communities. It is the gateway between Albuquerque and the Four Corners area. Its post office was established in 1887 during the Spanish American War.

Locally, the population of Cuba is a little less than 1,000, but if you add in the communities within a 30 mile radius, the population jumps to over 7,000.

The small town has several grocery and convenience stores, repair shops, motels, and restaurants. It is also the gateway to the famous Chaco Culture National Historic Park and the San Pedro Parks Wilderness Area.

Cuba Chamber of Commerce
P.O. Box 1000
Cuba, NM 87013
Phone: (505) 289-3514

On NM 550 South Outside of Cuba
MM 65.3

26-I

San Juan Basin

Thousands of feet of sedimentary strata have been down warped into the San Juan basin of northwestern New Mexico, a total area of some 20,000 square miles. The San Pedro and Nacimiento Ranges of the Southern Rockies rise in fault contact above the basin to elevations of more than 10,000 feet.

Gallup is built along the Rio Puerco on the rocks of the Crevasse Canyon Formation, strata that were laid down in Upper Cretaceous times. Underlying the town is one of three anticlines in the Gallup Sag. The Sag, a slight depression, or bay, extending from the San Juan Basin, held swamps and lagoons during periods when inland seas invaded the Basin. The vegetation that grew in these wet areas was buried by sediment to become coal. The Gallup Sag lies between the Zuni and Defiance Uplifts.

The Nutria Hogback, a rather startling group of upturned rocks at the east end of Gallup, is the western edge of the Zuni Uplift. The Uplift formed during the Laramide Orogeny in the late Cretaceous and early Tertiary time in the same place where an antecedent uplift had been. The earlier uplift may have been in place as early as the Precambrian. The older mountains were worn down and sedimentary rocks formed over them until the basement faults were reactivated, doming up the region.

In the Zuni Mountains, erosion has exposed Precambrian granite in the core of the dome. The red cliffs to the north of Interstate 40 are a part of the uplift, although as you drive by you see only the flat lying strata. When you drive north across them it is easy to see how the beds slope away from the mountains, dipping toward the San Juan Basin. The Zuni Mountains are included in the Cibola National Forest.

NM 550 North of Cuba
MM 71

26-J

Jicarilla Apache Reservation

The Jicarilla Apaches, primarily a hunting and gathering group, once occupied vast portions of northeastern New Mexico and southern Colorado. Pressure from Comanche Indians and European settlers eventually pushed them from their homeland. In 1887, the Jicarillas were given a permanent reservation in north-central New Mexico, near Dulce.

Anthropologists say that the Jicarilla (little basketmakers) came from Canada down the eastern flanks of the Rocky Mountains about 1300-1500 AD. All tribes deny the migration theories saying they are the First People, and have always been here.

Very successful as raiders, they were not recognized as being distinctive from other Apache tribes until about 1700.

Today, there is no question of their modern identity. Money from the wool of their thousands of sheep has been supplemented handsomely by the income from their gas and oil rich lands, and more recently, from the lucrative casino. They have been able to adapt to the cultural and environmental changes over the past 200 years while still maintaining their own cultural distinctiveness.

The capital of the Jicarilla Apache Reservation is in Dulce, NM. The Jicarilla are hospitable people and their visitor's center has a museum with exhibits of beadwork and basketry.

Jicarilla Apache Tribe
P.O. Box 507
Dulce, NM 87528
(505) 759-3242

NM 550 North of Cuba
MM 78 (Marker Missing)

26-K

Continental Divide

Rainfall divides at this point. To the west it drains into the Pacific Ocean, to the east, into the Atlantic. Elevation 7,379 feet.

Every continent has a continental divide. This is the point that determines which direction the rainfall and water shed will run.

The continental divide in the United States primarily follows the Rocky Mountain chain. This divide determines whether the water shed runs into the Atlantic or the Pacific Oceans.

This Divide begins in Alaska and runs through Mexico and into Central Mexico.

NM 550 South of Bloomfield
MM 90 (Marker Missing)

26-L

Alameda

This 18th century Spanish settlement was established on the site of an ancient Tiwa Indian Pueblo that was destroyed following the Pueblo Revolt of 1680. The pueblo was reestablished in 1702, but in 1708 the Spanish moved its Tiwa inhabitants to help resettle the Pueblo of Isleta. Here the Camino Real passed by cottonwood groves from which the community derived its name.

In 1710, the King of Spain issued the Alameda land grant which included the small town of Corrales. After the Pueblo Revolt and the re-establishment of Alameda in the early 1700's, this small town was built up around the ruins of an ancient Pueblo. As the city of Albuquerque slowly encroached upon it, the area became more and more modern. It is hard to tell where one ends and the other begins.

With the amenities of being so close to the major metropolis, the town of Alameda has grown and prospered and is today a modern, close knit community within the city.

I-25 in Alameda on NM 313
MM 0

26-M

Pueblo of Sandia Nafiat

This southern Tiwa Pueblo was established about 1300 A.D. The Pueblo and its Spanish Missions church complex were important sites along the Camino Real by 1614. Sandia was destroyed during the Pueblo revolt of 1680, and its Indian inhabitants sought refuge among the Hopi village in Arizona. The ancient pueblo site was re-occupied by descendants of the refugees in 1748.

Sandia Pueblo is perhaps the least known and understood of the dozens of pueblo cultures that once dominated the Rio Grande Valley. This is a bustling and thriving community dating centuries before Europeans entered the area.

Located 15 miles north of modern-day Albuquerque, it has been in existence at its present site since 1300. The first Spanish to "discover" it was Francisco Vasquez de Coronado who camped here with his Conquistadors in 1539.

Sandia was one of the Pueblos to participate in the bloody Pueblo Revolt that exploded throughout the area. The revolt culminated in decades of resentment or religious persecution, demands for tribute payment, involuntary labor, and conflicts between religious and civil authorities who demanded obedience from Pueblo Indians.

For many years after the Spanish re-conquered the area, the pueblo was repeatedly attacked and the Pueblo was forced to evacuate, until eventually they fled to Hopi lands in Arizona.

It was in 1748 that Spain's governor allowed them to resettle Sandia and it was completely rebuilt.

Sandia Pueblo
P.O. Box 6008
Bernalillo, NM
(505) 867-3317

I-25 North of Albuquerque
Junction 363 MM 3.5

26-N

Bernalillo

Archaeological research indicates that this fertile valley has been the focus of human occupation for at least 10,000 years. Soon after the Spanish colonized New Mexico in 1598, a series of estancias, or farming and ranching communities, flanked the Camino Real along this section of the Rio Grande. These settlements formed the basis of present-day Bernalillo, which was well established by the close of the 17th century.

From the Sandia Man to the Folsom Man, this area has been the center for occupation for many centuries. The fertile river valley brought herds of game for the ancient man to hunt, and provided many varieties of plant life to balance out their needs. The Rio Grande has provided the necessary water to make life possible in this hostile environment.

As the Pueblos grew from the wandering hunters and gathers of the past to farmers, this valley was chosen to plant their crops. They still gathered and hunted from the wilds, but now corn, beans, and squash became their mainstays.

The arrival of the Spanish would temporarily disturb the peace of the area as the Spanish set out to control the area and the Native Americans sought to hang on to their past. The Pueblos united and revolted in 1680 and drove the Spanish out. It was a temporary reprieve. In 1692, the Spanish returned in greater strengths, re-conquering the area and setting up farms and ranches as travel and trade grew.

The arrival of the white man did little to change Bernalillo for many years. It remained a small town that governed the local area.

Bernalillo Exit on 550 W
Then off 313 S MM 6.6

26-O

Pueblo of Sandia

Sandia is one of the pueblos of the Tiguex province visited by the Vasquez de Coronado expedition in 1540. Abandoned during the Pueblo Revolt of 1680, when many Tiwas fled to Hopi country, it was resettled by Tiwa-speaking refugees and a few Hopis in 1748. Its church, built in 1864, was renovated in 1976.

Sandia Pueblo is perhaps the least known and understood of the dozens of pueblo cultures that once dominated the Rio Grande Valley. This is a bustling and thriving community dating centuries before Europeans entered the area.

Located 15 miles north of modern-day Albuquerque, it has been in existence at its present site since 1300. The first Spanish to "discover" it was Francisco Vasquez de Coronado who camped here with his Conquistadors in 1539.

Sandia was one of the Pueblos to participate in the bloody Pueblo Revolt that exploded throughout the area. The revolt culminated decades of resentment or religious persecution, demands for tribute payment, involuntary labor, and conflicts between religious and civil authorities who demanded obedience from Pueblo Indians.

For many years after the Spanish re-conquered the area, the pueblo was repeatedly attacked and the Pueblo was forced to evacuate, until eventually they fled to Hopi lands in Arizona.

It was in 1748 that Spain's governor allowed them to resettle Sandia and it was completely rebuilt.

South of Bernalillo on Jct 313
MM 3.5

26-P

Las Placitas

The Sandia Mountains have been occupied by human beings for thousands of years. This area was settled by 1767, when Governor Pedro Fermin de Mendinueta made the land grant known as La Merced de San Antonio de las Huertas. The area is called "las placitas" because it contains several villages, also known as "plazas." Descendants of the stockmen and farmers who first settled the grant still live in the vicinity.

Camping, hiking and open-air concerts are popular in the rolling hills of the Placitas area. Mountain biking is great along Tunnel Springs Road in Las Huertas Canyon and on a 10k loop along Forest Road 445 between mile markers 2 and 3 on the south side of #165. Back country hiking is popular along several trails leading into the Sandia Ranger District of the Cibola National Forest and up Las Huertas Creek which is free-flowing all year long.

Visit Sandia Cave, a site of prehistoric inhabitation which now has camping and picnic areas. Here is proof that the Rio Grande Valley was inhabited as much as 10,000 years ago.

During "apple time," Placitas' organic orchards sell fresh apples and cider at roadside stands..

The Placitas Artists Series, running September through May, offers open air concerts.

Exit Bernalillo on SR 165-E
MM 3.5
Exit Bernalillo on SR 165-E
MM 3.6

26-Q

La Angostura

Near here the Rio Grande Valley closes into a narrow pass (angostura). Control of this pass was critical to the safety of the trade along the Camino Real, so this area has been the focus of fortifications since the early 17th century. The 18th century settlement of Algodones developed as a result of continuing Spanish efforts to control the pass and nearby fords of the Rio Grande.

One of the few natural passes of the Camino Real, Algodones was founded as a military garrison to provide protection for the merchant wagon trains traveling between Santa Fe and Chihuahua, Mexico. As late as the 19th century, it was the site of a military supply depot.

General Kearney and the Army of the West occupied it in 1846.

It was also the home to a stage coach stop and a train station. Today, the sound of the passing train establishes a unique and special link to the 19th century.

North of Bernalillo
on Rt 66   NM Hwy 313   MM 12.2

26-R

Pueblo of San Felipe

San Felipe, named for St. Philip the Apostle by Spanish explorer Francisco Sanchez Chamuscado in 1581, was abandoned during the Pueblo Revolt of 1680. Reestablished on the mesa top, this too was abandoned before 1706, when the pueblo was constructed on its present site. The mission church appears today much as it did in the 18th century.

San Felipe is one of the most culturally conservative of all the Keresan speaking people. They stubbornly retain their traditional religion and customs despite relentless pressures from the outside world. Community values and responsibilities are always subordinate to individual interests so that strong ceremonial structure and the traditional rituals have kept the San Felipe people a vital and distinctive entity with a proud heritage of ancient origin.

Although the Pueblo is less than thirty miles from Albuquerque, outsiders are not encouraged to visit except for certain times of the year. This has helped the people to resist the influence of modern life and to maintain their individuality.

Farming has been a principal occupation of the men of San Felipe as well as employment in various trades in Albuquerque. The revival of interest in native crafts and intricate bead work is once again available in local shops. Heishe of exceptional quality is again being produced by a few artisans at San Felipe.

San Felipe Pueblo
San Felipe, NM 87001
(505) 867-3381

Exit 252
West to Pueblo of San Felipe
MM 2.1

26-S

Pueblo of Santo Domingo Kiua

The Keresan people of Santo Domingo have occupied this area of the Rio Grande Valley since prehistoric times despite several floods that have forced relocation and reconstruction of the original pueblo. Strategically located along the roads that have led to La Bajada, this pueblo and its people have played an important role in the history of the Camino Real.

Santo Domingo Pueblo, New Mexico, lies about 35 miles South of Santa Fe. It is the home of a number of distinguished crafts traditions which have withstood centuries of European influence. Today, the traditional jewelry crafts of these Keres-speaking people remain the closest in form to pre-Columbus jewelry-making in the Southwest.

Using stone such as turquoise or jet, and shell, the families of the Pueblo shape and cut fine strands of beads, tab earrings(from thin slabs of stone or shell) and mosaic inlay jewelry strictly by hand. Some of these strands can contain individual shell, or coral beads worked as small as 1/32" in diameter cross-section.

Originally the colors and form of the jewelry was limited by the materials available locally or through their early trade contacts with neighboring cultures to the South in Mexico and Central America. Today, these art forms have blossomed through the addition of some modern tools, adhesives and access to many new sources of raw materials.

"Heishi" (he-she), a Keres word for shell, today often stands generically for this wonderful, traditional Southwestern Jewelry style. Although not all heishi available for sale in New Mexico is authentic, Santo Domingo Pueblo is proud of their handmade heishi. Imported heishi can be purchased in bulk from jewelers' supplies. Kiva is proud to offer only authentic, handmade Heishi, mosaic and tab jewelry from the artists of Santo Domingo Pueblo.

Santo Domingo Pueblo
P.O. Box 99
Santo Domingo Pueblo NM 87052
(505) 465-2214

Exit 259 on SR 22 West
North of Santo Domingo MM 4.4

26-T

Pueblo of Santo Domingo

Gaspar Castano de Sosa camped here in 1591, and in the 17th century, Santo Domingo served as headquarters of the Franciscan Order in New Mexico. It has had several different churches. The present one was built around 1890 by Father Noel Dumarest, and retains the traditional ecclesiastical architecture of this region.

One of New Mexico's largest Indian villages with a population of more than 2,000, Santo Domingo people adhere closely to their traditions and are well known for their jewelry. Visitors are welcome at the Indian Arts and Crafts Center, a small museum on the pueblo.

While adhering strictly to tribal authority, much of the pueblo productivity is devoted to the making of their famous jewelry. The pottery of Santo Domingo is strictly traditional, reproducing with care the ancient forms and decorations.

Like so many other Indian festivals, the Santo Domingo dances attract many visitors. Among others, the Corn Dance of the patron Saint's day is very popular, as well as the Sandaro, which is a burlesque with lots of clowning.

Off I-25
In Pueblo of Santo Domingo

26-U

Pueblo of Cochiti

Cochiti was established in the 1200's by Keresan-speaking Indians who came here from villages located at the present-day site of Bandelier National Monument. European contact was slight until Onate's colonization in 1598. In the 1960's, the mission church of San Buenaventura de Cochiti was restored to its nineteenth-century appearance.

Most of New Mexico's Pueblo Indians reside on reservations representing only a fraction of the lands that were theirs before the coming of the Europeans. These American Indians, who had peacefully occupied the river valleys for many centuries, were called Pueblos by the Spanish because they lived in closely clustered communities like the pueblos or villages of Spain.

Today's Pueblos cultivate their own industry and economy, and most still celebrate their unique and fascinating culture. An Indian pueblo is a complete entity with its own social organization, its own officers, and independence from all other pueblos. For that reason, the Pueblo Indians should not be called a tribe; a tribe is a political unity acknowledging a common authority.

The Pueblo Indians are world renowned for their weaving, jewelry and pottery. Arts and crafts are available at all of New Mexico's Indian pueblos, with the best from all 19 pueblos represented at the Indian Pueblo Cultural Center in Albuquerque.

Cochiti Pueblo is especially well known for their beautiful drums. There is also nearby Cochiti Lake for camping and recreation.

It is vital to remember a few points about visiting pueblos. If it is not possible to check in at the tribal office in advance, at least call the pueblo governor's office or the tourist center prior to visiting. Observe all posted requests or regulations, including photography or recording of any kind at some of the pueblos. Remember you are on Indian land and subject to Indian laws. When attending dances, remain silent and do not applaud afterwards. Dances are religious ceremonies, so be respectful.

Cochiti Pueblo
P.O. Box 70
Cochiti, NM 87072
(505) 465-2244

Exit 267 West on NM Hwy 16
to MM 22 S

26-V

La Bajada

This black volcanic escarpment is one of New Mexico's most important landmarks. The descent (bajada) of this escarpment marked the traditional division between New Mexico's upper (Rio Arriba) and lower (Rio Abajo) districts. Over the centuries, several trails and roads were developed to overcome this most difficult of the obstacles along the Camino Real.

La Bajada or "The descent" marks the division between the Rio Arriba or "upper river," and the Rio Abajo or "lower river," Section of New Mexico. This steep and dangerous grade was long an obstacle to caravan traffic going from the Rio Grande Valley to Santa Fe.

After long days on the trail, following the Rio Grande and the Camino Real, to the promised land of Santa Fe, they finally reached the landmark that was the beginning of the end of their journey.

And what a landmark it was! The towering escarpment had to be traversed before the newcomers could reach the end of the road. Many trails and roads have been developed through the years to make it past this difficult stretch of the Camino Real. Today, it is cruised past as if it was just a little hill, but think back to the days of oxen and horses, exhausted from weeks of travel, only to find this hill.

La Bajada, though it means descent, it was the climb back up to the top that weakened many hardy souls.

Exit 259 on US 22 West
to US 16 West MM 4.5
East 259 on US 22 West
to US 16 West MM 4.5

26-W

Pueblo Revolt Tricentennial

On August 10, 1680 the Pueblo Indians rose in revolt against Spanish rule. Forced to evacuate Santa Fe by the Tanos, Tewas and Tiwas, Governor Otermin led the retreating colonists south through the lands of the Keres pueblos, whose signal fires could be seen on the mesas, passing through the Pueblo of Santo Domingo on August 24.

Popé was a religious leader from San Juan Pueblo in present-day New Mexico. He organized and led the most successful Indian uprising in the history of the American West.

Provoked by a Spanish crackdown on native religion in 1675, Popé soon began conferring with other disaffected Pueblo leaders, some with Apache ties. They discussed the possibility of a large scale revolt against the Spanish.

Popé offered a millenarian vision to the Pueblos, stressing the complete expulsion of the Spanish military and religious authority and a return of Pueblo deities. Popé launched his revolt early in August 1680. He achieved stunning success due to the Pueblos vastly superior numbers. There were more than 8,000 warriors against fewer than 200 armed colonists. Despite language differences and distance, the Pueblos attacked everywhere at once, killing 21 Franciscan friars and more than 400 Spanish colonists.

When Diego de Vargas re-conquered New Mexico for Spain, it did not mean a return to the days before the uprising. Popé's revolt had permanently weakened the political power of the Franciscans. It was after his death that an alliance was made between the Pueblos and the Spanish. Though he would have disagreed with the alliance, he created the conditions for a new culture to emerge in the American Southwest, a blend of Indian and European influences which retains its distinctive character even today.

I-25 North of San Felipe

26-X

Kearney's Route

In 1846, U.S. forces under Brigadier General Stephen Watts Kearny invaded New Mexico and, on August 18, raised the U.S. flag in Santa Fe. Afterwards, he marched unopposed into Bernalillo and Albuquerque. As a result of this occupation, New Mexico passed from the jurisdiction of Mexico to that of the United States.

Born in 1794, Stephen Kearny lived in the wild and uncharted West during most of his remarkable 36 years of service. A soldier, explorer, builder, writer, and states man, Kearny commanded the Army of the West and is called "The Father of the U.S. Calvary."

By 1830, he had married Mary Radford, the step-daughter of General Clark (of Lewis and Clark fame) and had moved to Fort Leavenworth where he was charged with protecting the freight and travelers on the Santa Fe, Mormon and Oregon Trails.

When the Mexican War broke out, President Polk asked Kearny to muster an army and secure the Southwest in order to claim that region for the United States. Along the way, he was to organize territorial governments. Kearny was able to take the important northern commercial center of Santa Fe without firing a shot. He won over the local leaders and established a civilian government before he continued his march into Arizona and California.

On I-25
South of Santo Domingo

26-Y

Santa Fe County

Santa Fe County was created in 1852 and was named for a city in Spain built by King Ferdinand and Queen Isabella. Santa Fe is also the Capital of New Mexico, the oldest capital in the United States.

County Seat: Santa Fe
Communities: Tesuque, Galisteo, Stanley, Madrid, Edgewood, Glorieta

Roses of Santa Fe

3,714 Square Miles

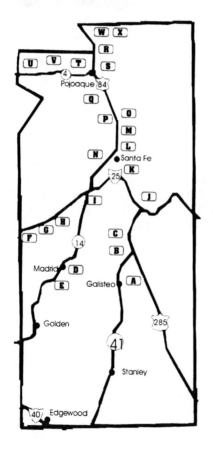

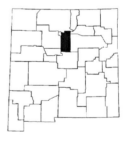

Galisteo Pueblo

Spanish explorers found several Tano-speaking pueblos in the Galisteo Basin in 1540. They were among the leaders of the Pueblo Revolt of 1680. 150 Tano families were eventually resettled in Galisteo Pueblo in 1706. Droughts, famine, Comanche raids, and disease led to its abandonment by 1788, with most of the survivors moving to Santo Domingo.

The Galisteo Valley contains the ruins of nine pueblos. There are two on the north side, and seven on the south. Five of these were occupied when discovered by the Spaniards. The best known, Galisteo, was located about one half mile above the present village. Originally called San Lucas by Castaño de Sosa in 1591, it was renamed Santa Ana by Oñate in 1598.

During the Pueblo Rebellion in 1680, an account was written that states, "There died also at the hands of the said enemies in Galisteo, Joseph Nieto, two sons of Maestre de Campo Leiva, Francisco de Anaya, the younger, who was with the escort, and the wives of Maestre de Campo Leiva and Joseph Nieto, with all their daughters and families."

After the Rebellion, the local pueblo people moved to Santa Fe until De Vargas drove them out in 1692. In 1706, Governor Cuervo y Valdez re-established the pueblo, but small pox and Comanche raids reduced the Tano Indians so greatly that in 1794, the few survivors moved to Santo Domingo.

Santa Cruz de Galisteo was one of the ten churches in the Province of New Mexico in 1617. Coronado came through here in 1541 on his way to Pecos. Espejo also visited in 1583.

On NM Hwy North
Of Moriarty- MM 56.4

27-A

Galisteo Basin

The extensive lowland south of here is called the Galisteo basin, a sag in the earth's crust where rock layers are depressed and thickened. It is one of the northernmost basins of the Basin and Range province in New Mexico and is bordered by the Rocky Mountains immediately to the north. Elevation 6,400 feet.

The Basin and Range province is an arid physiographic area occupying much of the western and southwestern part of the United States. The area has a varied and remarkable topography consisting largely of numerous small, roughly parallel mountain ranges separated by nearly flat desert plains, or basins. The basins are generally 4,000-5,000 feet above sea level, and the mountain ranges rise 3,000-5,000 feet above the level of the basins.

East of the Sonoran Desert and extending southward from the Colorado Plateau is the Mexican Highland section, which has many of the characteristics of the Great Basin and which covers parts of New Mexico, Arizona, and northern Mexico. To the east of this, the narrow, varied Sacramento section, in New Mexico and western Texas, is a plateau with blocks of eastward-dipping mountains.

The Basin and Range is a semi desert area with an extremely complex geologic history. Its 100 or so mountain ranges are the remains of crustal rocks that were upraised or uplifted by faulting along north-south lines, after which the resulting blocks were tumbled, eroded, and partly buried by debris that had accumulated in the desert basins at their feet. Most of the basins have no outlets for their drainage, and thus rainwater accumulates in the form of salt lakes, such as Walker and Pyramid lakes in Nevada and the Great Salt Lake of Utah, or in playas, which are mud flats occasionally covered by a few inches of rapidly evaporating water.

Marker Missing
North on NM Hwy 285
30.5 Meters from Lamy Exit

27-B

Southern Rockies

These foothills and higher glaciated peaks to the north are the southern tip of the Rocky Mountains. This particular segment is known as the Sangre de Cristo ("blood of Christ"), a formidable barrier that rises above 13,000 feet in a chain of peaks that trend from Santa Fe on the south side of Salida, Colorado on the north.

More than a half billion years ago in the Precambrian era, the core of the Rocky Mountains was formed in ancient ranges and later leveled by erosion. At the close of the Mesozoic era, during the Cretaceous Period more than 75 million years ago, the growth of the Rockies began. Perhaps the best way to describe what happened is to place your hands on a table cloth a few inches apart. Now slide your hands together. The wrinkles formed between your hands would represent the Rocky Mountains.

Through the years streams and rivers cut canyons and deep gorges through the ranges. During the Ice Age, snows accumulated on the mountains. Glaciers formed and moved down the valleys, further eroding the mountains. The sculpting of the Rockies by rain, wind, and ice continues today.

Rugged and massive, the Rocky Mountains form a nearly continuous mountain chain in the western part of the North America Continent. Along the crest of the Rockies is the Continental Divide, which separates streams that drain to the east from those that flow to the west.

An outdoor enthusiasts paradise, the Rockies have majestic views, challenging cliffs for climbers, and wildlife galore. Winter brings challenging winter sports at many of the local ski areas developed throughout the mountains.

Marker Missing
North on NM 28530.5 Meters from Lamy Exit

27-C

Garden of the Gods

Vertical beds of colorful sandstone and mudstone of the Galisteo Formation were deposited in streams 70 million years ago. Deposited as horizontal sheets, they have been tilted to their present vertical position by mountain building forces beneath the earth's surface. Elevation 6,000 feet.

The Garden of the Gods owes its beauty to the Earth's ever changing crust. Rivers deposited sand and mud here long ago. As the times changed, the sand and mud were baked into hard stones, then the tilt of the ever growing Mountains caused them to be lifted and transformed into the beautiful Garden of the Gods.

They have been further carved by wind, rain and erosion making them the colorful, soul stirring site that stands before you today.

Marker Missing
North of Santa Fe on Hwy 42
then West on NM 14- MM 33.5

27-D

Cerrillos

Before the arrival of the Spanish, the mineral-rich area around Cerrillos produced turquoise which was traded as far as the Valley of Mexico. An early settlement of Los Cerrillos harbored Spanish refugees from the 1680 Revolt, but the present community was not founded until the lead strike of 1879. Elevation 5,688 feet.

Though it is not known where Cerrillos had its official beginnings, it is known that this site has been mined as far back as 500 A.D. At that time the Basket Maker Indians inhabited the region and were in their prime. These ancient people used the gold and silver they mined and traded it for things they could not easily produce themselves.

It was nearly 1400 years later, yet before the California Gold Rush, that American prospectors rediscovered the ancient diggings at Cerrillos. Located on the Turquoise Trail, Cerrillos was soon brimming with hundreds of prospectors searching for gold and turquoise.

In 1899, it was reported New Mexico's production of turquoise was valued at $1,600,000, most of it coming from Cerrillos.

It was shortly thereafter that the town began to die off. The production of gold and turquoise slackened.

Today, Cerrillos is a small town that evokes the Old West feeling. It has been the setting for several major motion pictures and also offers a petting zoo, the Turquoise Museum, and Mountain Bike Adventures.

North on NM Hwy 14
MM 32.

27-E

Gold and Turquoise

The prominent hills to the east and to the left are the Cerrillos Hills, site of ancient turquoise mines worked by the Indians centuries before the arrival of the Spanish. The Cerrillos ("little hills") are regarded as the oldest mining district in the United States, and New Mexico is a major turquoise producer. Elevation 6,200 feet.

First gold placer mining west of the Mississippi began with the discovery of the precious metal in the rugged Ortiz Mountains south of here in 1828, 21 years before the California gold rush. Since then, the district has produced more than 99.000 ounces of placer gold. Gold is currently produced from lode deposits.

The Turquoise Trail, as Highway 14 has become known, is a scenic drive along the Eastern slopes of the Sandia Mountains between Albuquerque and Santa Fe. This National Scenic Byway passes through towns that once thrived on the coal, gold, and turquoise the mountains provided.

The first discovery of turquoise and gold mining was by the Basket Weaving Indians that populated the area around 500 A.D. Their ancient diggings were later discovered by Spanish, and still later by American prospectors.

It was in 1825 that the first gold rush west of the Mississippi brought hundreds of people to this area to seek their fortunes. Abandoned by the 1950's, the ghost towns became bargain property and were discovered in the 1970's by artists and craftsmen, converting the old buildings into shops, galleries and museums.

The Turquoise Trail is a fun way to spend a leisurely afternoon.

On I-25 SW of Santa Fe
at rest area- MM 269

27-F

La Bajada ("the descent")

La Bajada hill is a major break in topography situated along a geological fault zone that separates the downfaulted Rio Grande rift from the Santa Fe Plateau. The red formation tilted at various angles along the fault zone is the Galisteo Formation deposited in streams about 70 million years ago.

More recent volcanic lavas form the resistant caprock of the plateau above. Landslide deposits are prominent on the slopes below the lava cap. Total relief from the rim of the Santa Fe Plateau to Galisteo Creek at the foot of La Bajada is about 800 feet.

After long days on the trail, following the Rio Grande and the Camino Real, to the promised land of Santa Fe, they finally reached the landmark that was the beginning of the end of their journey.

And what a landmark it was! The towering escarpment had to be traversed before the newcomers could reach the end of the road. Many trails and roads have been developed through the years to make it past this difficult stretch of the Camino Real. Today, it is cruised past as if it was just a little hill, but think back to the days of oxen and horses, exhausted from weeks of travel, only to find this hill.

La Bajada, though it means descent, it was the climb back up to the top that weakened many hardy souls.

On NM Hwy 25
SW of Santa Fe

27-G

Bicentennial Celebration

This facility was built by the New Mexico State Highway Department to commemorate the bicentennial birthday of the United States. Located 15 miles south of the plaza in Santa Fe, the nation's oldest capital city, the site atop La Bajada (The Descent) affords a spectacular view of the Ortiz, Jemez and Sangre de Cristo Mountains.

La Bajada

La Bajada, or "the descent," marks the division between the Rìo Arriba, or "upper river," and the Rìo Abajo, or "lower river," sections of New Mexico. This steep and dangerous grade was long an obstacle to caravan traffic going from the Rìo Grande Valley to Santa Fe.

As a monument to the United States Bicentennial, the New Mexico Highway Department provided us with this beautiful rest area.

After long days on the trail, following the Rio Grande and the Camino Real to the promised land of Santa Fe, they finally reached the landmark that was the beginning of the end of their journey.

And what a landmark it was! The towering escarpment had to be traversed before the newcomers could reach the end of the road. Many trails and roads have been developed through the years to make it past this difficult stretch of the Camino Real. Today, it is cruised past as if it was just a little hill, but think back to the days of oxen and horses, exhausted from weeks of travel, only to find this hill.

La Bajada, though it means descent, it was the climb back up to the top that weakened many hardy souls.

On I-25 SW of Santa Fe
at Rest Area- MM 269

27-H

320

South End of the Rockies

Divided by the Rìo Grande, the volcanic Jèmez Mountains are the western New Mexico Rockies; the Sangre de Cristo ("blood of Christ") Mountains are the eastern chain. Ice Age glaciers carved their summits including Santa Fe Baldy, the prominent peak in the Santa Fe Range which rises to 12,622 feet above sea level.

Whether it is the volcanic slopes of the Jemez Mountains, or the majestic Sangre de Cristo Mountains, these barriers presented many hazards to the frontiersmen that sought to settle this country and gain their fortunes to the west.

Ancient people found homes and shelter in them. Food grew abundantly on the slopes. The winters were harsh, but the summers were cool. With fertile river valleys, and soul stirring vistas, these mountains have enchanted both visitors and residents for centuries.

In this ever changing world, it's nice to know that these mountains will still be here for generations to come.

Face Missing
North on NM 14 then West
on Santa Fe Frontage Road

27-I

Cañoncito at Apache Canyon

Strategically located where the Santa Fe Trail emerges from Glorieta Pass, this is where Mexican Governor Manuel Armijo prepared to defend New Mexico against the American Army in 1846. Here too, Union forces destroyed a Confederate supply train on March 28, 1862 while the Battle of Glorieta was in progress six miles to the east.

Both the Union and Confederate Officers thought they had won the battle for Glorieta Pass. It was not until the Confederates suddenly found themselves without crucial supplies that they began to retreat towards Santa Fe, and then further and further South, leaving the Union with a clear victory.

Though considered a minor encounter, the battle here was the deciding factor for New Mexico in the Civil War. There were an estimated 331 casualties during the Battle for Glorieta Pass, 142 from the Union and 189 from the Confederates.

Exit 294 South on I-25
to NM Hwy 300

27-J

Seton Village

Ernest Thompson Seton (1860–1946), naturalist, artist, writer, authority on Indian lore, and first Chief Scout of the Boy Scouts of America, lived here during the last part of his life. The village includes his home, art collection, library, and Indian museum.

At the turn of the 19th century, it was thought that children needed special kinds of education that the local schools couldn't or didn't provide. This led to several people designing youth groups. One of those groups was designed by Ernest Thompson Seton. He organized a group called the Woodcraft Indians and published a book in 1902 as a guidebook for his boys.

At the same time, Robert Baden-Powell was returning to his country, England, as a military hero from Africa. Baden-Powell had written a manual for his regiment on stalking and survival in the wild. In England, he found the book was being read by young boys. Branden-Powell began to gather ideas, from Ernest Thompson Seton, and other experts. He rewrote his military book as a nonmilitary skill book which he titled Scouting for Boys.

By 1910, the Boy Scouts of America (BSA) was begun here in the United States. Ernest Thompson Seton became the first volunteer Chief Scout where he served for 5 years.

He retired to this area in 1915 and lived out his life in the high mountains of New Mexico.

Exit 284 on NM Hwy 303
2.5 miles North

27-K

Santa Fe on the Camino Real

Santa Fe, the oldest capital city in the United States, was established in 1610 as the seat of Spanish colonial government for the Province of New Mexico. The Palace of the Governors, used by Spanish, Mexican, and Territorial governors, has flanked the historic plaza since its construction in 1610, and now comprises part of the Museum of New Mexico. Population 48,899. Elevation 7,045 feet.

For nearly 400 years, the Palace of the Governors has occupied a prominent role in Santa Fe's history. The Palace has changed over centuries but its history remains. Spanish, Mexican, Pueblo Indian, and American decisions that significantly influenced the future of New Mexico, have been made in the Palace of the Governors. From every point of view, it is the most important historical building in the state, if not the country.

Originally constructed in the early 17th century as Spain's seat of government for what is today the American Southwest, the Palace of the Governors in Santa Fe chronicles and documents the history of the city, as well as New Mexico and the region. Museum exhibits and collections, library and archive holdings, reflect the Spanish colonial, Mexican, U.S. Territorial and Statehood periods of history.

The Fray Angélico Chávez Library is the institutional successor of New Mexico's oldest library (1851) and now part of the Palace of the Governors. It preserves historical materials in many formats documenting the development and history of New Mexico, the Greater Southwest, the American West, and Meso-America from pre-European contacts to the present.

The adobe building was designated a Registered National Historic Landmark in 1960, and an American Treasure in 1999.

On I-25 Southwest
Exit on Cerrillos Road

27-L

Agua Fria

Caravans entering and leaving Santa Fe on the Camino Real wound their way through scattered agricultural settlements south of the capital. Although this section of the Santa Fe River Valley was initially utilized as pasture for livestock, in the 17th century farmers were attracted to its arable lands and to the fresh water springs from which the community derives its name.

Agua Fria, or Cold Water, was a popular name by the Spanish explorers. There are three small settlements that share this name. This small town that was once a community of farmers on the outskirts of Santa Fe, has since become part of the city itself.

Just 4 miles, "as a crow flies" from the capitol building, Agua Fria has enjoyed a rich history from the close association.

On I-25 SW Exit, Cerrillos road
North to Siler Road

27-M

San Isidro Catholic Church

This 19th century adobe church is dedicated to San Isidro the ploughman, patron saint of farmers and protector of crops. Christian tradition maintains that in order to allow San Isidro time for his daily prayers, an angel plowed his fields. Agua Fria annually observes this fifteenth day of May as "His Day of Goodwill" to honor his role in this agricultural community along El Camino Real.

Isidore, for whom this church was named, was a Spanish day laborer near Madrid, Spain. According to the Catholic Encyclopedia, he was born about the year 1070 and died May 15, 1130.

Isidore was in the service of a farmer in the vicinity of Madrid. Every morning before going to work, he would attend a Mass at one of the churches in Madrid. His fellow laborers complained to their master that Isidore was always late for work in the morning. When the farmer investigated, he found, according to legend, Isidore at prayer, while an angel was ploughing for him.

On another occasion, the farmer found an angel on either side of him, while he was at prayer, so that Isidore's work was equal to that of three of his fellow-laborers.

Agua Fria and the San Isidore Church celebrates his feast on the 15th of May.

In Cerrillos at Aqua Fria

27-N

Pueblo of Tesuque

The small Tewa-speaking pueblo of Tesuque was established around 1300, and was first visited by Europeans in 1591. The Pueblo Revolt, which drove the Spanish from New Mexico for thirteen years, broke out here in 1680. Its present church was built in the 1880's, on the foundations of an earlier structure.

Tesuque Pueblo is one of New Mexico's smallest pueblos with a population of only 400. Just 10 miles North of Santa Fe, the pueblo has been continuously occupied for more than 700 years.

The entrance to the pueblo lies just south of Camel Rock, a distinct natural sandstone formation that the wind has eroded into the shape of a camel. The casino operated by Tesuque Pueblo, The Camel Rock Casino get's its name from the formation.

The pueblo also boasts an RV park and store where Indian arts and crafts are sold. The RV park doubles as the pueblo's tourism center.

The Pueblo is closed on certain days of the month, so call ahead before visiting.

Tesuque Pueblo
Rt 5 Box 360-T
Santa Fe, NM 87501
505-983-2667

South On US Hwy 285-84
Just North of Pojaque

27-M

Santa Fe Opera
Entrance One Mile Ahead

The Santa Fe Opera, founded in 1957, has won world-wide acclaim for the high standards of its presentations and the success of its apprentice program. World and American premieres as well as standard operatic favorites are presented here. Most operas are sung in English.

John Cosby established the Santa Fe Opera with a company of 67 in a 480 seat open-air theater on July 3, 1957. The first production was Madam Butterfly.

Since that time, there have been many famous and soon to be famous faces and plays that have made their debuts here. Jack Benny, Jose Van Dam, Boulevard Solitude, Lulu, and Daphne, to name just a few of those gracing center stage.

On July, 27, 1967, a fire demolished the original theater, but the show must go on! The remainder of the season was performed in downtown Santa Fe. Within a year, on June 26, 1968, a new 1,889 seat theater was opened.

The theater was renovated in the late 1990's and in 1998 a new 2,128 seat theater opened.

John Cosby's final season as General Director was the 2000 season. His respect for the unique New Mexico environment has led to pioneering work in water recycling and wetlands projects on the opera grounds. He is the recipient of numerous awards and five honorary doctorates, most recently from Yale University in 1991. He was also awarded the National Medal of Arts by President George Bush the same year.

Mr. Cosby has created one of the country's leading state-of-the-arts facilities.

North of Santa Fe
on US Hwy 285-MM 171.4

27-P

Pueblo Revolt Tricentennial

The Tewa pueblos of San Juan, San Ildefonso, Santa Clara, Pojoaque, Nambè and Tesuque were responsible for directing the 1680 Pueblo Revolt after the Spaniards captured two Indian runners at Tesuque on August 9. Joined by Taos and Picurìs they formed into two divisions and on August 15 laid siege to Santa Fe.

Popé was a religious leader from San Juan Pueblo in present-day New Mexico. He organized and led the most successful Indian uprising in the history of the American West.

Provoked by a Spanish crackdown on native religion in 1675, Popé soon began conferring with other disaffected Pueblo leaders, some with Apache ties. They discussed the possibility of a large scale revolt against the Spanish.

Popé offered a millenarian vision to the Pueblos, stressing the complete expulsion of the Spanish military and religious authority and a return of Pueblo deities. Popé launched his revolt early in August 1680. He achieved stunning success due to the Pueblos vastly superior numbers. There were more than 8,000 warriors against fewer than 200 armed colonists. Despite language differences and distance, the Pueblos attacked everywhere at once, killing 21 Franciscan friars and more than 400 Spanish colonists.

When Diego de Vargas re-conquered New Mexico for Spain, it did not mean a return to the days before the uprising. Popé's revolt had permanently weakened the political power of the Franciscans. It was after his death that an alliance was made between the Pueblos and the Spanish. Though he would have disagreed with the alliance, he created the conditions for a new culture to emerge in the American Southwest, a blend of Indian and European influences which retains its distinctive character even today.

North of Santa Fe on Hwy 25

27-Q

Pueblo of Nambe

Occupied since about 1300, this Tewa pueblo was first described by Castaño de Sosa in 1591 as a square structure, two stories high, with a central plaza, whose people irrigated their crops. By the 18th century its population had dropped to 6 or 7 families. The present church of San Francisco de Nambè was built in 1974.

22 miles northeast of Santa Fe in the stunning foothills of the Sangre de Cristo Mountains, lies the Nambe Pueblo. Located just above the pueblo is Nambe Falls Recreation Area which offers swimming, fishing, camping, and a double-drop waterfall. The July 4th Nambe Falls Ceremonial, which includes dances and an arts and crafts fair, is a very popular festivity for both the pueblo dwellers and tourists.

There are several artist studios on the road to the pueblo that offer the renowned Nambe pottery and silver.

There is a fee for photography, sketching or tape/video recording at the Pueblo.

Nambe Pueblo
Rt.1 Box 117-BB
Santa Fe, NM 87501
1-505-455-2036

22 Miles NE of Santa Fe
on Hwy 503 to Nambe

27-R

Bandelier National Monument

Thought to be an early home of Indians from Cochiti and other Keres-speaking pueblos, the villages and cliff houses of Frijoles Canyon were occupied from the 1200's to before the arrival of the Spaniards in 1540. The monument named for Adolph F. Bandelier, explorer and pioneer anthropologist of the Pajarito Plateau.

In Frijoles Canyon south of Los Alamos, Bandelier National Monument, named after its Swiss discoverer Adolph Bandelier, is a feast of spectacular geology and archaeology.

Literally hundreds of masonry ruins are located throughout the monument, the most spectacular of which are among the best regarded in the country. Visit the Long House Ruin, Tyuoni, the Ceremonial Cave, and walk the Ruins Trail.

There are many good hikes in the canyons and woodlands of Bandelier National Monument Wilderness Area. Seventy miles of trails lead to intriguing destinations such as; the Shrine of Stone Lions, the Painted Cave, the Falls Trail and the mesa top prehistoric village in the Tsankawi area.

Tsankawi is about 12 miles from the Frijoles Canyon portion of Bandelier National Monument and it is a special place for a relatively easy hike. Start at the information center and then walk the 1.5 mile trail along prehistoric routes onto the mesa top. The trail has been used for centuries and thousands of feet have worn deeply into the soft volcanic tuff. A ladder must be climbed to clear the final ledge and reach the top and the pueblo ruins. The unexcavated 350-room pueblo was probably built during the 1400's and occupied until the late 1500's. Another ladder leads from the mesa top onto a ledge on the side of the mesa where caves were carved out of the volcanic tuff. Look for petroglyphs along the trails and enjoy far views of the Rio Grande Valley from the mesa top.

Bandelier National Monument
HCR 1, Box 1, Suite 15
Los Alamos, New Mexico 87544
505-672-0343

Marker Missing
On US Hwy 84
South of Las Alamos

27-S

Jemez Mountains

On the skyline to the west are the Jemèz Mountains where tremendous volcanic eruptions a million years ago created a huge caldera some 15 miles in diameter that now forms a beautiful Valle Grande set amid a ring of volcanic peaks. Geothermal energy has been tapped from hot rock beneath the mountains.

Flow and ash-fall deposits surround the volcanic range form the Pajarito Plateau, site of numerous, ancient cliff dwellings and the city of Los Alamos. The Jemèz Mountains are part of the Southern Rockies and form one of the western ranges of the Rockies in New Mexico. Elevations exceed 11,000 feet.

Jemez Springs cuts a canyon through the valley of volcanic ash. Some of the most interesting things are the numerous hot springs and pools. Many are large and safe for bathing. At the forceful waterfall, Soda Dam, the river drops 15 feet through a curious formation made of deposited minerals from nearby thermal springs.

The gaseous vents and tiny bubbling hot water fountains are near the roadside opposite the Dam, giving no doubt that there is something happening beneath the earth's crust.

Jemez Springs also has a State Monument, preserving the ruins of a 17th century Spanish mission and 13th century Indian Pueblo.

Most of the Jemez Mountains area is within the Santa Fe National Forest, so back-country camping is free, and commercial development is restricted.

On NM Hwy 502
East of Las Alamos

27-T

Pueblo of San Ildefonso

In the 1500's, migrants from the Pajarito Plateau joined their Tewa-speaking relatives at San Ildefonso. The pueblo is famous as the home of the late Marìa Martìnez and other makers of polished black pottery. The modern church, a replica of that of 1711, was finished in 1968.

San Ildefonso Pueblo is located about 22 miles northwest of Santa Fe. Known for its flourishing art community, thanks to the work of the late Maria Martinez and her family, the pueblo has an average of 20,000 visitors annually.

Since the early 1900's, when the arts revival began, San Ildefonso is renowned for its fine black pottery with black matte designs. Many artisan homes throughout the pueblo are open to the public for shopping. There is also a museum dedicated to Maria Poveka Martinez, or the San Ildefonso Pueblo Museum.

Not only is San Ildefonso known for its art work, but for its legends. Village history is found in the hearts of the people, through their wonderful stories and images of the past. Among their stories is the legend of the Black Mesa and its "giant", the local boogey man.

The visitors center sells maps and permits for non-commercial photography, sketching and recording, which is permitted except for ceremonies.

San Ildefonso Pueblo
Rt.5 Box 315 A
Santa Fe, NM 87501
505-455-3549

On NM Hwy 502
East of Las Alamos

27-U

Puye Ruins

This spectacular site on the Pajarito Plateau is located in the reservation of Santa Clara Pueblo. It includes a pueblo on the mesa top and rooms cut from the volcanic rock. Puyè, occupied from about 1250 to 1550, is considered the ancestral home of Santa Clara and other Tewa-speaking pueblos.

For over three centuries, this spectacular locale was the home of over 1500 Pueblo Indians. They built villages, lived, farmed, and hunted game here. The Santa Clara people state that their ancestors were the inhabitants of this area. They left when drought caused springs to dry up.

In the Tewa language, the name Puye translates as "pueblo ruin where the rabbits assemble or meet." The cliff dwellings are a National Landmark and are operated as a cultural monument by the Pueblo of Santa Clara.

There are two separate self-guided tours. The cave rooms were dug into the cliff walls and extend for over a mile along the south face of the Puye mesa.

Guided tours are available by reservation.

Puye Cliff Dwellings And Communal House Ruins
34 NM Hwy 5
753-7326

On NM Hwy 30
South of Espanola

27-V

Chimayo

Indians occupied the Chimayó valley centuries before the arrival of the Spaniards. The village of Chimayó, founded in the early 18th century, shortly after the reconquest of New Mexico, has been a center of the Spanish weaving tradition for over 250 years. The village retains the historical pattern of settlement around a defensible plaza.

Chimayó is located 40 miles south of Taos and 24 miles northeast of Santa Fe, about ten miles east of Espanola in the Sangre de Cristo mountains. It is on Hwy 76, often called the "High Road to Taos"—a scenic route through beautiful old Spanish villages and gorgeous Georgia O'Keeffe-esque landscape vistas.

Shortly after the Pueblo Revolt of 1680-92, several groups of Spanish colonists settled in the northwestern section of the fertile Chimayo Valley. The colonists were hard working and were frequently granted land, building lots, and subsidies for their new life of hardship on the frontier.

One of the oldest restaurants in New Mexico is located in Chimayo. Rancho de Chimayo is well known for traditional New Mexican cuisine. The village has several other traditional cafes and is home to a locally famous tortilla company.

Today Chimayo is well known for the woven craftsmanship of the Ortega and Trujillo families. Many shops contain their work as well as fine art and crafts from the region.

27-W

Santuario De Chimayo

In 1816, Bernardo Abeyta and the other residents of El Potrero, then a separate community, finished this massive adobe chapel honoring Nuestro Señor de Esquìpulas. It is noted for its 6-foot crucifix and its tradition of healing the sick. The Santuario remained in the Abeyta family until the 1920s.

It was around 1810 that a Chimayo Friar was performing penances when he saw a light bursting from a nearby hillside. He dug at the spot and found a crucifix.

A local priest brought the crucifix to Santa Cruz where it was dubbed Our Lord of Esquipulas. The crucifix, according to legend, vanished. It was found back in the hole where the friar had originally found it. Twice more, the crucifix traveled back to Santa Cruz, only to vanish and resurface in its original location.

A small chapel was built on the site. It was then that miraculous healings began. These grew so numerous that the chapel had to be replaced by the larger Chimayo Shrine, an adobe mission, in 1816. The crucifix still resides on the chapel alter, but for some reason its curative powers have been overshadowed by "El Posito", the sacred pit, from which the crucifix sprang. The dirt from the pit is said to have amazing curative powers.

Today, thousands of people make a pilgrimage to Chimayo to visit the Santuario each year during Easter. Whether they walk only a few feet, or hundreds of miles, they leave, taking away a bit of the sacred dirt from which the crucifix was found. The walls of the sacristy are hung with discarded crutches and before and after photographs as evidence of the healing.

It is believed, with over 300,000 visitors a year, that Santuario de Chimayo is the most visited church in the State.

27-X

Sierra County

Sierra County was named for the Sierra De los Caballos range of mountains. It was created in April 1884. The dry climate, cool lakes, and hot mineral springs draw thousands of visitors annually.

County Seat: Truth or Consequences
Communities: Hillsborough, Kingston, Caballo,
Elephant Butte, Monticello, Winston

4,231 Square Miles

Elephant Butte State Park

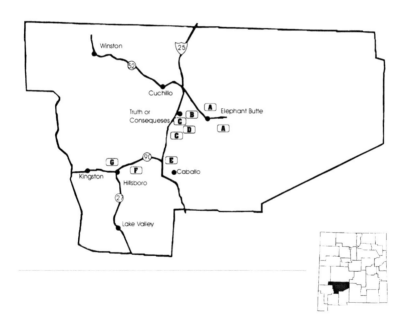

337

Elephant Butte Dam

Pueblo Indians had been irrigating and farming in the Rio Grande Valley for several hundred years before the Spaniards arrived to continue the tradition. The construction of Elephant Butte Dam, 1912–1916, represented the first large scale attempt to harness and control the river, and assured irrigation downstream.

New Mexico's largest reservoir is created by a dam constructed in 1916 across the Rio Grande. The reservoir is 40 miles long and has more than 200 miles of shoreline.

Constructed to provide for irrigation and flood control, the lake is New Mexico's premier water recreation facility.

Over 100 million years ago, the area was part of a vast shallow ocean. After the sea receded, the area became a favorite hunting ground for the largest land-dwelling predator of all time, tyrannosaurus Rex. Other local fossils include stegomastodon, which was discovered just west of the reservoir and was a relative of today's elephant.

The name "Elephant Butte" was derived from the eroded core of an ancient volcano, now an island in the reservoir, shaped like an elephant.

North East of T or C at Elephant Butte Dam
Marker Missing
I-25 South on NM Hwy 51
MM 4 East at dam

28-A

Elephant Butte Lake State Park

Situated beside the huge, 36,000-acre Elephant Butte Reservoir, this is one of the largest and most popular parks in New Mexico. It combines boating, waterskiing, fishing and other water-based sports with land activities such as camping, picnicking, and hiking. Fish caught year-round at Elephant Butte Lake include various species of bass, channel catfish and crappie.

In July of 1998, the town of Elephant Butte became New Mexico's newest city. With almost 1500 residents, it is home to retirees, families, and singles who like living minutes from the water. Located on the Southwestern shore of Elephant Butte Reservoir, Elephant Butte offers residents and visitors mild sunny winters, hot summers, and practically perfect weather in spring and fall.

The Park is the state's largest offering camping, boating, fishing, three marinas, numerous marine services along with a restaurant, a golf course, and lodging facilities.

Easter brings New Mexico's own version of Spring Break with up to 100,000 visitors coming for fun and the fireworks display. There are also numerous fishing tournaments, golf tournaments, and sailing regattas to provide competition along with the recreation.

During the winter, the Butte becomes a birdwatcher's paradise with great blue herons, sandhill cranes, osprey, seagulls, grebes, cormorants and pelicans. Golden eagles live in nearby McRae Canyon, and lots of ducks and other waterfowl seemed startled to find anything on the water besides themselves.

Elephant Butte Lake
P.O. Box 13
Elephant Butte, NM 87935
505-744-5421

In Town of T or C
On Business Loop 25 at Court House

28-B

Truth or Consequences

In 1581, Capitan Francisco Sánchez Chamuscado took possession of this region for the King of Spain, naming it the Province of San Felipe. Significant European settlement of the area, however, did not occur until the mid-1800's. Once called Hot Springs because of its curative natural hot springs, "T or C", in 1950, took its present name from the Ralph Edwards Radio program. Population 5,219. Elevation 4,576 feet.

The soothing hot mineral laced waters of Hot Springs, New Mexico, had a reputation of helping sufferers and the rehabilitation of crippled children. The year was 1950. One of the most popular game shows was Ralph Edwards Truth or Consequences. The show had been on the air for 10 years, and to celebrate the show wanted one town in America to willingly change its name to honor the show.

With a final vote of 1,294 to 295, Hot Springs became Truth or Consequences on April 1st, 1950. As a reward, Ralph promised to bring celebrities with him as his guests, every spring to a grand fiesta. Ralph has lived up to his word. The first weekend in May, The Truth or Consequences Show is performed live on stage followed by a concert performed by one of Ralph's guests.

At 4,260 feet above sea level and a population of 7,500, T or C is the county seat of Sierra County. It serves and an agricultural and ranching community and its hot springs still attract visitors who soak up in the mineral waters.

Sierra County Economic Development Organization
P.O. Drawer 489
Truth or Consequences, NM 87901
1-800-657-8575

In T or C on Business Loop 25
South of T or C by Williamsburg

28-C

Geronimo's Springs

The Indians knew of the great curative powers of the mineral waters of this spring long before the white man came. According to legend, Geronimo, famous Apache War Chief, often stopped here to bathe and relax.

Named for Apache leader Geronimo, Geronimo Springs is located within the Truth or Consequences city limits and said to have healing waters. Legend has it that this was a gathering place for his warriors. Use your imagination to see the warriors lounging in the hot mineral springs, celebrating a successful raid, and perhaps, planning the next venture.

The nearby Geronimo Springs Museum in Truth or Consequences includes a Ralph Edwards Room honoring the host of the television show. There is also a historic log cabin and a large mineral and rock collection, area relics, murals and exhibits from army forts and mining camps.

Prominently displayed in the museum is a quotation of General Sherman: "Every calculation based on experience elsewhere fails in New Mexico."

Geronimo Springs Museum
211 Main St.
Truth or Consequences, NM 87901
505-894-6600

In T or C Located at Geronimo Springs Museum
at Corner of Main and Jones

28-D

Caballo Mountains

To east beyond Caballo Reservoir are rugged Caballo Mountains, uplifted about 3 miles above downdropped Rio Grande through, along fault scarp at edge of mountains. Lowest slopes are ancient granites. Black ironstone beds are at base of high cliffs which are formed by Paleozoic dolomites and limestones. Elevation 4,390 feet.

The Sierra de Los Caballos, Mountains of the Horses, were named for the herds of wild horses which roamed the rugged hills. The horses are said to be the decendents of the ones brought by Coronado in the 1540's.

The area was first settled in 1908 when John Gordon arrived to homestead the area, the post office was later established in 1916. It was in 1938, when the Caballo Dam began to fill, that the homes of the early settlers were lost beneath the growing reservoir. The families moved their homes to the foothills on the west side of the Rio Grande and went on to raise their livestock.

Today, the area is filling with people purchasing small parcels of land for retirement. Caballo Lake State Park attracts thousands of visitors each year to enjoy boating, water skiing, fishing and camping. The state park's claim to fame are the majestic Bald and Golden Eagles that migrate here beginning in late October.

The lake is also home to largemouth bass, walleye, white bass, catfish, bluegill and the occasional rainbow trout.

Caballo Lake State Park
P.O. Box 32
Caballo NM 89731
505-743-3942

Exit 63 at Jct 152 South of T or C
MM 25

28-E

Percha Creek Bridge

This historic steel deck truss bridge, a Warren design, was built in 1927. It is the oldest of five remaining steel deck truss bridges in New Mexico. This structure has been preserved by the New Mexico State Highway and Transportation Department.

A Warren truss, patented by James Warren and Willoughby Monzoni of Great Britain in 1848, can be identified by the presence of many triangles formed by the web members which connect the top and bottom chords. These triangles may also be further subdivided. Warren truss may also be found in covered bridge designs.

Percha Creek is usually a trickle winding its way down to join the Rio Grande. But, on occasion, the trickle can become deadly.

The town of Hillsboro celebrates its Apple Festival on Labor Day weekend. It is three days full of apple pie, arts, crafts and fun on the banks of the Percha River. The town swells as three to four thousand people come in for the festival.

During the 1972 Festival, a deadly flood killed four, washed away seven businesses and destroyed 13 homes, leaving behind $750,000 in loss and damages. One witness said the devastating 12 foot wall of water "sounded like ten locomotives in a train switching station."

Today, the Apple Festival draws thousands of people from throughout the region. There are a few who can still hear the distant roar of 1972.

NM Hwy 152
West of T or C MM 152

28-F

Hillsboro Historic District

Hillsboro was founded in the 1870's after gold and silver were discovered in the surrounding Black Range. The town developed into an important mining and ranching center, and served as the Sierra County seat from 1884 to 1939. It was the site of several renowned trials, and is said to have had the last operating stage line in the United States.

In May of 1899, one of the most celebrated murder trials in New Mexico legal annals was moved from Las Cruces to Hillsboro on a change of venue. This trial brought national attention to the mining town.

The case involved the Territory of New Mexico vs. Ranchers Oliver Lee and James Gililland, charged with the murders of Col. Albert Jennings Fountain and his 8 year old son. Fountain was a widely known and respected attorney, legislator, and newspaper publisher.

Hundreds of people descended on the mining town for the trial, including reports from the nation's largest newspapers. For 18 days, the courtroom was mesmerized as 70 witnesses gave testimony, and defense attorney Albert Fall's fiery oratory and legal tactics shredded the prosecution's largely circumstantial case. Particularly damaging was the fact that the prosecution could not prove that a murder had actually been committed as there were never any bodies found. The defendants were acquitted.

Today, perhaps 75 people remain in Hillsboro, which lies beneath the majestic cottonwoods that line the main street.

On main street, the Black Range Museum, housed in the once-celebrated Ocean Grove Hotel, displays symbols of frontier days.

Black Range Museum
NM Highway 152
Hilsboro, NM
505-895-5233

West of T or C at Hillsboro on NM 152 W
MM 48.6

28-G

Socorro County

Desert Formation

Socorro County was created in 1850 and was the first County in New Mexico. It was named for the local pueblo that helped Don Juan Onate.

County Seat: Socorro
Communities: Magdalena, San Antonio, Bernardo,
San Acacia, Bingham, San Marcial,
Valverde

6,634 Square Miles

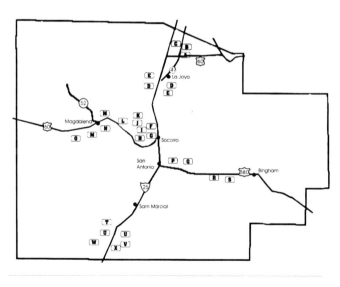

Las Nutrias

During the late 17th century, this area had become well known to the Spanish. Called La Vega de Las Nutrias, or meadow of the beavers, it was a welcome paraje, or stopping place, for caravans on the Camino Real. Eighteenth century attempts at settlement in this region failed, but by 1860 the current village had been established and a church had been built by the new settlers.

Beneath the shadows of the Sierra Ladrones to the west, Los Nutrias has long been a stopping place on the Camino Real.

The Sierra Ladrones, or Robbers Mountain, are so named for their historical use as a hideaway for Apache and Navajo Indians and later for smugglers and robbers to escape the trailing posses. The steep canyons and ruggedness held many places to hide the bounty of their plunder. Visibility extends up to 100 miles, and legends speak of buried Civil War cannons, lost treasure and mines, and desperado hideouts.

Though no longer a robber's roost, the Sierra Ladrones are now home to Desert Bighorn Sheep.

Geologically speaking, the mountain is an anomaly. Geologists cannot explain it's presence.

The Mountain is part of the Sevilleta Wildlife Refuge where chief research projects include Mexican Wolf Reintroduction, Long Term Ecological Research, as well as studies being conducted on weather, soil and vegetation. University students from all over the United States apply to conduct research at Sevilleta.

On NM State Hwy 304 North East of Bernardo
MM 10

29-A

Casa Colorado

A Spanish settlement, with houses built of red adobe or earthen bricks, was established in this vicinity in the 1740s. This community was soon abandoned, probably as a result of Apache raids, but was reoccupied in 1823 and developed into a bustling trade center along the Camino Real.

Dirt has always been readily available, even when other building materials were sorely lacking. The word adobe is derived from an Arab word, "at-tub", which refers to the earth bricks Arabs made as early as 7000 BC. With the components of sand, clay, water, and in some cases, straw, these ingredients were readily available for constructing homes on the Camino Real.

After bricks were formed and cured by drying under the hot New Mexico sun, they were stacked and held together with a mortar of mud. After the wall was completed, it was coated with a thick coat of adobe mud, then coated with a dry lime plaster. Every year, it was necessary to replaster the walls, but otherwise, there was little maintenance. The thick walls held in heat during the winter and kept temperatures down during the summer.

Once thought to be a poor man's brick, today adobe homes can bring millions of dollars and is truly a building material for all. The durability and cost effectiveness has helped to make apparent that the oldest remains of buildings world wide were made of adobe bricks.

NM St Hwy 204 North
MM 17

29-B

Las Barrancas

The area below these high bluffs, or barrancas, was settled by Andres Gomez Robledo in the mid- 17th century. Robledo's hacienda developed into an important stop along this section of the Camino Real until it was destroyed during the Pueblo Revolt of 1680. After the reconquest of 1692, Apache raids prevented Spanish resettlement of this area until Sabinal was established in 1741.

Up and down the Rio Grande, small communities rose and thrived on the fertile soils. During the summer and early fall roadside stands spring up, offering garden fresh squash, pumpkins, chili and just about anything else that can be imagined.

Sabinal, Los Nutrias, Veguita are just some of the small close knit communities along the river. First, people traveling the Camino Real needed safe rest places, then later, as modes of transportation increased, some areas grew while other became nearly deserted.

The agricultural opportunities of the valley continue to thrive as generation after generation has grown crops. Today, many residents have more lucrative careers in Albuquerque, Belen or Socorro. It was the advent of the tractor and other mechanical wonders that have made farming a part-time career for some, letting their traditions continue as they move through this modern, fast paced world.

St. Hwy 304 North
Just off of Sonenburg Rd MM 19

29-C

Acomilla

The Camino Real wound its way below the black basaltic buttes of San Acacia, seen to the southeast. Named Acomilla, or Acomita (little Acoma) by the Spanish, these buttes form the walls of a narrow passage for the Rio Grande, along which hostile Apache frequently waited in ambush. Travelers had to organize into well-armed caravans to assure their safety along this section of the Camino Real.

During the late 16th century, when Spaniards first arrived in the area, the Spanish established a military post in this area called "New Sevilla". It was near the end of their rule some 200 years later that the Community of Sevilleta was awarded the Sevilleta de la Joya Land Grant by the Governor of the New Mexico Province.

When Mexico became independent from Spain in 1821, the grant fell under Mexican rule.

It was after the Mexican-American war that the grant passed to yet another country's authority. Under the United States rule, a patent on the land was issued to the residents of the community. When New Mexico became a state in 1912, the community became responsible for taxes on the Grant. The taxes were never paid, and Socorro County bought the land in a public sale in 1928.

In 1936, General Thomas Campbell bought the land from the county. For the next 30 years, the Campbell family worked the land as a cattle ranch. Recognizing that the land was becoming over grazed, Campbell organized the Campbell Family Foundation in 1966. All grazing was stopped on the Sevilleta. The Campbell Family foundation offered to donate the La Joya Grant to the U.S. Government to be managed as a national wildlife refuge.

On December 28, 1973, for a fractions of the land's worth, the La Joya Land Grant became the Sevilleta National Wildlife Refuge.

On I-25 North At Rest Area MM 166.5
I-25 South of Bernardo at Rest AreaMM 166.74

29-D

Rio Salado Sand Dunes

Sand blown northeastward from normally dry bed of Rio Salado forms dunes along this part of Rio Grande Valley. Rio Grande is deep down-dropped trench with uplifted Los Pinos Mountains to east and Ladron Mountains to northwest. Rocks on crest of Ladrons are 4 miles deep below sand dunes. Elevation 4,850 feet.

Closed to the public most of the year, the Sevilleta National Wildlife Refuge surrounds both sides of the Rio Grande in this area. Sevilleta is a beautiful place where higher learning goes hand in hand with the rehabilitation of the land.

The refuge is slowly returning to the natural conditions that might have been seen around the turn of the century. Native animals have become more abundant and visible. There is also a program where the endangered Mexican wolf is being acclimated to its historical habitat to be reintroduced.

Sevilleta NWR has a wide range of ecosystems which makes it a unique place to study further. There are the Chihuahuan Desert, Great Plains Grassland, Great Basin Shrub-Steppe, Pinon-Juniper Woodland, Bosque Riparian Forests, Wetlands and Montain Coniferous Forests ecosystems within the boundaries of the protected Refuge.

In the future, a Visitor Center and a hiking trail will be opened.

Sevilleta National Wildlife Refuge
P.O. Box 1248
Socorro, NM 87801
505-864-4021

I-25 North, just South of Bernardo
MM 166.5
On I-25 South of Bernardo
MM 166.7

29-E

Points of Interest

On most of the historical markers, there is text describing geological, historical, or other interesting facts about the area you are visiting. On the back of most of these signs are Points of Interests maps. These maps lead you to other Historical Markers in the area.

New Mexico has a rich and fascinating history. It's Tri-culture influence can be seen throughout the state. Whether you're taking a break from a long car ride, or exploring, the historical markers will give you a chance to explore and learn about this great state.

I-25 South
Exit 150 in Socorro on Terry St.

29-F

Garcia Opera House

Using the gold he had left her, the widow of Juan Nepomuceno Garcia began construction of the Garcia Opera House in 1884. It was completed three years later in 1887.It served as the main center for cultural and community events including theatrical productions, balls, marriages etc. The curved shape of the massive 34-inch walls strengthened the building and improved acoustics. The "rake" stage is one of very few still in existence in the U.S. Restoration began in 1983 and was completed in 1985 by Holm Bursum, Jr. The Garcia Opera House is a National Historic Site.

During the restoration of the Garcia Opera House, one of the major concerns was that earthquakes would cause the dome to collapse. Historical and recent records of earthquakes in New Mexico show that, although the area along the Rio Grande from Socorro to Bernardo occupies only two percent of the total area of the state, it accounts for about 45 percent of all of New Mexico's earthquake activity.

The relatively high earthquake activity in the Socorro area can probably be attributed to the ongoing inflation of a thin, yet extensive, horizontal layer of molten rock. This Socorro magma body resides about 12 miles below the middle Rio Grande valley. The minor quakes measuring up to 2.1 will usually last days or weeks, with only some being strong enough to be felt.

When restoring the Opera House, the seismic activity was of a great concern. Thus the dome was reinforced with visible supports.

Exit 150 In Socorro
California St, South of Abeyta

29-G

Jumbo

This is a fragment from Jumbo, a huge steel vessel designed to contain the explosion of the first nuclear device at the Trinity Site some 35 miles southeast of here on July 16,1945. Jumbo was 25 feet long, 12 feet in diameter, and weighed 214 tons. Its steel walls were 14 inches thick. Although Jumbo was not used in the tests, it was 800 feet from ground zero at the time and escaped without damage except for a steel superstructure around it which was crumpled by the blast. Jumbo was used in later experiments which resulted in the ends being blown out. This piece of Jumbo is a souvenir of the world's first nuclear explosion.
Dr. Marvin Wilkening an observer in 1945

In 1944, plutonium, one of the key ingredients in the atomic bomb, was extremely rare and expensive to produce. To contain the plutonium, in case the Trinity bomb did not explode properly, the concept of Jumbo came to be. It was thought that by placing the explosive inside Jumbo, they could salvage the plutonium in case something went wrong.

Jumbo was built by the Babcock and Wilcox Steel corporation in Ohio at the cost of $12,000,000. Shipping the 428,000 pound steel container to New Mexico by rail, it arrived 30 miles from Trinity in April of 1945. Jumbo was then loaded on a 64 wheeled trailer, then pulled and pushed the 30 miles to Trinity by four Caterpillar D-8 tractors.

After it arrived at the site, it was decided that it would not be a good idea to have 214 tons of highly radioactive material flying around in the atmosphere. Also, plutonium was, by then, more readily available, and the Project scientists were sure the Trinity device would probably work.

Not knowing what else to do with the massive containment device, it was decided to suspend it from a 70 foot steel tower 800 yards from ground Zero. Jumbo survived, but the tower was flattened. To hide Jumbo from a possible congressional investigation committee, eight 500 pound conventional bombs were detonated within the container. The resultant explosion blew both ends off Jumbo.

Unable to totally destroy Jumbo, the Army, in its great wisdom, buried it in the desert. It was later recovered and moved to it's present site as a monument to the world's first atomic explosion.

29-H

In Socorro on Manzanares St at Plaza Park

Socorro

In 1598, Juan de Oñate's Spanish colonization expedition arrived here at the Piro Indian Pueblo of Pilabo, They renamed it Socorro owing to the food and shelter provided by Pilabo's inhabitants. The pueblo and its Spanish mission were destroyed during the Pueblo Revolt, and the area was not resettled until 1815. A west bank road connected Socorro to the Camino Real on the east side of the Rio Grande.

Crossing the inhospitable region known as Jornado Del Muerto, the"Journey of Death", they arrived at a small pueblo. Here the people greeted them with food, water and shelter. Juan de Oñate named the Pueblo Socorro, which means "Help".

During the Pueblo Revolt of 1680, the area was abandoned as both natives and newcomers fled South to Texas. When the Spanish returned to New Mexico in 1692, this area remained empty. It wasn't until the late 18th Century, when the trail needed better protection, that Santa Fe Officials began planning to resettle this area.

The land around Socorro is very fertile and the Rio Grande brings an abundance of water. Farming and ranching has historically been important to this valley. In the 1880's and 1809's, extensive mining in the mountains and surrounding hills, with smelters to handle the ore, made Socorro boom.

Today, Socorro continues to thrive. The New Mexico School of Mines remains one of the state's leading centers for education and research. Socorro is Socorro's county seat.

Socorro Chamber of Commerce
P.O. Box 743
Socorro, NM 87801
505-835-0424

North of Socorro on Jct 60 West
In Socorro, North on Manzaners St In Historic Plaza Park

29-I

NM Bureau of Mines and Minerals Museum

Based on personal collection willed to the New Mexico Schools of Mines by C.T. Brown in 1928, this museum displays thousands of mineral specimens from around the world with special emphasis on minerals found in New Mexico. Highlights include smithsonite from Kelly (Magdalena District), linarite from Bingham, Grants District uranium, Carlsbad potash, Silver City copper, Harding pegmatite minerals, and numerous fossils.

The New Mexico State Legislature approved an Act establishing a Bureau of Mines and Mineral Resources in 1927. The Bureau was responsible for research into the geology and mineral resources of the state. The Bureau conducts studies on geology, mineral and energy resources, water resources, geologic hazards, environmental problems, and extractive metallurgy.

Information is then impartially shared non-proprietary information from its research with all companies, individuals, agencies and institutions.

The museum was Socorro's first museum of any kind. It has been nurtured by dozens of scientists over the years and the collection has more than 10,000 pieces today. The collection provides ongoing aesthetic, scientific, and research benefits for all of society.

Located in the Workman Addition on the NMIMT campus, visitors are welcome seven days a week, academic and regular holidays excluded.

In Socorro at NM School of Mines
in Mineral Museum Parking Lot

29-J

New Mexico Tech

Founded in 1889 as New Mexico's School of Mines, New Mexico Institute of Mining and Technology offers degrees through the doctorate in a number of science and engineering disciplines. In addition to its academic functions, the institute also conducts extensive research and development activities.

New Mexico Institute of Mining and Technology, or New Mexico Tech for short, is over 100 years old. The state legislature established it in 1889. The purpose of the school was to provide for higher education in the earth and related sciences.

New Mexico Tech is one of the nation's leading schools. Small enough for individualized attention, and large enough to offer a well rounded curriculum, it strives to promote science and technology to those who grace its campus

In Socorro
at NM Tech Campus

29-K

Magdalena Fault

Magdalena Mountains to west are topped by South Baldy at 10,783 feet; La Jencia plain to east down dropped with rocks in Water Canyon 3 miles below this sign. Bench along edge of mountains is Magdalena fault dividing uplifted mountains from downdropped plains. Elevation 6,110 feet.

The Cibola National Forest's Water Canyon Campground has an interesting hiking trail up Copper Canyon. Parallel to a pleasant little stream and bypassing private property, you hike up towards the crest. At the top, you'll unexpectedly cross a dirt road. This road leads to Langmuir Lab.

In 1963, with funds from the National Science Foundation, New Mexico Tech located in Socorro, built Langmuir Laboratory for Atmospheric Research. This facility studies lightning, cloud physics, precipitation and astronomical observations. The facility has also undertaken groundbreaking research in ozone and cosmic rays. It is open to the public from 8 am to 5 pm during the summer months. Tours can be arranged. (505) 838-5424 for more information.

Closer still to Magdalena is The Lady on the Mountain. For centuries, she has gazed down from Magdalena Peak. Legend has it that this has been a sacred spot for the Indians, protecting those who sought her refuge from attack from other tribes.

US 60 West of Socorro
MM 124.5

29-L

Magdalena

Magdalena is located in a mineral-rich area which became a center of silver mining in the 1860's. In 1885, a railroad was built to the smelter in Socorro, and Magdalena became an important railhead for cattle, sheep, and ore.

The first non-Indians known to be in the Magdalena area was a small party of Spanish soldiers and a priest. This small group left the Spanish army in 1540 and turned West. They were harassed by Indians. Hot by day, cold by night, the group sought shelter and discovered a mountain with a face. The face of a woman looks to the blue skies of New Mexico. It reminded them of their home in Spain and the called the mountain "La Sierra De Maria Magdalena," after Mary Magdalena. Though the area was named, no attempt was made to colonize it during the early Spanish rule.

It would be years later when silver was discovered at nearby Pueblo Springs and mining began, that this area was opened for settlement. As years went by, the town was moved from Pueblo Springs to its present day site. The railroad was brought in and mineral rich ores were transported down the mountain to the railhead where it was then shipped for processing in Socorro.

Magdalena had one major problem though. Water was very scarce. Early residents carted water by the barrel full from Pueblo Springs. It would be a number of years until their own water system was developed. This left the town very vulnerable to fires. As the mines' productivity declined, so did property values of Magdalena. Many buildings were lost to fires, not all of them were "accidental".

Today, Magdalena is once again a thriving community. Ranching plays an important part in its economy, and the "Lady Magdalena" on the mountain continues her watch on the skies above.

Magdalena Chamber of Commerce
P.O. Box 281
Magdalena, NM 87825
1-866-854-3271

In Town of Magdalena
MM 112.9 Hwy 60
In Town of Magdalena
MM 111.918

29-M

Kelly

Kelly was central New Mexico's most prosperous mining town from the 1880s until the early 20th century. Silver had been mined at Kelly since the 1860s, but in 1903 it became a major source of zinc carbonate, a vital ingredient in the manufacture of paint. Located 3.5 miles south of Magdalena on NM 114, Kelly is now a ghost town, but former residents still hold a festival every June.

Silver was first discovered here in the late 1800's by soldiers turned miners exploring the area. Prospecting was a good way to pass time when not on duty. It was also a dangerous pass time as wandering Indians made several prospectors vanish.

The town of Kelly was established in 1883 when the post office was opened. Kelly grew and prospered as it was the center of several mines in the area. The railroad was needed though and the Atchison, Topeka and Santa Fe finally built a spur from Socorro to Magdalena and to within a mile of Kelly. Engineers took one look up the narrow twisting canyon in which Kelly sits and threw up their hands. "If you want the railroad, you'll have to come to it." And they did. Cart loads of ore were shipped down to the rail head. This spur of 30 miles became the most lucrative of all during the period it was used.

After the bottom fell out of the silver market, attention was then turned to the zinc. This mineral had been left in the "dumps" when silver had been the metal of the day. Recovering the zinc which had already been mined made this a very prosperous affair as the zinc was needed to manufacture paint. Over $21,000,000 of Zinc was mined from this area.

Down below, the town of Magdalena prospered as miners left the narrow confines of the canyon to spread out and enjoy their paydays.

Today, no one is left in Kelly. The ruins of the mines and a few crumbling buildings are all that remain. Visitor passes are available and one can collect small stones containing remnants of silver and the "green rocks" containing zinc carbonate. Luckily, unlike the original miners and settlers, you won't have to worry about hostile natives looking for scalps.

In Kelly on Highway 60 West
MM 112.617

29-N

Plains of San Agustin

Northeast part of Plains of San Agustin, occupied some thousands of years ago by large intermountain lake, is downdropped graben bordered by uplifted volcanic masses. San Mateo and Luera Mountains and Pelona Mountain on southeast and Horse Mountain and Datil Mountains on northwest. Elevation 7,030 feet.

The San Agustin Plains are the home to the Very Large Array (VLA). This is a huge radio telescope operated by the National Radio Astronomy Observatory. The VLA was used in the movie "Contact" starring Jodie Foster.

The visitor center has an automated slide show of the VLA itself. It is the starting point for a self-guided tour of the region.

The telescopes are designed to collect radio waves and distribute this information through a correlator and then analyze the output. There are 27 antennas, each measuring 81 feet in diameter and weighing approximately 200 tons. These antennas are formed in a Y shape and are moved and reconfigured using a set of train tracks.

Near Pie Town, NM, is the home of VLA-Pie Town link which is a project to link the Very Long Baseline Array antenna located there with the VLA located on the San Augustine Plains through optical fibers.

The VLA is located 50 miles west of Socorro on NM 52, then West on the VLA access road to the Visitor's Center. They are open from 8:30 am to sunset daily.

US Hwy 60 West of Magdalena
MM 89.5

29-O

San Antonio—On The Camino Real

In the mid-19th century, San Antonio was the last outpost on the Camino Real before the Mesilla Valley to the south. Today it is known as the birthplace of Conrad Hilton and the site of the first Hilton Hotel, located in his family's adobe house near the train station.

If seeing wild animals and spying the plumage of a rare preening bird in their natural habitat, is to your liking, then the Bosque del Apache Wildlife Refuge is a must. Between Socorro and San Antonio, the Bosque is located in New Mexico's Middle Rio Grande Valley. Here, temperatures hover at 60 degrees in the middle of winter, beckoning you to get out of your vehicle with camera and binoculars to study the herons, hawks, cranes, geese and hundreds of other species.

For the price of $3 at the visitor's center, you can explore the Marsh Road Loop. A parking area is provided where you can leave your vehicle to explore the Marsh Overlook Trail on foot. There are many "blinds" where you can watch the animals do what animals do best.

There are other roads and trails to explore. Coyotes will howl with the oncoming darkness. A buck may lift his proud head to study you a moment, before turning and vanishing into the underbrush. Overhead, geese coming in for the evening will fly in the classic V formation, the sounds, nature's own symphony.

I-25 S Exit 139
Just before San Antonio

29-P

San Pedro

By the mid 19th century the village of San Pedro was established nearby and had become a welcome and important trading center along the Camino Real as it passed along the east bank of the Rio Grande. San Pedro, once renown for its extensive vineyards and produce, is now abandoned and in ruins. Like many similar villages, its existence and historic role are largely forgotten.

Local residents who live near the area are hard put to point out exactly where the forgotten town once was. The few crumbling walls are all that is left of the tiny community. The vineyards have long since blown away. San Pedro never was a large community, but the ghost town had the distinction of being the closest town to the Trinity Site where the atomic age was born.

It was Joe McKibben who threw the firing switch that changed the world. First came the light, it turned the night skies of the desert with an eerie brilliance. The unearthly glow illuminated every peak ridge and canyon as though the sun had abruptly risen. The fireball boiled up from the desert floor.

The chief of the Manhattan project, as the Trinity device was known, had a major problem on his hands within seconds of the explosion. He had to maintain the tight veil of wartime secrecy around the bomb. The device was to bring the end of the war. It would kill approximately 70,000 people within the next few weeks and would bring an abrupt end to World War II.

As the blinding light, the roar and the fury of the blast faded, Maj, Gen. Groves reminded his aides, "We must keep this thing quiet."

One of the aides said, "But Sir, I think they heard the noise in 5 states."

Another said, "Can you give us an easy job, general, like hiding the Mississippi River?"

Those were only slight exaggerations. The blast was seen and heard across two-thirds of New Mexico, the Texas Panhandle and portions of Eastern Arizona. Houses were shaken and windows were blown out in Gallup, 235 miles away. Deming and Silver City also reported similar damages.

The remains of San Pedro witnessed history in those predawn moments. It will forever keep its secrets.

Exit 139 on NM 380 MM 2.1

29-Q

Carthage-Tokay-Farley

Important coal-mining towns from the 1880's to 1925 when the mines closed. Originally developed by the Santa Fe Railroad and later operated by the Carthage Fuel Company mainly to fire the Kinney brick kilns in Albuquerque. Farley was a limestone quarry. The Hilton Mine belonged to the father of Conrad Hilton.

"In the 1884 there were short railroad lines that went from San Antonio to the coal mines at Carthage. Father Peter Joseph Pelzer was the priest serving the valley near Socorro in addition to his regular church at Socorro. He made his missionary visits to all the small parishes nearby, including San Marcial, Magdalena, Kelly, Chloride, and the little coal town of Carthage.

"Sometimes the railway men carried Mexican nationals who had hired out to work the mines. When new houses were built for those who hired out, these were equipped with modern plumbing, complete with bath tubs. The new arrivals stored wood and coal in the tubs to keep them from theft. The railroad company hurried to put up wood sheds after that." (From "the Horny Toad Line" by Patricia O'Neal, Burroughs, 1935)

Neither Carthage, Tokay or Farley were large commercial towns. These mining towns have long since been abandoned, and today, cattle and antelope call it home.

Exit 139 on NM 380
East of San Antonio

29-R

Trinity Site

The world's first atomic explosion occurred on July 16, 1945, at the Trinity Site near the north end of the historic Jornada del Muerto. It marked the beginning of the nuclear age, and the culmination of the Manhattan Project. The site, now part of the White Sands Missile Range, is closed to the public.

Out of the Second World War arose the birth of the Nuclear age. If the need to end the war had not been so dominant, the atomic bomb would not have been developed. If the bomb to end the war had not been developed, today's advances and benefits from the nuclear age would have been much longer in coming.

Today, a sixth of the world's energy supply comes from nuclear powered plants. If California's rolling blackouts are any indication, then even more shall become necessary in the near future.

Over 5 million cancer patients per year are treated with radiation therapy. There are approximately 575 nuclear-powered ships and submarines. And as time goes on, more benefits will be born from the loss of life that ended a global war.

Just think, without Trinity and the events thereafter, how could we ever have had a cartoon character like Homer J. Simpson, a hopelessly inept nuclear-power-plant operator?

This site is open to visitors only on the first Saturday in April and October.

I-25 South, Exit 139 on NM 380 EMM 12.4   **29-S**

Fort Craig Rest Area

Fort Craig is on alluvial gravelly sands, derived from mountains to west, sloping toward Rio Grande to east. Magdalena Mountains to northwest and San Mateo Mountains to west are mainly thick piles of volcanic rocks. San Andrés Mountains on southeast horizon are of older limestones and shales. Elevation 4,810 feet.

In 1866, the U.S. Congress designated all-black regiments. These regiments were under the command of white commissioned officers. They became known as Buffalo Soldiers. Indians named them because of their hair which closely resembled buffalo hair and for their fighting integrity.

Most of the Buffalo Soldiers were former slaves and Civil War veterans.

Buffalo Soldiers served at most of New Mexico's forts, including Fort Craig. These soldiers were used to help control Indian raids, build roads, repair and build post buildings, escort stages, and protect stages, travelers and civilians.

The role of the Buffalo Soldiers is slowly being revealed with the help of historians. They played a definite part of the creation of the West.

I-25 North of Elephant Butte
at southbound Rest Area   MM 114

29-T

Paraje De Fra Cristobal

The mountain range seen along the east bank of the Rio Grande is named after Father Cristobal de Salazar of the 1598 Juan de Onate expedition. An encampment at the northern edge of the mountain, whose profile is said to resemble that of the good friar, was a place of rest for caravans on the Camino Real as they entered or exited the Jornada del Muerto.

After nearly 100 miles of non-stop travel, Paraje De Fra Cristobal was a welcomed site. This is where the Camino Real rejoined the Rio Grande. Water and wood was once again easily available, and the routine of 15 miles per day could be re-established.

The Camino Real was not merely a conquest route. It brought new ideas and social institutions which would alter the southwest, and, in later years, the entire United States.

It was along the Camino Real that the first breeding herds of horses, cows, sheep goats, pigs, oxen, mules and chickens would make their way into the interior of the United States.

The horse was the most important. As Indians adapted to the horse, it brought a balance of power between the invading Spanish and Americans to the Native Americans. Spain was the only European country to herd cattle on horseback. Mexico, with it's wide open spaces was perfect for this type of ranching. As the Anglo-Americans began to penetrate Mexico's northern boundaries, they learned these new techniques, thus the American Cowboy has its roots in Hispanic culture.

I-25 North of Elephant Butte
Rest Area MM 1139
I-25 south of Elephant Butte

29-U

Espejo's Expedition on the Camino Real

In 1582 and 1583, Antonio de Espejo and his party paralleled the Rio Grande north to the Bernalillo area. He was trying to learn the fate of two Franciscan friars who had stayed with the Pueblo Indians after the Rodriguez-Sánchez Chamuscado expedition returned to Mexico in 1581.

Mesa Del Contadero

The Chihuahua Trail passed by the large volcanic mesa on the east bank of the Rió Grande, marking the northern end of the Jornada del Muerto (Journey of the Dead Man). "Cantadero" means "the counting place," or a narrow place where people and animals must pass through one-by-one.

On June 5, 1581, three Franciscans-Agustín Rodríguez, Francisco López, and Juan de Santa María-left Santa Bárbara, Mexico, to explore missionary possibilities in the country to the north. They were accompanied by an armed escort of eight soldiers under the command of Francisco Sánchez (also called Chamuscado), nineteen Indian servants, ninety horses, and 600 head of stock.

    The Rodríguez-Sánchez expedition continued along the west bank of the Rio Grande through the area of present El Paso and in August 1581 arrived at the Piro and Tigua pueblos of New Mexico. On August 21 the party took formal possession of the land for the king of Spain. For the remainder of the year the party explored extensively in all directions, covering much of the same territory viewed by Francisco Vásquez de Coronado forty years before. In the meantime, Fray Santa María had ill-advisedly set out on his own to report to the viceroy and was killed by Indians in September 1581, though his companions did not learn of his fate until sometime later.

    In early 1582 Sánchez and his men discussed returning to Santa Bárbara to report to the viceroy, but the two Franciscans announced their intention of pursuing further their missionary endeavors in New Mexico. They did not heed Sánchez's warnings of the great dangers involved and on January 31, 1582, stayed behind when the rest of the explorers returned to Santa Bárbara, Mexico. Glowing accounts of great wealth in New Mexico, together with the concern about the safety of the friars, led to preparations for an expedition led by Espejo to the new land.

On I-25 South in Rest Area
MM 114

29-V

Vasquez De Coronado's Route

In 1541 an expedition from the army of Francisco Vásquez de Coronado, New Mexico's first explorer, marched south 80 leagues to investigate the pueblos along the lower Rio Grande. The group reached that part of the infamous Jornada del Muerto, now covered by Elephant Butte Lake, where the river disappeared underground.

Francisco Vasquez de Coronado was born into a noble family in Salamanca, Spain in 1510. At the age of 25, he came to the Americas as an assistant to New Spain's first viceroy.

An ambitious man, he married the daughter of the colonial treasurer, put down a major slave rebellion, and became the governor of a Mexican province within three years of his arrival. But he wanted more. Rumors of earlier explorations by Cabeza de Vaca about 7 cities of gold inspired him to lead a royal expedition to explore the north into what is now the American West.

The expedition explored, bringing Catholic ideals to the pueblos they encountered, and the Spanish influence that is still very present today.

When they did not find the "Seven Cities of Cibola", parties were sent out, some traveling all the way to the border between Arizona and California where they explored the Grande Canyon. Coronado himself led a party into what is now Kansas.

Returning to Mexico without locating a single golden city, the Viceroy branded Coronado's expedition an abject failure. His career quickly declined and in 1544 he was removed from office as a governor and moved to Mexico City where he worked in a modest position for the city. He died in 1554, though his legacy is seen throughout the west.

On I-25 Northbound Rest Area
MM 114

29-W

Fort Craig

Fort Craig, which replaced Fort Conrad located about nine miles north, was established in 1854 to control Indian raids along the Jornada del Muerto. Troops from Fort Craig were defeated by Confederate forces at the Battle of Valverde, 7 miles distant, in 1862. Named for Captain Louis S. Craig, the fort was deactivated in 1885.

Valverde Battlefield

The first major battle of the Civil War on New Mexico soil occurred at Valverde on February 21,1862, when a Confederate force of Texas Volunteers under General H. H. Sibley defeated Union forces commanded by Col. E.R.S. Canby stationed at Fort Craig. From here, Sibley marched north and was defeated in Glorieta Pass near Santa Fe.

Built originally to protect settlers from the Navajo and Apache Indians, Fort Craig is little more than piles of eroded adobe bricks and volcanic rock today.

In its day, the commander of a group of scouts, Captain Paddy Grayton, was said to have used an unusual method for filling his ranks. It was perhaps the first "Involuntary induction" system used. According to the legends, when one of his men was killed or deserted, the captain would scout the area. He would find an indigent person who he would call by the name of the missing scout. The Captain would then haul the unfortunate person back to the fort, where he had his new "recruit" on duty. The luckless recruit would be closely watched so he would not desert a second time.

Union forces were defeated at Valverde Battlefield where they retired within the fort while the Confederates moved on to take Albuquerque and Santa Fe. It was at the Battle of Glorieta where the Confederates were defeated and irreplaceable supplies destroyed.

On I-25 North of Elephant Butte
MM 113.9

29-X

Taos County

Kit Carson

Spanish explorers discovered an inhabited pueblo here. When the County and County seat were named for the nearby pueblo in 1852.

County Seat: Taos
Communities: Questa, Ranchos de Taos, Talpa
Arroyo Seco

2,257 Square Miles

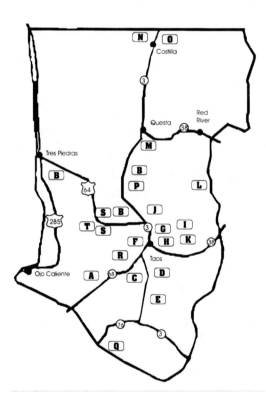

Pilar

In 1795, twenty-five families were granted land along the Rìo Grande at Pilar, then known as Cieneguilla. The Battle of Cieneguilla was fought at Embudo Mountain near here in March 1854. A large force of Utes and Jicarilla Apaches inflicted heavy losses on sixty dragoons from Cantonment Burgwin near Taos.

Pilar is located on the Southwestern edge of the Orilla Verde Recreation Area. The BLM managed recreation area is nestled along the banks of the Rio Grande and offers visitors a wide variety of recreation opportunities.

The local terrain is comprised of rugged, wide open mesas and chiseled steep canyons. Because of the dramatic change in elevation of 800 feet in places, the diversity of life draws many species of wildlife including raptors such as eagles and hawks, songbirds, waterfowl, beaver, cougar, deer and much more.

The Rio Grande has been attracting humans since prehistoric times. Scattered throughout the recreation area are petroglyphs and many other archaeological sites.

The visitors station is open 7 days a week throughout the summer. Day use is $3.00 per car load and camping is $7.00 per night. There are 5 developed campgrounds.

Orilla Verde Visitor Station
(505) 758-4060

Marker Missing
Southeast of Taos
On Hwy 68

30-A

Rio Grande Gorge

The Rìo Grande cut this spectacular gorge through layers of basalt, a volcanic rock that erupted between 2 and 5 million years ago. This basalt was highly fluid and flowed many miles. The enormous landslide blocks downstream were caused by undercutting when the river was much larger during the Pleistocene glacial age.

The Rio Grande flows out of the snowcapped Rocky Mountains in Colorado and journeys 1,900 miles to the Gulf of Mexico. It passes through 800 foot chasms of the Rio Grande Gorge, a wild and remote area of northern New Mexico. The canyon provides a wide variety of recreational opportunities, luring fishermen, hikers, artists, and whitewater boating enthusiasts. Access in the upper canyon is restricted by the terrain, but several trails lead to the rivers edge. The two most popular whitewater segments are the Taos Box, 17 miles of Class IV whitewater (runnable season generally from the end of April to mid-July), and the 5 mile Racecourse, a Class III segment (high use season is generally May through August). The lower canyon is paralleled by state roads, and receives the majority of the recreational use.

The Rio Grande and Red River designation was among the original eight rivers designated by Congress as Wild and Scenic in 1968. The designation was extended by legislation in 1994 to include an additional 12 miles of the Rio Grande. The designated area includes 60 miles of the Rio Grande from the Colorado/New Mexico state line to just beyond BLM's County Line Recreation Site, and the lower 4 miles of the Red River.

On NM Hwy 68
North of Embudo-MM 24.9

30-B

Jemez Mountains

Formed from cataclysmic volcanic eruptions some one million years ago, the Jèmez Mountains are a part of the westernmost New Mexico Rockies that enter the state from Colorado near Chama. Chicoma Peak (11,561 feet), prominent on the western horizon, is the highest in the Jèmez Mountains. Elevation here is 5,800 feet.

Sangre De Cristo (Blood of Christ)

From left to right along the eastern horizon, two of New Mexico's highest mountain ranges are visible, the Truchas Range and the Santa Fe Range. Both are part of the Sangre de Cristo Mountains of the Southern Rockies where glacier carved alpine peaks rise to elevations exceeding 13,000 feet.

Jemez Springs cuts a canyon through the valley of volcanic ash. Some of the most interesting things are the numerous hot springs and pools. Many are large and safe for bathing. At the forceful waterfall, Soda Dam, the river drops 15 feet through a curious formation made of deposited minerals from nearby thermal springs.

The gaseous vents and tiny bubbling hot water fountains are near the roadside opposite the Dam, giving no doubt that there is something happening beneath the earth's crust.

Jemez Springs also has a State Monument, preserving the ruins of a 17th century Spanish mission and 13th century Indian Pueblo.

Most of the Jemez Mountains area is within the Santa Fe National Forest, so back-country camping is free, and commercial development is restricted.

On NM Hwy 68
North of Embudo-MM 33.6

30-C

San Francisco De Asis Church
Ranchos de Taos, New Mexico

This Mission Church is one of the oldest churches in America dedicated to San Francisco de Asis. It was constructed between 1813 and 1815 under the direction of the Franciscan Fray Josè Benito Pereyro. It is an outstanding example of adobe mission architecture. This Church continues to this day to be a place to worship and an integral part of the community.

Ranchos de Taos is a village just south of Taos that was settled in 1716. San Francisco de Asìs, the mission church built in 1772, is probably the most photographed and painted church in the United States. With its massive adobe buttresses, high ceilings with vigas and hand-carved corbels, it has sparked the imagination of such great artists as Georgia O'Keeffe and Ansel Adams, to name a few.

The retablos, paintings of religious figures such as the Virgin Mary, and bultos, angels or spirits, on the northeast screen, were created by an early 19th century santero (Saint painter), Molleno. The church also has the largest altar screen in New Mexico.

In the rectory is a painting by artist Henri Ault. "The Shadow of the Cross" has optical illusions of making the cross disappear.

The Ranchos de Taos plaza has many galleries and shops to explore.

On US Hwy 68
To Taos-MM 413

30-D

Cantonment Burgwin—1852-1860

Never officially designated a fort, this post was built to protect the Taos Valley from Utes and Jicarilla Apaches. It is named for Capt. John H.K. Burgwin, who was killed in the Taos uprising of 1847. It was abandoned in 1860 and is now the site of the Fort Burgwin Research Center.

As more and more settlers moved west, the US Army was called upon to move with them. Though sometimes the Army would fortify existing buildings, most of the time the soldiers were required to build their own forts. Army posts were established on the basis of anticipated use. The fast changing needs of the country had the Army setting up posts and then abandoning them when they were no longer needed. In order for a post to be designated a fort, a contingent of troops had to be permanently assigned to it.

Troops from Company "I" of the 1st Dragoons of the Cavalry established a post south of Taos. Later, Company "F" helped to protect the Taos Valley, but neither company was permanently assigned to the Cantonment, which usually signifies temporary quarters. With several thousand Indians in the area, the garrison was involved in many serious encounters. The cavalry was here from 1852-1860.

Today it serves as the Fort Burgwin Research Center of Southern Methodist University. The research center was established as a permanent research and education facility operated by Southern Methodist University. Its central focus is on archaeological research and it has conducted summer field schools which focus on sites located in the northern Rio Grande Region. Excavated materials are curated at the center.

Permission is needed before visiting the site.

Marker Missing
On NM Hwy 518
Southeast of Taos

30-E

Taos Plaza
End of Camino Real

Spanish settlers lived in the Taos Valley before the Pueblo Revolt of 1680, but the town of Fernández de Taos was not founded until the 1790's. The Camino Real, or King's Highway, from Mexico City reached its end in this plaza and in nearby Taos Pueblo.

After months on the trail, through all types of weather, constant threat of attack from hostiles, heading into the unknown, people traveled along the Rio Grande, following the Camino Real to their final destination: Taos. They arrived at the Plaza, rejuvenated to have come so far, and now their dreams of a new home, land of their own, and adventure awaited them.

The late 1800's brought an increasing number of artisans, making Taos one of the most well known and respected hubs of modern art.

Taos Plaza, the heart of Taos, is home to numerous shops and galleries. As you browse through the shops, keep an eye out for Taos-made products. There's something for everyone from Native American drums and moccasins to chile ristras to southwestern clothing and jewelry, leather work, pottery, packaged food items and more! Specialty items and gifts satisfy every taste and pocketbook.

Marker Missing
On NM Hwy 68 in Taos
at Taos Plaza

30-F

Kit Carson Park

This municipal park was acquired by The Town of Taos in 1988 from the State of New Mexico. It is dedicated to the citizens of Taos and to the historic figures of our Community who have made this a great place to live and visit.

Please help us keep it clean and safe!

Kit Carson State Park is open daily from 8 to 5 with free admission. Located just two blocks north of Taos Plaza, the park includes a cemetery that is the final resting place for Kit Carson, the legendary mountain man and explorer who played crucial roles in the growth of the United States.

Also laid to rest here is Padre Antonio Severino Martinez who was a merchant and one of Taos' first mayors. He owned a large 21-room fortress-like home built in 1804 that is located two miles west of Taos Plaza.

There are other historical figures who were laid to rest here.

On US Hwy 68
North in Taos

30-G

Kit Carson Memorial State Park Cemetery

In 1868, Christopher "Kit" Carson, the legendary guide, scout, soldier, and trapper, died in Fort Lyons, Colorado. The next year, his body and that of his wife Josefa were brought home to Taos. Others buried here include soldiers killed in the 1847 rebellion protesting the U.S. annexation of New Mexico.

It was in 1842 that Christopher (Kit) Carson would meet John C. Fremont. Fremont would be instrumental in turning Carson into a national hero. In popular fiction of the day, Carson was portrayed as a rugged mountain man capable of superhuman feats.

In real life, Carson was indeed an amazing person with a knack for being in the right place to become an important part of settling the United States.

Carson lead Fremont to Oregon and California and it was Fremont's widely read reports that began what would become Carson's legendary life.

Events in which he was associated with include California's short-lived Bear Flag rebellion. Carson also lead General Stephen Kearney from New Mexico to California. He also helped to conquer the Navajo Indians who were forced in what was called "The Long Walk" from Arizona to Fort Sumner.

Later years found Carson increasing his ranch, expanding into Colorado where he died in 1868. He and his wife were moved the following year to this cemetery near his old home in Taos.

On NM Hwy 68 North
East of Kit Carson Park

30-H

Pueblo of Taos

Parts of Taos were occupied when Hernando de Alvarado visited here in 1540. Taos served as the headquarters from which Popè, of San Juan Pueblo, organized the Pueblo Revolt in 1680. In 1846, the pueblo was a refuge for Hispanics and Indians resisting the annexation of New Mexico by the United States.

Archeologists say that ancestors of the Taos Indians lived in this valley long before Columbus discovered America and hundreds of years before Europe emerged from the Dark Ages. The main part of the present buildings were most likely constructed between 1000 and 1450 A.D. and appear much as they do today. The Pueblo was one of the fabled golden cities of Cibola.

The Pueblo is made entirely of earth mixed with water and straw. The adobe was then either poured into forms or made into sun-dried blocks. The outside surfaces of the Pueblo are continuously maintained by replastering thick layers of mud. The Interior walls are carefully coated with thin washes of white earth. The Pueblo is actually many individual homes, built side-by-side and in layers. They share common walls, but have no connecting doorways.

Though many of the houses outside the Pueblo have modern conveniences, inside, their traditions dictate there is no electricity or running water. Around 150 people live within the Pueblo full time, while others come and reside there during ceremonial times.

This Pueblo is considered to be the oldest continuously inhabited community in the united States.

Taos Pueblo Tourism
P.O. Box 1154
Taos, NM 87571
(505) 758-1028

Marker Missing
On US Hwy 68 North
At Taos Pueblo

30-I

Taos

The Spanish community of Taos developed two miles southwest of Taos Pueblo. It later served as a supply base for the "Mountain Men," and was the home of Kit Carson, who is buried here. Governor Charles Bent was killed here in the anti-U.S. insurrection of 1847. In the early 1900's, Taos developed as a colony for artists and writers. Population 3,369. Elevation 6,938 feet.

Named for Don Fernando de Taos, Taos has developed from the end of the Camino Real, to the center for tourism and the arts. Taos actually consists of three distinct villages: The original Spanish settlement, the Pueblo de Taos which retains much of the pre-European culture of the Taos Indians, and Ranchos de Taos, a farming community that is home to one of New Mexico's most scenic mission churches.

Located at the base of the Sangre De Cristo Mountains, it's a city of contrasts, where mountains meet mesas, where history meets cutting edge art, recreation and technology.

If one word were used to describe Taos culture, it would be diverse. There are native Americans, Hispanics, Anglos and a collection of various other ethnic groups. The individuals in this community are artists and scientists, entrepreneurs and business people, professionals, farmers and cattle ranchers. Each holds a piece of the history that makes Taos and New Mexico unique.

Taos is also the county seat of Taos County.

Taos County Chamber of Commerce
P.O. Box I
Taos, New Mexico 87571
(505) 758-1028
1-800-732-TAOS

On US Hwy 68
In Taos- MM 3

30-J

Taos Canyon

In 1962, after having been driven from New Mexico by the Pueblo Revolt of 1680, the Spanish began to re-establish their rule. In one of the last battles of the reconquest, in September 1969, Governor Diego de Vargas defeated the Indians of Taos Pueblo at nearby Taos Canyon.

Named for Kit Carson, noted frontier scout, the Carson National Forest offers some of the most beautiful mountain scenery in the West. The Supervisor's office is located in Taos and the district includes the Sangre De Cristo Mountains, Wheeler Peak (New Mexico's highest point at 113,161 ft) as well as part of the Pecos Wilderness.

Taos and the surrounding areas have a lot to offer in the way of stream, lake and ice fishing, hunting, hiking, horseback riding, rafting and birdwatching. With four wilderness areas as well as the Valle Vidal Unit, which provides 100,000 acres of some of the best big game hunting in the state.

Marker Missing
On NM Hwy 64
South of Taos68

30-K

Vietnam Veterans National Memorial

This Chapel was erected in 1968 by Dr. Victor Westphall in memory of his son and all other U.S. personnel killed in the fighting in Vietnam. It was first dedicated as the Vietnam Veterans Peace and Brotherhood Chapel, and on May 30,1983, it was rededicated as DAV Vietnam Veterans National Memorial.

Dr. Victor Westphall, founder and Director Emeritus of Angel Fire, began planning the memorial with its Vietnam Veterans Peace and Brotherhood Chapel, just five days after Dr. Westphall's son and namesake, Victor David Westphall III, died in an enemy ambush in Quang Tri Province Vietnam on May 22, 1968. The proceeds from his military insurance policy provided seed money from which the Vietnam Veterans Peace and Brotherhood Chapel would grow to symbolize the sacrifice as well as the futility and tragedy of war.

David's parents and brother wanted to "memorialize all Vietnam veterans—the living, the dead and the maimed in body and spirit"—and in 1968 led the nation in this fitting and contemplative token of love, honor and respect. "We had no idea of changing the mores of a nation. All we wanted to do was assure that our son, and all his buddies, were properly recognized."

Until 1977, it subsisted entirely on the Westphall family resources and public contributions.

An inscription at the entrance to Angel Fire's Vietnam Veterans Peace and Brotherhood Chapel reads:

The Ultimate Curse
Greed plowed cities desolate
Lusts ran snorting thru the streets
Pride reared up to desecrate
Shrines, and there were no retreats.
So man learned to shed the tears
With which he measures out his years.
— Victor David Westphall III

On NM Hwy 64
South of Eagles Nest

30-L

Palo Flechado Pass

Palo Flechado (tree pierced with arrows) was a pass much used by Indians, Spaniards, and Anglos traveling from the plains by way of the Cimarron River (called La Flecha-the arrow-in 1719). The Flecha de Palo Indians (Apache band) in 1706 inhabited the plains east of the mountains.

Finding the "Easy" route through the Rocky Mountains was a challenge. This pass on the Cimarron River was not one of the easiest or most used, but it was used often by those seeking a route to the other side.

Traders needed to be able to get their goods to the people who needed them. A pass through the mountain could be a blessing or a curse. Some narrowed and allowed enemies to attack from above.

Others, allowed for quicker trip, making the goods a bit more valuable.

Just think of the old western movies. Two traders start out at the same time. One takes the "Easy" route, though longer, and considered safer. The other takes the Harder route where news of Indian attacks have been reported.

Who will get there first? You'll never know till the end of the movie.

Marker Missing
On NM Hwy 64
Northwest of Taos

30-M

Welcome To New Mexico
Land of Enchantment

These signs are the first thing to greet visitors to the great state of New Mexico. Found at all major entry points, some offer special extras, such as free coffee, and all give a weary traveler a place to get out and stretch their legs, get a fresh breath of air, before resuming their journey. So, whether you are passing through, planning an extended visit, or moving here permanently, welcome to New Mexico.

Taos County
On NM Hwy 522 North
On NM/Col Border

30-N

Points of Interest

On most of the historical markers, there is text describing geological, historical, or other interesting facts about the area you are visiting. On the back of most of these signs are Points of Interests maps. These maps lead you to other Historical Markers in the area.

New Mexico has a rich and fascinating history. Its Tri-culture influence can be seen throughout the state. Whether you're taking a break from a long car ride, or exploring, the historical markers will give you a chance to explore and learn about this great state.

On NM Hwy 522 North
on Colorado Border

30-O

Lawrence Ranch
University of New Mexico

The Kiowa Ranch, home of novelist D.H. Lawrence and his wife Frieda in 1924–25, was given to them by Mabel Dodge Luhan, Freida continued to live at the ranch after his death, and later married Angelo Ravagli. In 1934 they built a shrine for Lawrence's ashes. Aldous Huxley was among the many visitors to the ranch.

The author of such classics as "Women in Love and Lady Chatterly's Lover," D.H. Lawrence first came to this area at the invitation of Mabel Dodge Luhan. He and his wife, Frieda traveled here several times until his death. They were accompanied by Dorothy Brett, an English painter and admirer of Lawrence. She often typed his manuscripts for him.

Frieda built the small shrine in which to hold the ashes of D.H. Lawrence. She feared that the ashes would be stolen, "now let's see them steal that." was her comment as she dumped the ashes into a wheelbarrow of wet concrete.

The concrete was used to build the alter.

Freida died in 1956 on her 77th birthday. Her wishes were to be buried here, and her grave is just outside to the left as one enters the memorial.

On NM Hwy 522
South of Quest,NM

30-P

Las Trampas

The village of Las Trampas was established in 1751 by 12 families from Santa Fe, led by Juan de Argüello, who received a land grant from Governor Tomás Vèlez Cachupìn. The Church of San Josè de Gracia is one of the finest surviving 18th-century churches in New Mexico

Land has always been a precious commodity. The Spanish and Mexican land grants in New Mexico are the most enduring legacies of their colonial experiences.

There were several types of land grants. The three most common to New Mexico were Pueblo grants, which are also the oldest. They were grants of land made to Indian communities in New Mexico. All of New Mexico's Pueblos currently exist within a reservation which has its basis in a Spanish land grant.

Another type of Grant was the Private Grant. This was a grant made to individuals as rewards for their service to the government. The difference being, these were for personal use of individuals and their families and became private property which could be sold by the owner.

A community grant was made to a group of people who promised to settle and defend the granted land. Each individual of the group was given a parcel of land on which to build a home. The remainder of the thousands of acres often granted were reserved for common use and benefit of all settlers. The common lands of the grant remained community property and could not be sold.

There were many requirements to obtaining deeds to the homes they built on these grants, and most of today's residents are direct descendants of the original grant holders.

North of Truchas
On NM Hwy 76-MM 24.2

30-Q

Rio Grande Gorge Bridge

Second highest bridge on the National Highway System, rises 650 feet above the stream of the Rio Grande. Dedicated Sept. 10. 1965, it is a lasting monument to the untiring efforts of Governor Jack M. Campbell and the citizens of Northern New Mexico to open this scenic area to the public.

As you leave the mountains and travel across the flat stretch of High Way 64, you have no idea of what is coming. It isn't until you are almost upon the wide gaping chasm that you realize there are cars parking and people going to observation points to view the magnificent Rio Grande Gorge.

You park your car, step out, and look back to the mountains towering behind you and in front. You take a slow stroll towards the observation point, your eyes widening as you get closer and view the reds, blacks, blues, and greens of the deep chasm, set off with the sparkling silver of the river nearly 650 feet below.

It is a magnificent site, the second highest bridge on the National Highway System, the colors, so vibrant as the sun moves across the azure sky, lighting and giving nature a chance to shine as this enchanting land once again weaves its spell over you.

On NM Hwy 64
On NM Hwy 522
North of Taos-MM 274

22-R

Rio Grande Gorge Bridge

Second highest bridge on the National Highway System, rises 650 feet above the stream of the Rio Grande. Dedicated Sept. 10. 1965, it is a lasting monument to the untiring efforts of Governor Jack M. Campbell and the citizens of Northern New Mexico to open this scenic area to the public.

Jack M. Campbell Highway
Taos To Tierra Amarilla

This road passes through some of the most spectacular scenery in the American Southwest. It is a key section of the east-west highway which brings visitors to this region from throughout the United States. Since this route became a reality through the leadership and perseverance of Governor Jack M. Campbell (1963–1966), the members of the New Mexico State Highway Commission voted unanimously on September 23, 1965 to name this portion of US 64 in his honor.

Governor Campbell, who died in June of 1999 at the age of 82, will always be remembered as the "bridge builder."

At his funeral, Incumbent Governor Gary Johnson as well as his predecessors stretching back to the late 1960's sat together in the front row of the church.

Governor Campbell was known for his love of the outdoors and for his many accomplishments in public office. He was credited for strengthening a low that provided for nonpartisan civil service for state government, which ended a political patronage system that had meant most rank-and-file state workers lost their jobs when new governors took office. The state Capitol building was also built during Campbell's administration.

Always a "bridge builder", he also helped found New Mexico Technet, an early operation in what is now known as the Internet and information superhighway. He was its president from 1986 to 1988.

After leaving the governorship, Campbell never ran for another elective office.

19 ½ miles East On US Hwy 64 by Rest Area

22-S

Rio Grande Gorge State Park

With spectacular views and some of the finest public fishing in New Mexico, this park runs along the banks of the Rio Grande. From the Colorado border through the park, the "great river" offers exciting white-water boating through a deep canyon. There are four major camping/picnicking areas along the river.

Recently renamed Wild Rivers National Recreation Area, this site area was set aside so visitors could experience the beauty of two national Wild and Scenic Rivers protected by Congress.

This area is Public Land, administered by the Bureau of land Management, and it is here the Rio Grande and the Red River meet at La Junta Point.

The Wild Rivers Back Country Byway winds its way along the rim of the Rio Grande Gorge, offering access to spectacular overlooks of the canyon ecosystem. From rim to river, the ecosystem descends 800 feet. Ancient pinon and juniper forests are home to 500 year old trees. Wildlife such as mule deer, red-tailed hawks, and prairie dogs thrive.

Information on activities is available at the Visitor's Center. The Visitor Center is open from Memorial Day through Labor Day, 10:00 AM to 4:00 PM, and additional hours as staffing permits. Outside displays are available.

Wild Rivers Recreation Area
P.O. Box 9,
Cerro, NM 87519
(505)239-7211

On US Hwy 64\
19 ½ miles East at Rest Area

30-T

Torrance County

Torrance County was created in 1903 and was named for Francis J. Torrance, a promoter who took part in building New Mexico Central Railroad.

County Seat: Estancia
Communities: Clines Corners, Encino, Manzano,
Moriarty, Mountainair, Tajique, Willard,
McIntosh

Quarai of Salinas National Monument

3,355 Square Miles

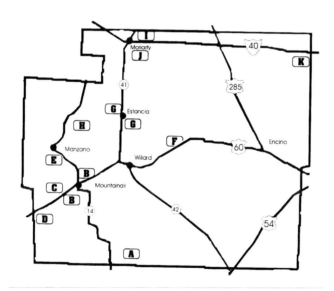

Quivira Ruins
Salinas National Monument

1 Mile South

The Tompiro Indian "Pueblo de las Humanas" (ca. 1300— 1670's) had 1,500 to 2,000 inhabitants and was a trading center with Plains Indians. The village evolved for centuries on the fringe of the Mogollon and Anasasi culture. There are two large Spanish Franciscan mission churches, San Isidro built in 1629, and San Buenaventura constructed in 1659.

Salinas, or salt, was very necessary to the early Indians as a preservative and trade good. Quivira is the oldest and largest of the three monuments, having been recognized as a National Monument since 1908. Its gray stones make an interesting contrast to the red stone work of the other two monuments that comprise Salinas National Monument. The Spanish explorers called the Pueblo, Las Humanas, meaning that the pueblo was thriving when Oñate first approached it in 1598.

The natives resisted the newcomers at first, but they reconciled themselves and then borrowed freely from the Spanish as they did from other cultures. The pueblo's black-on-white pottery took on new forms.

In the 1660's, friars burned and filled kivas in an effort to exterminate the old religion. Hurriedly altered above-ground rooms converted to kivas attest to the Pueblo priests' response.

A second church was begun, but was never completed, partly because Apache raids had begun. In 1672, further weakened by drought and famine, the inhabitants (only 500 by that time) abandoned the pueblo.

Salinas Pueblo Missions National Monument
P.O. Box 517
Mountainair, NM 87036
(505) 847-2585

At Intersection of Hwy 55
South & East-MM 37

31-A

Mountainair

Founded in 1902, Mountainair developed as a major center for pinto bean farming in the early 20th century until the drought of the 1940's. The region had been occupied earlier by Tompiro and eastern Tiwa pueblo Indians from prehistoric times through the mid-17th century, when it served as a major center for Spanish Franciscan missionaries. Population 1,170. Elevation 6,535 feet.

At one time known as the "Pinto Bean Capital of the World", Mountainair owes much of its beginnings to being in the right place. Abo Pass, one of the few natural passes through the Rocky Mountains, led to this enclosed valley.

The first business, a grocery store, was opened here in 1903. It was the steel rails that made up the Belen Cutoff that sealed the survival of the small town.

Today, there has been a major influx of artists into the community bringing a unique combination of old world charm and modern ideas to this once sleepy ranching community.

Nicknamed Gateway to Ancient Cities, Mountainair proudly welcomes thousands of visitors to Salinas Pueblo Missions National Monument every year.

Mountainair Chamber of Commerce
P.O. Box 595
Mountainair, NM 87036
(505) 847-2795

On US 60 South in Mountainair
On US 60 West in Mountainair-MM 204.3

31-B

Abo Ruins
Salinas National Monument

3/4 Mile North

Located adjacent to the major east-west trade route through Abó Pass, the Tompiro Pueblo of Abó (ca. 1300s–1670s) was one of the Southwest's largest Pueblo Indian villages. Extensive Indian house complexes are dominated by the unique buttressed walls, 40 feet high, of the Spanish Franciscan mission church of San Gregorio de Abó, built around 1630.

On an expedition to investigate the Salinas district in 1853, Maj. J. H. Carleton came upon Abó at dusk. "The tall ruins," he wrote, "standing there in solitude, had an aspect of sadness and gloom..The cold wind..appeared to roar and howl through the roofless pile like an angry demon." Carleton recognized the remains as a Christian church, but didn't know that the "long heaps of stone, with here and there portions of walls projecting above the surrounding rubbish," marked the remains of a large pueblo.

Located on a pass opening onto the Rio Grande Valley, Abó had carried on a lively trade with people of the Acoma-Zuñi area, the Galisteo Basin near Santa Fe, and the plains. Salt, hides, and piñon nuts passed through this trading center. Springs provided water for households, crops, and flocks of turkeys.

Abó was a thriving community when the Spaniards first visited the Salinas Valley in 1581. Franciscans began converting Abó residents in 1622, and by the late 1620s the first church was finished. Later, a second church was built with a sophisticated buttressing technique unusual in 17th-century New Mexico. It had an organ and a trained choir.

But the good times did not last. Battered by the same disasters that struck the other Salinas pueblos, the people of Abó departed, sometime between 1672 and 1678, to take refuge in towns along the Rio Grande.

Salinas Pueblo Missions National Monument
P.O. Box 517
Mountainair, NM 87036
(505) 847-2585

West on US 60
West of Mountainair-MM 195

31-C

Abo Pass Trail

This route through the southern edge of the Manzano Mountains links the Rio Grande Valley to the salt lakes and the Salinas Pueblo missions east of the mountains.

The road began as a Pueblo trade route to the eastern plains and later connected the Spanish -period Camino Real to the region. Evolution of the route continued when the Santa Fe Railway completed its Belen Cutoff route through the pass in 1908 and with subsequent construction of a modern highway.

The Rocky Mountains has long been a obstacle preventing easy travel from one side of the mountains to the other. One of the few natural passes in either direction, allowed for ease of travel and has helped to shape the valleys on either side of the Mountains. The Rio Grande with its fertile land and water on one side, and the salt lakes and vast plains to the east.

The word "pass" is just a little deceiving for this rugged five and a half mile passage. As modern trains cross the seven bridges and roll past the rugged outcropping of Abo Canyon, one can appreciate the beauty of the steep rugged walls of the canyon.

The setting sun lighting half of the canyon appears to be an entirely different planet as scrub juniper trees give way to the open vastness of the plains on the Western side where the Rio Grande lazily follows its bed to the Gulf of Mexico.

South of Mountainair
On US Hwy 60

31-D

Quarai Ruins
Salinas Pueblo Mission National Monument
1 Mile West

On the edge of the Plains stands the abandoned Tiwa Pueblo Indian village of Quarai (ca. 1200–1670's), the southernmost of the Tiwa villages, located along the eastern flanks of the Manzano Mountains. The Spanish Franciscan mission church of La Purìsima Concepción (1630) is the most complete remaining example of the large Salinas churches.

Like Abó and Las Humanas, red-walled Quarai was a thriving pueblo when Oñate first approached it in 1598 to "accept" its oath of allegiance to Spain.

Its towering cottonwoods and one-mile hiking trail make this an interesting place to spend a relaxing afternoon.

The red of the high rock walls of the church contrast against the green of the cottonwoods and the blue of the New Mexico sky. An interesting feature of this church was that it was built in the shape of a cross.

The mile long trek starts out with crossing a small bridge. From there it wanders along the hill, through trees, cacti, and grass, leading to the Spanish Corral Site. The only architectural features on this hill are stone walls and this foundation called the "Spanish Corral." There has been little archaeological study of these features. Historians feel that this area may have been used by settlers, in the 1800's, as a holding pen for sheep or for sheepshearing.

Spanish Conquistadores introduced sheep into New Mexico in 1540. Sheep were used for food on the journey, but some were also brought for breeding purposes. They provided mutton, but the primary demand changed to wool. Income from the sale of sheep had its ups and downs, and a few people monopolized the trade. The peak years were from 1821 through 1846.

Salinas Pueblo Missions National Monument
P.O. Box 517
Mountainair, NM 87036
(505) 847-2585

On US Hwy 55 North
MM 70

31-E

Salt Lakes

The Pedernal Hills form the eastern edge of Spanish New Mexico's 17th-century "Salinas Jurisdiction." Pueblo Indians used salt from these salinas in trade with Plains Indians. This salt was also prized by the Spaniards because of its use in silver processing for the rich Chihuahuan mines farther south in Mexico.

Numerous salt ponds and lakes, of which Laguna del Perro is the largest, occur in the lowest part of Estancia Basin, closed depression between Manzano Mountains to west and low Pedernal Hills east. This Basin was filled by a 150 foot deep lake in the late Pleistocene time and later was used by the Paleo Indians for mining salt.

The salt mined from here was a big commodity for the early Indians. They were able to use it to preserve their own food and to trade it for things they could not provide themselves.

There is no natural drainage for the Estancia valley, and these low lakes are seldom completely dry.

North of Encino
on US Hwy 60

31-F

Estancia

Incorporated in 1909 and county seat of Torrance County since 1905, Estancia is located in an enclosed valley or basin. It was ranching country until the early 20th century, when the coming of the railroad opened it to homesteaders and farmers. Pinto beans were the best known local crop until the 1950s. Population 830. Elevation 6107 feet.

Estancia, meaning small farm, is the county seat of Torrance County. Torrance was named for Francis J. Torrance who helped to build the railroad through Central New Mexico. The nearby village of Manzano is the site of the first apple orchard in New Mexico.

Estancia's population has been growing steadily due to its proximity to Albuquerque. People seeking a rural home, yet needing the proximity of the career oriented city, find this a good place to raise children.

The county was established March 16, 1903, nearly nine years before New Mexico obtained statehood.

While Mountainair and Moriarty host annual 4th of July celebrations, Estancia celebrates Old Timer's Day late in the summer. With Fiddler's contest, dances, parades, and a barbeque, Old timers, new and old, get together and enjoy a weekend of celebration.

Estancia Chamber of Commerce
P.O. Box 1000
Estancia, NM 87016
1-505-384-2372

Marker Missing
On NM Hwy 41
South of Estancia-MM 10.6
Marker Missing
On NM Hwy 41
South of Estancia-MM 12.4

31-G

Tajique

The pueblo-mission of San Miguel de Tajique was established in the 1620's. In the 1670's, famine, disease and Apache raids caused the abandonment of the Jurisdicción de las Salinas (1598–1678) which included Tajique. Modern occupation of Tajique began in the 1830's with a land grant made to Manuel Sanchez.

Near Tajique, in the Manzano Mountains, is the Manzano Mountain Cross-Country Ski Center. Boasting 25 miles of trails suitable for all levels of skiers, the center has a full-service ski school, as well as a rental shop and separate skating lanes. There is also a snack bar for warming up before and after hitting the slopes.

The Ski Center is open from December 1 to March 30th and a day pass is $8.50.

Nordic Skiing,
Ski School Children's Programs
Equipment Rentals
Group Rates
Snack Bar
Ski Packages

Manzano Mountain Cross-Country
Ski Center
Tajique, New Mexico
384-2209

On NM Hwy 55 in Tajique

31-H

Gregg's Trail

Josiah Gregg, merchant and pioneer historian of the Santa Fe Trail, made four expeditions to Santa Fe. On his last, in 1839–40, he blazed a new route from Van Buren, Arkansas, which followed the Canadian River north of here. The new trail became popular with California-bound gold-seekers in 1849.

Josiah Gregg was born in 1806, a direct descendant of William Gregg who was a Quaker immigrant of 1682. Josiah was a sickly boy and had a very grave outlook towards life. He had a tendency towards intellect. He tried to apprentice to a Doctor at a young age, but was refused. About this time he was struck down with consumption, and was bed ridden from September to the following Spring. His Doctor recommended that he travel to Santa Fe where the air would assist him to heal.

He started the trip out lying in a bed in the back of a wagon. By the time he reached Santa Fe, his health had improved greatly. He traveled on to California, then returned to New Mexico. While he traveled back to the "States" several times, he also enrolled in a medical school and graduated, returning to New Mexico to practice medicine.

It was during his travels that he collected, measured, and kept track of every detail of his surroundings, which made his notes for his book "Commerce on the Prairies", published in 1844.

Josiah died in 1850 in California, where he was still exploring and surveying his surroundings.

On I-40 East of Moriarty
Exit 197- MM 198

31-I

Lake Estancia

This large valley was occupied by ancient Ice Age Lake Estancia some 12,000 years ago. To the north, the Southern Rockies rise to altitudes of 13,000 feet; to the northwest are the Ortiz and San Pedro Mountains; to the west are the Sandia Mountains, and to the southwest are the Manzano Mountains. Elevation 6,200 feet.

The Estancia Valley is, in fact, a drainless basin. There is no natural drainage from the valley. This might have its drawbacks in ancient times, but historically it was a highly desirable valley.

Two Land Grants given to two different families, came to a head in a bloody shoot out in Estancia in the summer of 1883.

New Mexico was still part of the Spanish Empire in 1819 when a man named Bartolome Baca applied for a grant of more than a million acres in the Estancia Valley. For unknown reasons, he neglected to acquire legal papers giving him final title as he grazed huge flocks of sheep on the princely grant.

The year before New Mexico passed from Mexican to American rule, Governor Manuel Armijo made a new grant consisting of 300,000 acres in the very center of the old Baca Tract. Both the original owners sold their claims.

When one of the new owners rode into Estancia to drive the "upstarts" out, a shootout erupted. Two men died and the Territory was left in an uproar.

The real tragedy of the affair was that soon after, the courts finally ruled on the land grants which had started the trouble. Both land grants were declared invalid and the valley was placed in the public domain and opened for homesteading.

Thus, the bloody shoot-out at Estancia Spring had all been for nothing!

Marker Missing
On Interstate 40 East of Moriarty

31-J

Edge of Plains

Grassy plains meet pine dotted uplands in this transition from Great Plains to Basin and Range provinces. Plains to the east are capped by caliche, sand, and gravel which are deeply eroded into underlying bedrock in places. To the west, faulting has produced alternating highlands and intermountain basins of the Basin and Range province. Elevation 6,500 feet.

How small and insignificant one can feel when looking across the great plains. As far as the eye can see, it seems to go on forever.

In contrast, looking up to the top of the mountain ranges beyond, feeling so small, needing to pass the mountains to see what's on the other side.

It took a lot of courage to pack up the family and head out in a wagon. Ahead were Indians to fight, desert thirst, and then mountains and winter storms. Mother Nature has always had a way of testing so that only the strong survive.

And survive, we did.

East of Moriarty

31-K

Union County

Clayton Lake State Park

The Union County Courthouse was built in 1909 in Clayton, New Mexico.

County Seat: Clayton
Communities: Folsom, Des Moines, Grenville, Mt. Dora, Capulin, Gladstone, Amistad, Stead

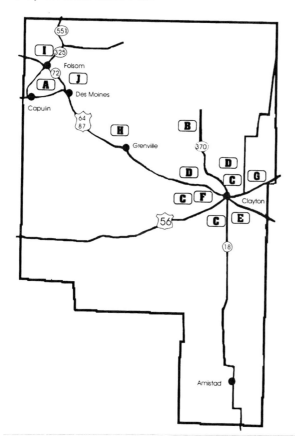

Capulin Volcano National Monument

An outstanding example of an extinct volcano cinder cone. Capulin Mountain was formed as early as 10,000 years ago. In cinder cones, lava pours from cracks in the base rather than over the top. Capulin itself was the escape hatch for gases that blew lava fragments into the air where they solidified and landed red hot on the cone.

Capulin Volcano, a nearly perfectly-shaped cinder cone, stands more than 1200 feet above the surrounding High Plains of Northeastern New Mexico. The volcano is long extinct, and today the forested slopes provide habitat for mule deer, turkey, black bear and other wildlife. Abundant displays of wild flowers bloom on the mountain each summer.

A two-mile paved road spiraling to the volcano rim makes Capulin Volcano one of the most accessible volcanoes in the world. Trails leading around the rim and to the bottom of the crater allow a rare opportunity to easily explore a volcano.

Entrance fee is $4.00 per private vehicle, and $2.00 per person on a motorcycle. Call for commercial fee rates and education groups may apply for a waiver by writing prior to visit.

Capulin Volcano National Monument was established in 1916 to preserve this striking example of a volcanic cinder cone.

Capulin Volcano National Monument
P.O. Box 40
Capulin, New Mexico 88414
(505) 278-2201

Interstate 25 North Bound Lane
Mile Marker 360.4

31-A

Clayton Dinosaur Trackway

One of the best dinosaur track sites in the world can be viewed at Clayton Lake State Park. More than 500 fossilized footprints, made by at least eight kinds of dinosaurs, are visible on the lake's spillway. These tracks were embedded in the mud over 100 million years ago, when most of New Mexico was a vast sea.

One of the most unique aspects of Clayton Lake State Park is the Clayton Dinosaur Trackway. The tracks were discovered by amateur paleontologists after a season of high water washed away the layer of sediment that was covering the tracks at the spillway of the dam across Seneca Creek.

The tracks, also known as traces, were made in the middle of the Cretaceous period about 100 million years ago. The tracks were made by both herbivores and carnivores, though most of the tracks were made by bipeds, dinosaurs that walked on their hind legs. There are also traces of ancient crocodiles. There are 8 different species of tracks and about 500 different tracks.

The best time to view the tracks is early morning and late afternoon. There are interpretive markers that identify significant tracks and paleontological features on the walk.

Clayton Lake State Park
Rural Rt. Box 20
Seneca, NM 88437
(505) 374-8808
Hours: 6 am - 9 pm

US Highway 87
Mile Marker 4.5

32-B

Clayton

Trade caravans and homesteaders traveling the Cimarron Cutoff of the Santa Fe Trail passed near here. Clayton was founded in 1887 and named for the son of cattleman and ex-Senator Stephen W. Dorsey, one of its developers. It became a major livestock shipping center for herds from the Pecos Valley and the Texas Panhandle. Population 2,968. Elevation 4,969 feet.

In the early 1880's Ex-US Senator Stephen W. Dorsey acquired the land and helped to lay out the town of Clayton. Founded in 1887, Clayton was a major shipping point for livestock. Today, Union County produces twice as many cattle as any other county in New Mexico.

Clayton is proud of its clean, well-paved streets and the easily accessible commercial district on South First Street.

The Union County Courthouse was built in 1909 and is still in use today. Interesting places to visit are the Eklund Hotel and the Union County Historical Park as well as Clayton Lake State Park.

The Shrine of Testaments is a museum dedicated to Jan Maters, a Dutch-born, classically trained artist. His life-long ambition was to illustrate the Holy Bible. Admission is free. Call to find hours or make an appointment to visit (505) 374-9693

Clayton Chamber of Commerce
1103 South First Street
P.O. Box 476
Clayton, NM 88415
(800) 390-7858
(505) 374-9253

US 56
MM 81.1

32-C

Rabbit Ear Mountains

These two striking mounds were the first features to become visible to Santa Fe Trail traffic crossing into New Mexico from Oklahoma, and so became important landmarks for caravans. From here, traffic on this major 19th century commercial route still had about 200 miles to travel before reaching Santa Fe.

Land marks such as these mountains were a welcome site after days of endless praries. Being one of the first of the Rocky Mountain foothills, it stood as a landmark, letting people know that their journey was drawing to a close.

These mountains have a very colorful history. A Cheyenne Indian Chief, Orejas de Conejo, roamed the area with his tribe in the early 16th century. Killed in battle, the chief was buried on the large peak of the mountains in a secret cave. The English translation of Orejas de Conejo is Rabbit Ear, thus the mountains were named after the Chief.

These same mountains were the site of one of the bloodiest Spanish-Comanche battles in early Western history. In 1717 a volunteer army of 500 Spaniards from Santa Fe, determined to end the Comanche raids, staged a surprise attack and killed hundreds of Indians, taking 700 prisoners. The result of the surprise attack was a truce, freeing the vast open lands of this area.

However, this was still Indian country. In later years, Indian scouts watched from the top of the Rabbit Ears as wagon trains made their slow progress along the Santa Fe Trail. When the wagons reached a water hole, the Indians would swoop down to raid, stealing livestock, slaves, and whatever they found, before retreating back to their homes, till the next wagon train was spotted.

On US 56

32-D

Santa Fe Trail-Cimarron Cutoff

The Santa Fe Trail was the major trade route between New Mexico and Missouri from 1821 until the arrival of the railroad in 1880. The Cimarron cutoff, a major branch of the trail, passed through this portion of Northeast New Mexico. Some of the best preserved segments of the trail route are located at the nearby Kiowa National Grasslands along the Santa Fe National Historic Trail.

What a decision to make. People traveling along the Santa Fe Trail must have pondered this important decision for several days before arriving at the junction in Kansas. The two routes had very different hazards. Should they take the shorter, easier route across the desert, and face a 50-mile stretch of waterless prairie and higher probability of Indian attack, or the Mountain Branch which followed the Arkansas River to Bent's Fort, then turned southwest to climb over the treacherous Raton Pass?

Those taking the Cimarron Cutoff left behind ruts clearly visible today. Six of the famous watering places along the route (known as the Clayton Complex) are all within a 50 minute drive from town.

Time, weather, and erosion have not erased the deep wagon ruts stretching across the Kiowa National Grasslands. From here, the weary traveler could see Rabbit Ear Mountains, one of the first landmarks to break the flat "sea of grass", to let them know they were reaching the end of their trail. As travel was just 12 to 15 miles per day, watching the mountains would have been like a homing beacon, just as the limestone "Kansas fence posts" which marked the trail were located and followed.

32-E

Santa Fe Trail

William Becknell, the first Santa Fe Trail trader, entered Santa Fe in 1821 after Mexico became independent from Spain and opened its frontiers to foreign traders. The Mountain Branch over Raton Pass divided here. One fork turned west to Cimarron, then south and joined a more direct route to Rayado.

The difficulty of bringing caravans over rocky and mountainous Raton Pass kept most wagon traffic on the Cimarron Cutoff of the Santa Fe Trail until the 1840's. Afterwards, the Mountain Branch, which here approaches Raton Pass, became more popular with traders, immigrants, gold-seekers, and government supply trains.

William Becknell left Old Franklin, Missouri, on September 1, 1821. He headed west to trade with the Indians, but didn't have much luck. In New Mexico, he encountered Spanish dragoons. Instead of taking him prisoner for having entered Spanish Colonial Territory illegally, the soldiers urged him to bring his goods to Santa Fe.

He arrived there on November 16 and quickly sold all he had brought. Mexico had declared its independence from Spain, and American traders were now welcome in Santa Fe.

Within a few weeks, Becknell had organized another expedition. He took several wagons crammed with $3,000 worth of trade goods. His profit in Santa Fe was 2,000 percent, and the Santa Fe Trail was born.

The Santa Fe Trail was the first of America's great pathways from the Mississippi River area to the West. It preceded the Oregon and California trails by more than two decades.

I-25 NBL
MM 434.0

32-F

Clayton Lake State Park

The rolling grasslands around Clayton Lake were once a domain of the huge buffalo herds that ranged the Great Plains. Many years prior to this, dinosaurs ruled the area, as indicated by a series of tracks embedded in the rock near the lake. Clayton Lake is stocked with rainbow trout and channel catfish, and also provides good bass and walleye fishing. The lake serves as a wintering area for waterfowl.

12 miles north of Clayton on Highway 370 is Clayton Lake State Park. It was created by the New Mexico Game and Fish Department in 1955 as a fishing lake and winter waterfowl resting area.

A dam was constructed across the Seneca Creek and the lake is a popular spot for anglers hoping to catch trout, catfish, bass and walleye. The area is also a popular spot for waterfowl. Mallards, pintails and teals frequent the lake and Canada geese and bald eagles are often seen here.

The park offers camping and picnicking facilities, a group shelter and a modern comfort station. Also, be sure and check out the trails to see the dinosaur footprints by the spillway. The locals say the best time to view the prints is in the morning and late afternoon.

Clayton Lake State Park
RR Box 20
Seneca, NM 88437
(505) 374-8808

US 87
Mile Marker 4.5

32-G

Sierra Grande

Largest extinct volcano in northeastern New Mexico, Sierra Grande rises to an elevation of 8,720 feet, one of many volcanoes, cinder cones, and flows that cover more than 1,000 square miles of area in northeastern New Mexico and the southeastern Colorado eastward to the Oklahoma state line.

Situated about 10 miles southeast of Folsom is Sierra Grande. It is the largest single mountain in the United States. This extinct volcano is 40 miles in base perimeter and covers 50 square miles, with an altitude of 8.720 feet.

The rocks in this area are mostly lava or "malpie" from the nearby volcanoes. Near here, a company screens red and black cinder rock according to size, before they are loaded on trucks and hauled all over the United States to be used extensively for landscaping, roofing, barbeque grills and structures.

The small town of Des Moines has a wonderful view of the Sierra Grande. It is on an unprotected plateau leaving it colder in winter and cooler in summer than any other town in Union County.

Sierra Grande is known as a shield volcano because of its resemblance to a shield laying upon the ground. Considering that the lava reached nearly to Oklahoma, it is a sight to behold.

US 64/87
Mile Marker 392.0

32-H

Folsom Archaeological Site

Near here was the site of the discovery of a spear point between the ribs of an extinct species of bison. This find established man's presence in North America about 10,000 years ago, prior to the extinction of large mammals at the end of the last Ice Age.

In the early 1900's, George McJunkin, foreman for the Crowfoot Ranch, discovered large bones in a dry arroyo. No one was interested until 1926, when scientists excavated and found 23 ancient Bison skeletons and 19 projectile points. The points were named Folsom Point after the nearest town to the site. So far, no human bones of the Folsom Man have been found, but here was proof that man was here long before anthropologists supposed.

Folsom was named for Frances Folsom who married President Cleveland in the White House. Folsom was incorporated in 1914, a hub of activity in this area.

In 1908, a disastrous flood washed away most of the town. Sarah Rooke, the telephone operator, stayed at her switchboard warning people of the coming flood until her building was swept away. Seventeen people lost their lives and most of the businesses were gone, never to be rebuilt. Sara Rooke was honored as a heroine. Switchboard Operators from across the nation donated to her memorial.

On NM 72
MM 27.1

32-I

New Goodnight Trail

Charles Goodnight, the great Texas cattleman, used the Trinchera Pass branch Goodnight-Loving Trail until 1875. In that year, he blazed this trail northward from Fort Sumner to near Tucumcari and Clayton. This was the last trail created by Goodnight marking the end of his operations in New Mexico.

Born in Illinois on March 5, 1836, Charles Goodnight migrated to Texas at the age of 9. Legend says he made the trip bareback with his mother and step-father. Ten years later, he entered the cattle business on the northwest Texas frontier. He also served with the local militia in their long-running battle against Comanche raiders.

At the age of 21, he joined the Texas Rangers and fought for the Confederacy in the Civil War. When the war ended, Goodnight returned to Texas where he helped to gather all the stock that had roamed free during the four long years of war. Having recovered his herd, the next problem was in getting it to market somewhere outside the war-ravaged South.

He decided to head West towards New Mexico and Colorado, despite the fact that a huge waterless stretch of west Texas would make it a very risky venture. He met up with Oliver Loving and, in 1866, they set out with two thousand head of cattle to blaze a trail from Belknap, Texas to Fort Sumner, New Mexico. In 1867, after Loving was killed holding off a band of Comanches, Goodnight extended his activities, blazing the Goodnight Trail from Alamogordo Creek, New Mexico to Granada, Colorado.

By 1876, Goodnight and a new partner, John G. Adair, owned a ranch controlling over a million acres in the Texas Panhandle.

A pioneer in cattle breeding, Goodnight crossed the tough but scrawny Texas longhorns with the more traditional Herefords to produce a longhorn breed that was both independent and commercially lucrative. He also crossed cattle with buffalo to produce the first "cattalo" other wise today known as "beefalo."

While he lived every aspect of the cowboy myth to the fullest, Goodnight was at the same time a shrewd and immensely successful entrepreneur. After selling off his ranch, he invested in Mexican mining operations, and even tried his luck as a movie producer, and enjoyed the acclaim of his community at a small ranch near Goodnight, Texas. He died December 12, 1929 and is buried in the Goodnight Cemetery near the town named after him.

US 64/87 to Raton MM 384.8

32-J

Valencia County

Valencia County was created by the Republic of Mexico as one of the nine original counties by the territorial legislature. It is named for the village of Valencia.

County Seat: Los Lunas
Communities: Belen, Bosque Farms, Los Chaves, Tome, Jarales, Valencia, Vegita

Early Spring in Valencia   1,458 Square Miles

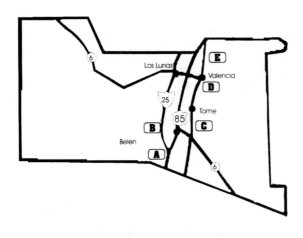

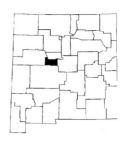

Belen
On the Camino Real

By the mid-18th century, Spanish colonization had begun along the Rio Grande north of Albuquerque. The Belen land grant was made to encourage this expansion, and colonists from Albuquerque settled here around 1740. The early community also included a group of genizaros, or Hispanicized Indians. Belen is Spanish for Bethlehem. Population 5,617. Elevation 4,800 feet.

The El Camino Real from Chihuahua, Mexico to Santa Fe, New Mexico traveled along the east side of the river through Valencia County. In Rio Communities, east of Belen, there is a visitor's center that commemorates El Camino Real. The visitor's center features information about the trail as well as other materials.

In 1880, the Atchison, Topeka and Santa Fe Railroad built the first section of its line through Valencia County from Albuquerque. Although the line did not have an immediate impact on the growth of Belen, the railroad brought many people into the area.

It was in 1907 when the Belen Cut-Off, linking Amarillo, Texas and Belen was completed. Belen became a railroad center and an important shipping point for the productive Rio Grande Valley. This Cut-Off alleviated traveling over Raton Pass, which required two to three large engines because of the 7,000 foot elevation.

Today, the importance of the railroad continues as Belen remains a refueling and servicing stop for many trains.

Belen Chamber of Commerce
712 Dallies Avenue
Belen NM 87002
505-864-8091

Hwy 314 North of Belen
MM 2.5

33-A

Vasquez de Coronado's Route

In the fall of 1540, Francisco Vasquez de Coronado's army traveled from Zuni to his chosen winter headquarters in the Tiguex province on the Rio Grande. Here the advance guard of the army followed the river from the Isleta area to Alcanfor, a pueblo near Bernalillo, where it camped for two winters.

Francisco Vasquez de Coronado was born into a noble family in Salamanca, Spain in 1510. At the age of 25, he came to the Americas as an assistant to New Spain's first viceroy.

An ambitious man, he married the daughter of the colonial treasurer, put down a major slave rebellion, and became the governor of a Mexican province within three years of his arrival. But he wanted more. Rumors of earlier explorations by Cabeza de Vaca for 7 cites of gold, inspired him to lead a royal expedition to explore the north into what is now the American West.

The expedition explored, bringing Catholic ideals to the pueblos they encountered, and the Spanish influence that is still very present today.

When they did not find the "Seven Cities of Cibola", parties were sent out, some traveling all the way to the border between Arizona and California where they explored the Grande Canyon. Coronado himself led a party into what is now Kansas.

Returning to Mexico without locating a single golden city, the Viceroy branded Coronado's expedition an abject failure. His career quickly declined and in 1544 he was removed from office as a governor and moved to Mexico City where he worked in a modest position for the City. He died in 1554, though his legacy is seen throughout the west.

NM 314 South of Isleta
MM 11.9

33-B

Tome

For centuries, the prominent cerro, or steep hill, of Tome was a significant landmark for travelers along the Camino Real. Settled as early as 1650, this area was abandoned following the Pueblo Revolt of 1680 and remained uninhabited until the Tome Land Grant was established in the 1739. During the late 18th and early 19th centuries, Tome was the center of government for the Rio Abajo district.

Tome Hill, which dominates the landscape in this area, has been used as a religious site, a refuge from hostile Indian attacks, and from floods. It was also a great observation point to watch and see what was coming.

The Immaculate Conception Catholic Church is in the Oldest Hispanic settlement in Valencia County. Among the most interesting things to see is Tome Immaculate Conception Church and Museum, known as the Tome Catholic Church, with a history exhibit and hand-carved wooden saints.

Here, the countryside is pure New Mexico pastoral, with horses grazing in cultivated fields fed by ancient acequias, or irrigation ditches.

Just south of Tome Hill, you'll find a massive sculpture, La Puerta del Sol, celebrating the three cultures of this region: Indian, Spanish, and early European settlers. La Puerta del Sol is the beginning of a 10 acre park which will include pathways, picnic tables, native plants, bike paths and interpretive panels telling the story of Cerro del Tome and the people of Tome.

NM 47 North in Tome
MM 25.4

33-C

Valencia

This community traces its beginnings to the hacienda established by Captain Francisco Valencia along this section of the Camino Real by the mid-17th century. Abandoned during the Pueblo Revolt of 1680, the area was resettled in 1740 by Christian Indians called genizaros. These settlers played an important role in the defense of the Spanish frontier.

The small town of Valencia, which grew up around the Valencia hacienda, is one of the oldest Spanish-American settlements in the county. At one time the Town of Valencia was the county seat.

After the Pueblo Revolt of 1680, the descendants of Valencia returned to re-occupy the area. On January 9, 1852, the County of Valencia was confirmed by the New Mexico Territorial Legislature.

The genizaros was the name give to many non-Pueblo Indians who did not belong to a specific tribe. They had no tribal identity to any specific tribe so they eventually became Hispanic. These people were very important in helping to settle this area. They helped to defend and develop the irrigation ditches, and to raise the crops, as well as provide knowledge on the seasons and temperament of the local tribes to those arriving on the Camino Real.

There are at least seven, historic churches around the Los Lunas area, dating back to the 1600's. Although the earliest mention of Peralta has been found in Catholic documents dated 1835. Located now on NM Highway 47 (Main St.) as you enter Peralta traveling east and north. The church originally was, it is said by local historians, "...right on the Camino Real."

Hwy NM 47 North of Tome
MM 30.5

33-D

Peralta

One of the last skirmishes of the Civil War in New Mexico took place here on April 15, 1862. The Sibley Brigade, retreating to Texas, camped at the hacienda of Governor Henry Connelly, a few miles from Peralta. Here the Confederates were routed by Union forces under Col. Edward R.S. Canby.

Canby ordered troops from Fort Union to march toward Santa Fe while his men continued their march north from Fort Craig toward Albuquerque. He hoped these movements would force the Confederates to abandon Santa Fe and concentrate their strength at Albuquerque to protect the remaining Confederate supplies stored there. This plan worked as the Confederates abandoned Santa Fe and fell back to Albuquerque.

Although a major clash in or near Albuquerque seemed imminent, the Confederates decided to abandon the campaign and withdraw from New Mexico.

The Union commander, Canby was often criticized for not battling the Confederates as he had far more numbers and was much better equipped. Canby was more interested in getting the Confederates to leave New Mexico, and by harrying them instead, he would not have to be responsible for feeding a large number of prisoners.

Union troops did fight the Confederates in a skirmish sometimes referred to as the Battle of Peralta a few miles south of Albuquerque, but this is viewed as further Union encouragement for the Confederates to depart New Mexico Territory.

The collapse of Sibley's New Mexico campaign ended the Confederacy's grand scheme of expansion to the Pacific. For the duration of the Civil War, New Mexico Territory remained firmly in Union hands.

NM Hwy 47 North of Valencia
MM 32.6

33-E

About the Authors

Phil T. Archuletta, owner and CEO of P&M Signs, Inc and P&M Plastics, Inc, has been in the sign manufacturing business for over 30 years. His experience with the Historical Markers as well as his love of New Mexico and its history have been life-long. He has traveled the state, logging each marker, helping to preserve New Mexico's colorful history.

Sharyl S. Holden has always dreamed of writing and has several published articles. Born and raised in Mountainair, New Mexico, the wide open spaces have enchanted her all her life. When she became Phil's Office Manager in 1999, Phil had just won a state contract to replace some of the Historical Markers. This guide is their joint effort.

Phil and Sharyl would like to give a special thanks to:

Aimee Watts, who typed, outlined, and proof-read more hours than she'd care to think about.

Larry Archuleta, who tirelessly traveled all the back roads and by-ways in search of the elusive markers.

Charles Parker for his editing and proofing.

Maybel Ocana, President of P&M Signs, Inc.

Peter Green and the staff of **New Mexico's Energy Minerals and Natural Resources Department** for letting us use their photographs.

And to the following websites that aided in the research:
www.zianet.com/snm.
www.nps.gov
www.nenewmexico.com

Printed in the United States
62447LVS00003B/4-12

9 780865 344006